THE
AMERICAN
SMALL
BUSINESSMAN

THE
AMERICAN
SMALL
BUSINESSMAN

BY

John H. Bunzel

ALFRED A. KNOPF   NEW YORK

1962

L. C. catalog card number: 62–11051

THIS IS A BORZOI BOOK,

PUBLISHED BY ALFRED A. KNOPF, INC.

FIRST EDITION

A portion of Chapter III, "The General Ideology of American Small Business," appeared in different form in *Political Science Quarterly* in March, 1955. Part of Chapter V appeared in different form in *The Western Political Quarterly* in September, 1956, as "Comparative Attitudes of Big Business and Small Business."

FOR

Cammie and Reed

—AND THE TROOPS

Preface

→

A number of years ago I received a letter from a responsible official of the United Auto Workers (AFL-CIO) in which he expressed an interest in my study of the American small businessman and went on to say: "But I challenge your thesis that he cannot be counted upon to support liberal groupings such as organized labor. If you can show that the small businessman is not a friend of ours I will be willing to revise my thinking."

This feeling, I soon discovered, was shared in one form or another by a variety of people who looked upon the small businessman as a kind of modern-day American underdog. For one thing, his present economic situation was known to be tight and often desperate, and it is very much in keeping with our own traditions to react with sympathy or outrage, as the case may be, when it is felt the "little guy" is being pushed around. More important, however, is the fact that the small businessman has always been identified with all of the homely virtues of Main Street America and thus is in something of a charmed if not sacred category along with Motherhood and the American Flag.

I would be less than honest if I did not admit that this almost universal admiration prompted in me a sense of deep skepticism. I also became quickly aware that very little was actually known about the small businessman, and it was this finding more than any other which led me to take a closer look at the man as well as the legend.

When a writer has finished a book he recognizes, perhaps

better than anyone else, that he could have written a different one. I was especially sensitive to the wide range of possibilities inasmuch as most of the literature on small business consisted mainly of either scattered collections of statistical data or books of a "how-to-start-one" variety. This realization resulted in the arbitrary decision on my part not to concentrate on the strictly economic aspect of small business' problems, since most of this data were easily available to anyone who cared to peruse, say, the files of the House and Senate Committees on Small Business. I have not ignored this aspect of the problem—it would be impossible to do so. I have described many of the empirical realities characterizing small business in Section 2 of Chapter Two, which, if it does not exactly read like a novel, will, I hope, give the interested reader a fairly comprehensive picture of the place of small business in our economy today. I also decided that because of my long interest in the business community of this country I would focus my attention on the *American* small businessman rather than undertake a comparative analysis of small businessmen in three or four different countries. This latter study should someday be done because it will open up a rich mine of information on everything from the varying effects of two-party as against multi-party systems on the political expression of small businessmen to the multiplicity of other factors which lead some of them to back left or liberal political parties and others to become reactionaries. Still another kind of study could give extended treatment to a more specialized problem of our advanced economy. For example, a significant development in recent years has been the role of technology in breaking up old businesses and in many cases creating new small ones. In the electronics industry almost all businesses, until recently, have been small. Here is an important entrepreneurial laboratory, and the pattern of survival would be an interesting one to explore. My own interests and purposes, however, lay elsewhere.

In the last decade or so a rash of social criticism has dealt with the top managerial groups of our society, drawing attention to the large and efficient corporate organizations which now determine so much of the economic life of this country. Small business, on the other hand, has largely been ignored because it was considered inefficient or dying, even though small business-men still account for the greater part of all entrepreneurial activity and for this reason are a potent political force. Thus the book I had in mind was essentially an anatomy of the small businessman, and my principal interest, after describing his economic position, was to analyze the roots and qualities of his political behavior. The study was intended to be suggestive rather than definitive, since I was far more interested in depicting and even speculating about the small businessman in our present society (supported wherever possible by the data available) than in codifying definitions or distinctions. In Chapter Three, for example, I have made use of the ideal-type analysis of Max Weber as a suggestive and ordering device to identify a complex of traits which seemed to me to be meaningful and essential for an understanding of the contemporary small businessman.

I am in debt to many people who helped in the writing of this book. Two graduate students of mine, Katherine Hinckley and Alan Gross, gave me invaluable research assistance and listened patiently to a variety of ideas which I tried out on them for size. Two research grants, one from the Committee on Research in Public Affairs of Stanford University and the other from the Rabinowitz Foundation, made it possible for me to complete the study. I am all the more grateful to them because, at a time when big foundation money is more readily available to team research on a vast scale, they were expressly interested in giving assist-ance to an individual working alone. Miss Shirley Sonne and Mrs. Dorothy Schoenberger deserve special thanks for typing the manuscript in its final form. I also wish to express my appreciation to the editors of the *Political Science Quarterly* and the *Western Political Quarterly* for permission to draw on articles of mine which first appeared in their journals.

My biggest debt of gratitude is to Norman Jacobson, teacher and friend in the profoundest sense of both words. My initial interest in the American small businessman grew out of many long conversations with him, and one idea after another from his active and provocative mind has found its way into many pages of this book.

JOHN H. BUNZEL

Stanford University

Contents

→

THE
AMERICAN
SMALL
BUSINESSMAN

CHAPTER 1

Background

E arly in 1938 President Roosevelt, at the suggestion of the Department of Commerce, extended an invitation to the "rank and file" of small businessmen to hold a conference in Washington and then confer with him at the White House. The President had already talked with a hundred business and labor leaders about the economic recession in the country and what to do about it. Now it was the small businessman's turn.

Until the small businessman came to Washington the White House parleys had been characterized by solemnity and restraint. The conferees would hold preliminary sessions behind closed doors, and whatever plans or programs were then carried to the President remained secret. Co-operation was the keynote of these meetings, and when communiqués were issued after the conferences ended they stressed the fact of mutual understanding.

On February 3 one thousand small businessmen with one thousand ideas descended on a bewildered nation's capital. It was reminiscent, according to *The New York Times,* of the advance on Washington during the NRA code-making days. The delegates gathered in the Department of Commerce auditorium and for three days conducted some of the most tumultuous sessions ever held in that city. Practically no organization or program had been worked out prior to the meetings, and it was soon apparent that opposition to a large portion of the New Deal was the chief bond uniting those who had accepted the President's invitation.

The conference from start to finish was a scene of almost constant turmoil, interrupted only fitfully by a few moments of orderly procedure in response to the emotional appeals of a tired and aging chairman.[1] Parliamentary rules had no standing with the delegates. Men and women who a day or two before had been quietly minding their own stores back home were now all shouting at once and sometimes even in unison. But more frequently they shouted and bid against each other in presenting first their individual grievances and then their personal solutions to the business recession. It took one hour after the gavel fell, calling the first meeting to order, before someone was able to read President Roosevelt's message of greeting. A moving man from Rutherford, New Jersey, tried to open the conference with a prayer but was shouted down in the general bedlam. He yelled above the crowd: "If we can't have a prayer in this God's country, then where can we?" But the chair, either unable to hear the gentleman's call for worship or simply convinced that the Lord would not get the hearing to which He is normally accustomed, refused to recognize him.

The meeting was hardly under way when the public address system broke down. The Secretary of Commerce, in the midst of his welcoming address, was seen to move his lips but could not be heard even by those in the front rows. When deafening

[1] I have drawn liberally from the accounts of this conference that appeared in *The New York Times* on February 1, 2, 3, 4, and 13, 1938.

shouts of "louder" filled the hall the Secretary pleaded for everyone to sit down, only to be told "No" by a group in the rear. When the loudspeaker system was repaired, the booming voice of the Secretary was heard as he said to a battery of surrounding cameramen: "Why take pictures of me? Why don't you take pictures of this splendid group of American citizens?" The Assistant Secretary of Commerce innocently introduced a Cleveland shoe wholesaler and proposed him as temporary chairman of the conference. The uproar that ensued, according to *The New York Times,* was a harbinger. A metal products dealer from Springdale, Pennsylvania, sprang to his feet and charged that the shoe salesman was "hand picked" by the administration to guide the discussion along favorable lines. Demands were made that the chairman-elect state his qualifications, and, above the din of the debate and gavel pounding, he was finally able to satisfy the conference by saying he employed only fifteen workers.

The first speaker to gain the recognition of the chair introduced himself as the representative of the National Council of Independent Business Associates. He had not gone far into a speech about small businessmen and how little they received "when supping at the government table" when someone shouted: "Give that speech to the newspapers." A lady from Brooklyn tried to demand equal rights for women, but her voice was drowned out by shouts from men. "All the men want to do is talk," she said. "We women have something to offer"—which must certainly be viewed as a generous and courageous gesture under the circumstances.

The conference suddenly flared into a disruptive climax over what reporter Milton Bracker called the old issue of New York *vs.* The Rest of the Nation. According to Bracker, while throats strained and a baffled chairman pleaded futilely, a phalanx of seventeen delegates from the metropolitan area spread themselves across the front of the Department of Commerce auditorium and demanded to be heard on behalf of the millions whom they said they represented. With equal raucousness and superior numbers, non-New Yorkers popped up all over the floor, chanting: "New York, sit down. New York, sit down." Ultimately a Philadelphian, who defended the delegates from the metropolis because they were among his customers, went to the aid of a hysterical clothier with such gusto that it required Captain E. J. Sullivan and two patrolmen to throttle his oratory and drag him outside. A vibration control man from New York City, cigar in hand and spats on his shoes, tried unsuccessfully to offer a proposal. It was never heard. A woman marched to the head of the center aisle and shouted: "I want one man and one woman from each State to be allowed to speak. Am I right?" Apparently she was wrong, for Captain Sullivan, "resplendent in gold braid," had to escort her to her seat.

The afternoon session started as if everyone was talked out.

Nathan Schlessel, Brooklyn sportswear man, actually dozed for a moment, with a cigar in his mouth, while speakers from States beginning with A and C had three-minute says. A flashlight bulb woke him.

The New Yorkers showed their first sign of impatience when Michigan was called.

"New York!" a fretful delegate yelled.

"Mr. Chairman, I'm from Brooklyn, N.Y.," began another.

"You got plenty time," grunted someone on the other side of the room.

Then at 4:20 Mr. Roth (the Chairman) called New York and the seventeen who wanted to speak jumped into line like an overmanned football team.

"Sit down!" roared a Westerner.

"Pass up New York!" ordered a Southerner.

"Mr. Chairman, I represent 500,000"—began a man from nobody knows where.

"Brooklyn, Brooklyn," thundered another in the rear.

Mr. Roth banged the gavel and remarked that New York had had at least three speakers in the morning.

"Remember—New York got 12,000,000 people," one of them argued.

"For the time being we'll pass up New York," ruled the Chairman.

Protest swelled wildly.

"New York, sit down," began the chant.

"Take the Conference to Brooklyn."

"That's unfair, Mr. Chairman."

"Aw, forget it."

Mrs. Catherine R. Dobbs of Barberton, Ohio, threw in a word for the big city men. Then, at the end of the front row, a short, dark man began the yelling which precipitated the climax.

"I've spent my last dollar to get here and I'll be heard," he screamed. "Gentlemen of the press, gentlemen of the New York press, I appeal to you—"

"Mr. Trotsky, sit down," advised the small-towners.

The New Yorker, Harry Cashdan, tapered off a bit. But a thick-set man in a brown suit, with his name on a placard held in front of him, took up the battle.

"I'm not from New York, I'm from Philadelphia," he began. "But I do business with the men from New York and I—"

The "throw him out" chorus surged everywhere. The Philadelphian, who said he was A. S. Shafer, building contractor, waved his arms and yelled louder. He was engulfed. He fought back. Captain Sullivan and his men sped from the platform. Thus Mr. Shafer was ejected.

R. L. Freid of Pittsburgh chided the non-New Yorkers with: "If our President was good enough to invite so many from New York, they ought to be heard," and someone countered with: "Mr. Chairman, New York thinks he's the whole United States."

Ultimately a New Englander broached a plan whereby the starting time of the main conference will be moved up from 10:30 to 10 tomorrow morning. The extra time, among other things, was expected to allow for a few more New York speeches.

Mr. Dobbs suggested a night session, but Mr. Roth

told his audience they needed a good night's sleep more than anything else, and he probably was right.[2]

The Washington "town meeting" of small businessmen revealed the inherently difficult problems small business faces while at the same time pointing out the multiple ingredients of the small businessman's ideology. SMALL BUSINESS BAITS NEW YORKERS, ran a headline on the front page of *The New York Times*. DOMINATION IS CHARGED. CALIFORNIANS AND OTHERS FROM FAR WEST STALK OUT IN UPROAR AGAINST BIG CITY MEN. All this is part of the frontier agrarian tradition. It reflects the distrust of city life that in the past led Tom Watson to point his pitchfork at the hordes of immigrants—"the scum of creation" —who were invading our urban centers, or William Jennings Bryan and Henry George to preach their respective sermons about the evil city, the home of moral corruption. The alien ways of the big city are still regarded by many with suspicion and fear in much the same way that anything new or foreign haunts the nativist American mind. Most of the small businessmen and women attending the Washington conference wore little American flags, shaped like bows. Then someone made the discovery that they had been made in Japan, *The New York Times* reported, "cutting noticeably the visible display of patriotism."

Thus the ingredients are all there in the antics of the President's conference: the Populist ferment of plain citizens as they shout in behalf of the independent proprietor; the energy and incessant activity that are impatient of all restraints and finely drawn distinctions; the protests of Main Street against Wall Street and the iniquities of the big metropolis; the demand for direct and positive action to halt the bureaucratic bungling of an omnipotent, impersonal government. A traveling salesman

[2] Article by Milton Bracker: *The New York Times*, February 4, 1938.

at the conference, claiming authority to speak for at least twelve Southern States, complained that the main thing wrong with the nation was that "forty-eight States are a-pullin' and a-haulin' and a-cuttin' at each others' throats instead of a-pullin' and a-haulin' together." The best thing for the country, he said, was to repeal some of the laws already enacted and enact no more. This is part of the cry and the appeal of the small businessman as he registers his anger at the concentrated might that has entrapped all America in its industrial vortex. The agrarian justice of a simpler day has been traduced by an organized power structure that, he feels, has clipped the wings of the little man in order to feather its own nest. Miss Julia M. Ring, the proprietor of an agency furnishing watchmen for ships in Philadelphia, echoed the sentiments of small business-men everywhere when she asked that the government pay a little more attention to the plight of the middle class and a little less to that of the underprivileged. "The middle class," she said, "is the backbone of the nation." If there is a moral it can be put quite simply: the small businessman represents the last stand of the self-made man who at one time, as Frederick Jackson Turner said, was the frontier man's ideal as well as the kind of man all men might become.

In one of his reports to the Senate Small Business Committee Senator James Murray remarked that to the people of this country "small business is a combination of social values, a pattern of civic life, a free society, and a healthy competitive community. It is the small businessman who is the foundation of the home town's growth and development." [3] It is a familiar portrait, one that is painted in broad, sweeping strokes with

[3] *U.S. Senate Small Business Committee—Its Record and Outlook* (Progress Report of the Special Committee To Study Problems of American Small Business, 79th Congress, 1st Session, Report No. 47, February 12, 1945).

generous splashes of red, white, and blue. As a living expression of the American Dream and its democratic promise the small businessman is seen as a mainstay of the middle class whose investment in political democracy and free enterprise is unequaled and whose very survival is at stake. Moreover, small business is viewed as a social and political stabilizer by virtue of its very numbers, which act as a safeguard against the total control of society by big business.[4] Since only the continued existence of a vigorous and independent small business community can prevent the development of concentrated power in any form, the small businessman emerges as one of the great bulwarks of a democratic society.

Yet there is more than a touch of irony in this picture. What do we actually know about the small businessman? What are his hopes—and his fears? What does he believe in, both for himself and his country? A paradox of the present political scene is that the small businessman, to whom so many appeals and testimonials are continuously being made by office seekers of every complexion, is really an ambiguous and in many ways unknown political quantity. In the pages that follow an attempt is made to look at the small businessman against the background of our industrial social order with the aim of discovering the political values and beliefs to which he is fundamentally committed. He may be, as many have contended, a younger brother of the big businessman, a capitalist in his own right, merely trying to make a profit. But as description this falls far short of providing a picture in depth. It lacks the various perspectives to bring him ultimately into sharper relief.

A serious economic problem for small business today, and one which serves to illuminate the larger dilemma facing all small businessmen, is the supermarket revolution. While there

[4] A. D. H. Kaplan: *Small Business: Its Place and Problems* (New York: McGraw-Hill; 1948), pp. 3–4.

are still some 200,000 mom-and-pop food stores in the country, they do only 6 per cent of the grocery business and are vanishing at the rate of about 6,000 a year. It was not too long ago when a persevering young man could start a career in retailing with a small store or even a pushcart. Time was, too, when the butcher, the baker, the candlestick maker—and the grocer—were pillars of the community.[5] Now the same young man is much more likely to get a job with big business as a corporation employee. To the small businessman the trend toward consolidation and chains spells nothing less than disaster. "It spells the day when no young man in this country may be able to stop in the middle of a block, look at an empty building, and say: 'Here I will build my future.' "[6] To be deprived of such an opportunity, he feels, is to be deprived of the benefits of free enterprise, of freedom of choice. In keeping with this feeling a national small business organization at the end of the Second World War circulated a story of a veteran returning home only to find that the shop on West 100 Main Street where he used to work was out of business. "Johnny" looked up his old boss, who told him how the government had forced the shop to go out of business. His boss told him, however, that he might be able to get unemployment compensation.

> But, Boss, I don't want no unemployment compensation, and I don't want no job from Uncle Sam. . . . Y'mean to tell me that all I've got to look forward to is unemployment compensation or a straightjacket job in a government-run plant, where I'll be just a number instead of a free American citizen? Nuts! I want a chance to work and own a factory of my own someday, like you did, and

[5] See Sidney Margolius: "Super Business of Supermarkets," *The New York Times* (Sunday Magazine Section), March 29, 1959.

[6] Edward Wimmer: *Freedom Depends on Business Independence* (pamphlet distributed by the National Federation of Independent Business, Inc., based on a talk delivered before the National Conference of Independent Shoe Retailers, in Chicago, on October 24, 1953).

be somebody in town, like you were. . . . Let me tell you one thing, Boss: if other people want to live the way we lived before the war, they can if they want to badly enough to work for it, like my Dad did, and like I had to work for my jalopy and my tootlehorn and my Sunday suit and extras. If they won't work for things they won't get them.

And believe me, Boss, those of us that went abroad were plenty broadened by our contact with the foreigners we saw, and most of us are pretty well fed up with the idea that we want to live with them, share and share alike, and call them brothers. And we can't tell them how they've got to run their countries when we let a bunch of screwballs run ours to hell.[7]

The anxieties of the small businessman are manifested in a number of significant ways, leading to the constant and urgent demand that something be done to preserve the liberty and freedom of the individual. He clings to an image of an earlier time when free individuals acted in their own behalf, unhindered by the State. Yet he lives in a society stratified into a large number of organized economic groups and classes, wherein the government is recognized as a problem-solving institution performing useful and constructive services. Just what it is he wants and how he proposes to get it is both the hope and the despair of the contemporary small businessman. Still thinking in terms of his jalopy, tootlehorn, Sunday suit, and extras, he poses the very real question of whether or not he is out of step with our modern industrial society.

[7] Undated circular entitled: *When Johnny Yank Comes Home* (printed and distributed by the Conference of American Small Business Organizations).

CHAPTER II

Small Business

and the

American Heritage

1
                         The small businessman, in one
sense at least, is in an enviable position. If the folklore that has
been built up around him is any indication, he appears to have
few enemies and is, in fact, something of a national hero. In his
own way he represents the independence, freedom, and perseverance that have long been identified with the American way of
doing things. Living in a country that places heavy emphasis on
material success and pecuniary rewards, the small businessman
has managed to be a symbol of success even in times when he
has not, in point of fact, been financially successful. If the myth
is sometimes stronger than the reality, it is only because it re-
inforces the tradition of individualism upon which so much in
American life has been dependent.

    In many ways the small businessman today is in a better
position than the farmer to win the sympathy of those who still
applaud the individual efforts of an industrious man as well as
the fruits that may come from bitter struggle. When A. W. Griswold remarked that "a self-sufficient farm in our time is more

likely to be a haunt of illiteracy and malnutrition than a well-spring of democracy," he was commenting on much more than the decline of the farmer as the central figure in American society. If his words reflect a feeling of personal disappointment, they also express a mood of caution and apprehension in the face of the severe changes which have been wrought by the industrial revolution. However, it is unnecessary here to describe the development of the farmer's way of life in the past fifty or sixty years. It is a story that has been told and documented many times and its central theme is quite clear: farming today is no longer Hamlin Garland's man with a hoe working on his own few acres of land, but an industry that has become an important segment of the business world. The image of the farmer as the clearest representative of the spirit of independence and self-sufficiency, if it has not disappeared, has certainly become somewhat blurred.[1]

C. Wright Mills makes the point that at the beginning of the twentieth century it was the new "captain of industry" who emerged as a hero because, through determination, ambition, and audacity, it was he who was shaping the new society. He was following in the tradition of the self-made man who once again made good in the American way, with the added advantage and good fortune that this time *his* spoils were colossal. Today, however, he has been replaced by such impersonal and unheroic figures as the absentee owner and the professional manager, and as a result the rugged and determined individualism of a bygone day has long since vanished. With the passing of the family farm and the independent farmer from the center

---

[1] "Farming, until recently regarded as the epitome of independent individual enterprise and the free market, has been brought under a system of production controls, subsidies, price supports, and integrated marketing, all of which add agriculture to the other nationally managed areas of our society. Small business is thus left as the only relatively 'unadministered' sector of the economy." Kaplan: op. cit., p. 3.

of the American scene it is the small businessman who remains
to perpetuate the tradition and preserve a place for the "independent people," waging an uphill, if not impossible, fight
against the odds of bigness, organization, and power. Upon his
shoulders "rests the hope of those who hold to the Jeffersonian
ideal of a typically small and self-sufficient proprietor as the
mainstay of our political and economic democracy." [2] But the
picture is overdrawn, for the truth is that the small businessman
is handicapped from the start. In much the same sense that
some men today are a hundred years ahead of their time in
their ideas and beliefs, the small businessman in many ways has
been lingering on for fifty years or so *after* his time. Consequently he can never really live up to the heritage that has been
invented for him.[3]

The small businessman had an important stake in the
American Revolution. The British system of mercantilism had
effectively prevented the growth of any colonial business in
spite of America's abundant supply of willing workers, raw
materials, a buying market, and potential capital. The colonial
economy was tied to England's through the powerful Board of
Trade, which exercised almost complete economic authority
over everything from investments to recommendations on legislation.[4] Both big business and small business gave support to the
movement for American independence, although the hope of
the former was essentially to achieve equality with England in
commerce and to be free of restrictions. When the big bour-

[2] Joseph D. Phillips: *Little Business in the American Economy*
(Urbana, Ill.: University of Illinois Press; 1958), p. 7.

[3] I wish to acknowledge here my indebtedness to Professor Mills's
study, *White Collar* (New York: Oxford University Press; 1951). His
section on the "old Middle Classes" is an excellent portrait of the small
entrepreneur and his world of "middle-class capitalism," and much of my
own discussion draws on his observations.

[4] Louis M. Hacker: *The Shaping of the American Tradition* (New
York: Columbia University Press; 1947), pp. 124–30.

geoisie did not get the relief they hoped for, they were caught between the wishes of the great majority of the people for complete freedom and their own desire to maintain an economic dominance which could best be insured by a continued alliance with England. The big bourgeoisie gave up the fight, as Lewis Corey has said, because they only wanted freedom from the restrictions imposed by an alien ruling class. Democracy was excluded; the aim was an oligarchy of big property. It was the small businessmen who were left to carry on the conflict to its ultimate revolutionary end. "The middle class wanted freedom of enterprise in terms of independence of the privileges and restrictions imposed by the colonial ruling class. The aim was democracy of small property." [5]

The mythology that surrounds the small businessman has its origin not only in the pioneer virtues of ambition and self-reliance that marked the frontier civilization of nineteenth-century America, but in the system of property arrangements which underlay the structure of that society. Private property in the period around 1830 was widespread and the recognized basis for power as well as for freedom. There were people, it is true, who owned no property at all, just as there was a part of the country where slavery was commonly accepted as God's and nature's way of handling things. Nor should it be forgotten that the new ruling class recognized the importance of birth,

[5] Lewis Corey: *The Crisis of the Middle Class* (New York: Covici-Friede; 1935), p. 77. The Sons of Liberty movement of Samuel Adams was composed mostly of these middle-class businessmen. In order to assure the wealthy merchants that the movement of independence was not really so radical, the "proletariat mechanics" were excluded. Ibid., p. 80. Gradually the lower classes came to the support of the middle class in order to gain their own freedom to advance to the middle-class level. They resented the increasing power of the established shopkeepers and craftsmen who had formed something of a guild system. It was the support of the lower class which spurred the British on to even stronger restrictions and spurred the Americans on to more radical movements. See Hacker: op. cit., pp. 167–9.

education, and wealth as aristocratic qualities peculiarly fitting them, in contrast to the lower orders of society, for their claim to power and rulership. Yet, as Mills has said: "The most important single fact about the society of small entrepreneurs was that a substantial portion of the people owned property with which they worked." [6]

The ideal of universal small property was one to which Thomas Jefferson in particular was dedicated. To him the farmers were "the chosen people of God, if He ever had a chosen people," because they exemplified, in Lockean terms, the happy mixture of a man's personality and his property, and, as a result, they were free. Thus the moral importance of the farmers in America and "of their rightful claim upon that society for their fair share of its production, power and prestige" consists in the familiar assumption that "the essential nature of American society at its best derives from the rural community of free, independent land-owning, God-fearing farmers." [7] In his first inaugural address Jefferson summarized his economic philosophy by calling for "a wise and frugal government, which shall restrain men from injuring one another, which shall leave them otherwise free to regulate their own pursuits of industry and improvement, and shall not take from the mouth of labor the bread that it has earned." He was voicing the conviction that, by letting nature take its course, the natural forces of economics would restore freedom and equality. Although his ideas were aimed at the farmers, it was a philosophy which the small entrepreneurs could easily adopt.

The observation has been made that it would be interesting and revealing to discover when, how, and why the change in

[6] Mills: op. cit., p. 7.

[7] John M. Gaus and L. O. Wolcott: *Public Administration and the United States Department of Agriculture* (Chicago: Public Administration Service; 1940), pp. 17–18, quoted in V. O. Key, Jr.: *Politics, Parties and Pressure Groups* (New York: Thomas Y. Crowell Co.; 1947), p. 18.

ideology occurred that substituted the businessman for the Jeffersonian ideal of the independent farmer.[8] However, this presumed "change" is in many respects more of an extension than an alteration since the farmer cannot claim to be the exclusive heir to the virtues of self-interest and independence that were characteristic of this free-market society. Many of the antecedents of small business are deep in the same traditions of American rural life. Furthermore, the American farmer was always an enterpriser, and entrepreneurial success as well as individual initiative were valued and nourished in the rural Yankee world. Unlike the European peasant, the American farmer did not emerge from a long struggle out of feudalism, but almost from the beginning invested his energies in the infant economic order that permitted and encouraged him to add to his capital holdings, to speculate—to become, in the words of Veblen, a "cultivator of the main chance as well as of the fertile soil." [9]

But the man of enterprise was not only the farmer. He was the general country storekeeper like Peter Smith of Utica, whose friend John Jacob Astor imported British goods in return for the furs and ginseng that Smith collected for Astor. He was the shipowner-captain who collected his own cargoes and sold them at whatever port he could find buyers, the Missouri trader who loaded and accompanied freight wagons for the Santa Fe, and the Illinois farmer who brought his pork, wheat, and lumber by flatboat down the Mississippi to New Orleans. The merchant, the moneylender, the shipper, the tradesman, as well as the farmer, were all part of the world of the small entrepreneur, committed to the belief that individual freedom and enlightened self-interest were the true basis for a just social order.

[8] Kurt Mayer: "Small Business as a Social Institution," *Social Research* (September 1947), pp. 340–1.
[9] See Mills: op. cit., p. 4.

The potential for a burgeoning capitalist economy was present, and small business thrived and reached the peak of its strength in the 1820's. The main form of production was "cottage production," which meant that the producers in this period were not a "factory population." It was not a system of social production but one of independent producers whose class loyalties, to use Hacker's terms, were those of the petty bourgeoisie. With 80 per cent of the population in this class, the predominance of the laissez-faire theory of governmental control was obvious. About 75 per cent of the people were farmers, yet many combined farming with production in the home or in small stores.

> Out of this society of small producers rose the American Dream. It was a dream of liberty and progress moving irresistibly onward to new and higher fulfillment. Most vital was the ideal, determining all the other ideals, of the liberty and equality of men owning their independent means of livelihood.[1]

Andrew Jackson came to power in this age of individual enterprises, swept along by the democratic upsurge which was closely linked to the ambitions of the small capitalist. His veto of the United States Bank, far from being part of a radical leveling philosophy or a proposal to reconstruct the society along different lines, was designed as another move to assist aspiring capitalists in making the most of their opportunities. Unlike the years of the New Deal when regulation of business monopoly became an urgent consideration, the Jacksonian period crystallized the philosophy of a rising middle class and sought to release the energies of independent and creative enterprise. The Jeffersonian philosophy was given an urban garb.

To be enlightened about one's self-interest is at the core of the American tradition, and its seed is in what Mills aptly calls

[1] Corey: op. cit., p. 113.

the "self-balancing society" of the 1820's and 1830's. What a man could do by himself, through his own energy and determination, was the yardstick by which his capacity to advance was ultimately measured, and what he would do for himself, it was firmly believed, was almost certain to be better done than anything done in his behalf.[2] The Protestant ethic of hard work and individual initiative, as Franklin and others had vigorously maintained, produced a breed of men whose independence and freedom were equally matched by strength of character and nobility of purpose. In one of the standard works on small business, which is dedicated simply to "The American Way of Life," it is made clear that the small businessman is the personification of what is most free and enterprising in this country. "For the development of self-reliance, for *making men* as well as money, small business excels. Small business suits the personality and independent attitude of many. Thousands of individuals who would chafe under the restrictions of employment" find the idea of being their "own boss" much to their liking.[3]

Thus the traditional outlook and values of the small businessman have roots deep in the rural society of yeoman farmers and their suppliers and merchants. It was the American Civil War, as Lewis Mumford has written, that "cut a white gash through the history of the country." In a stroke it dramatized the changes that had taken place during the preceding twenty

[2] In this connection Laski, among others, claimed that this "enlightened self-interest" is "the parent of experimentation," wherein "an accumulation of small acts of self-denial enables any energetic citizen to advance his fortunes. This is perhaps why it seems to take a great crisis—world war, for example—to evoke great sacrifices from Americans; the drama needs to be staged on a vast scale before the average man thinks far beyond the cultivation of his own garden." Harold J. Laski: *The American Democracy* (New York: Viking Press; 1948), p. 15.

[3] Pearce C. Kelley and Kenneth Lawyer: *How To Organize and Operate a Small Business* (New York: Prentice Hall; 1949), p. 11. My italics.

or thirty years. Industrial production had begun to develop with startling new advances in technology. A number of corporations, savings banks, and insurance companies made their appearance. Transportation facilities were expanding rapidly, opening up vast new potential markets. Imports were increasing with new capital from the Western gold strikes, and the influx of immigrants in the 1840's brought cheap labor into the American economy. The depression of 1837–43 illuminated the weaknesses of independent capitalism, and by the middle of the century there were clear signs that the time of the small businessman as the dominant economic force in America would soon be passing.[4] The new technology made the centralization of industrial power easy by requiring factory production. As Corey put it:

> The accumulation of capital inexorably destroys the conditions of independent enterprise. Either small capitalists became bigger or new capitalists started new and bigger enterprises, or both: but, in either case, it meant the progressive slaughter of small capitalists.[5]

The Civil War ended the domination of the American economy by small-scale capitalism, and in the period immediately following, business was free to expand along with the new technological advances. For all practical purposes the old America was demolished. Industrialism had come swiftly, had transformed the practices of agriculture, had encouraged "a mad exploitation of minerals, oil, natural gas and coal, and had made the unscrupulous master of finance, fat with war profits, the central figure of the situation." [6] In terms of the traditional rivalry between Hamilton and Jefferson, it signaled the com-

[4] Hacker: op. cit., pp. 248–9.
[5] Corey: op. cit., p. 124.
[6] Lewis Mumford: *The Golden Day* (New York: Boni & Liveright; 1926), pp. 158–9.

plete defeat of Jefferson and the beginning of the triumph of industrial capitalism.[7] To the small entrepreneur, whether farmer or small businessman, the most significant economic change was the increasing industrialization of private enterprise, with the corporation replacing the individual as the principal unit of production. "There is no other period in the nation's history," Richard Hofstadter has written, "when politics seems so completely dwarfed by economic change, none in which the life of the country rests so completely in the hands of the industrial entrepreneur." [8]

In spite of the rapid shift of economic power to big business, the American Dream was still a symbol for many people. The tremendous influence of the big businessman in the 1890's brought William Jennings Bryan to the front of the political stage, and his Democratic platform of 1896 echoed much of the Jeffersonian ring. It was not a call for a sweeping revision of the nation's economic life through government intervention but rather an appeal to the government to keep its hands off. Bryan's plea to return to bimetallism was an attempt to improve the monetary plight of the small entrepreneur and to preserve American individualism. The entire Populist movement exemplified the confusion of the middle classes. A farmer

[7] See S. E. Morison and H. S. Commager: *The Growth of the American Republic* (New York: Oxford University Press; 1942), Vol. II, p. 123. "Within two generations of Jefferson's death the value of American manufactured products was about treble that of the agricultural, and the spokesmen of big business were appealing to his laissez-faire principles against the regulatory ideals of his rival Hamilton. For a hundred years America has progressed economically in the direction that Alexander Hamilton wished: that of a diversified, self-sufficing nation, ruled by the people who control the nation's property. When the census of 1920 recorded over nine million industrial wage-earners producing commodities of the value of some sixty-two billion dollars, and over fifty per cent of the population crowded into towns and cities, surely Hamilton was able to collect some bets from Jefferson in the Elysian Fields!" Ibid.

[8] Richard Hofstadter: *The American Political Tradition* (New York: Alfred A. Knopf; 1948), p. 162.

movement basically, it enlisted the support of urban groups and demanded state action to protect small property and create more favorable conditions of competition for small enterprise. But the urban workers were rapidly becoming economically dependent upon big business. Consequently they were unable to give unqualified support to either the free competition of Populism or the bimetallism of Bryan. The material power of big business had so expanded over the past few decades that it had seriously affected the previously strong status of small business.

> By the 1900's, the society of independent producers was almost completely destroyed, while the middle class was a minority of the people and no longer included all its old elements. . . . Workers were separated economically from the middle class. . . . Dependent salaried employees now greatly outnumbered the independent enterprisers. . . . Most of the salaried employees and professionals were a product of large-scale industry and directly dependent upon it.[9]

The last decades of the nineteenth century and the turn of the twentieth represented more than the passing of the frontier and what Parrington was fond of calling its "coonskin democracy." A country whose way of life had been predominantly agricultural and mercantile was rapidly becoming a nation of bustling industrialism. Americans now had to adjust themselves to economic and social changes far more abrupt and pervasive than ever before. At the same time they were confronted for the first time in their national experience with a challenge to many of their most cherished beliefs and philosophical assumptions.

> They were now to be required not only to articulate their economy to a new technology and adjust their society to

[9] Corey: op. cit., p. 141.

new ways of life—that was a familiar task—but to make their politics and morals conform to new scientific and philosophical precepts. Under the impact of these new forces, the note of confidence which had long characterized the American accent gave way to doubt, self-assurance to bewilderment, and resolution to confusion.[1]

Political corruption, slums, monopoly, racial minorities, inequality of wealth, urbanization, big business power—these were some of the problems with which Americans were now faced. The 1890's were marked by bitter class conflict, including a series of violent strikes, the Haymarket riot, and the panic of 1893. It is not surprising that workers, farmers, and small businessmen, in the words of Henry Adams, "died like flies under the strain." The Populist movement emerged as the last refuge of discontent and protest, with the independent farmer and shopkeeper as its heroes and concentrated wealth and bigness as its enemies. The protest was made "not merely against injustice to farmers but against injustice to all common men. Agrarianism spoke in the name of all. The enemy which it challenged was power." [2]

The advance of industrial capitalism did more, however, than sweep over the angry protests of dirt farmers and small shopkeepers. It dealt the final blow to a way of life whose primary virtues were simplicity, independence, and unrestricted freedom. In the America of 1820, approximately 80 per cent of the people owned something called "property" and made a living from it that was relatively peaceful and private. A little over a century later 80 per cent of the people drew a wage or

---

[1] H. S. Commager: *The American Mind* (New Haven: Yale University Press; 1950), p. 43.

[2] Grant McConnell: *The Decline of Agrarian Democracy* (Berkeley & Los Angeles: University of California Press; 1953), p. 8. For one of the most insightful and rewarding discussions of "the folklore of Populism," see Richard Hofstadter: *The Age of Reform* (New York: Alfred A. Knopf; 1956), pp. 60–93.

salary check, worked for someone else, and were a part of some factory or similar business organization. The picture of a middle-class democracy or of small independent producers was now growing dim.[3] The "old middle class" had become the "new middle class" of "technical-managerial, professional, and clerical employees new in its numbers, in the variety and significance of its occupation, and in being a typical class product of large-scale collective economic activity." [4]

It was inevitable that the mushroom growth of big business would produce a reaction on the part of the independent enterprisers and others of the middle class who were deprived of so much of their former power. Theodore Roosevelt, drawing a line "against misconduct, not against wealth," sought to regulate rather than destroy big business.[5] Woodrow Wilson, on the other hand, resented the ethics of big business and its size. His New Freedom was an attempt to restore competitive conditions in business, so that the little man could rise up the economic ladder. The political discussion in this period, or at least a large part of it, was between two different methods of holding property. If Roosevelt took a more realistic approach, Wilson better expressed the ultimate hopes of small business. Yet the idealism of Wilson was doomed along with the rest of the "small business philosophy" by the relentless

---

[3] "The middle class of small independent enterprisers grew in absolute numbers from 1870 to 1910 but underwent a relative decline; since 1910 the numerical size of the class has remained virtually stationary while it has considerably shrunk as a proportion of all gainfully occupied persons. Its economic power has shrunk even more than its numerical strength because of increasing monopoly domination." Lewis Corey: "The Middle Class," *Antioch Review* (Spring 1945), p. 2.

[4] Ibid., p. 10.

[5] Although Theodore Roosevelt was not a vigorous supporter of small business property he nevertheless recognized the fears of the middle class and took early steps to calm them. See Hofstadter: *The American Political Tradition*, pp. 226–31.

press of technology, money, and war. Specifically, the strong position of big business was demonstrated by the failure of the antitrust movement, a failure accounted for "by the impracticability of divorcing a recognized principle from the consequences to which it necessarily leads." [6] It was a matter of big business beating small business at its own game, with the doctrine of freedom of individual enterprise in this case encouraging the concentration of power. Small businessmen increasingly faced the alternative of either giving up their tenuous economic position or suffering stiffer competition than ever from big business. Herbert Hoover was a prominent victim of this problem. He had grown up in an era which had witnessed the phenomenal growth of the American economy under a relatively uncomplicated system of laissez-faire and was a strong spokesman for its virtues. The result was that he was disinclined to deal effectively with the depression crisis through the use of governmental action.

The enormous changes which transformed the United States economically and socially as it moved from a pre-industrial to an industrial society posed many urgent problems for the small businessman. The entrepreneurial world of the nineteenth century was radically different from the modern world of big business or what is sometimes called "mass society." Agriculture had been replaced by industry, with an accompanying complex interdependence and a new employer-employee relationship. Locke's theory of property ownership as the basis of individual freedom had been adopted by big business to justify its own position. In a more specific sense, new large-scale monopoly replaced the old monopoly (a monopoly which the local merchant once held effectively over the economy of his own town) by the spread of syndicated stores and lower

[6] "Middle Class," *Encyclopedia of the Social Sciences*, p. 410.

prices.[7] A century ago there were no severe political restraints imposed on a man's activities for the simple reason that there was no political power in society strong enough or centralized enough to impose such restraints—and, what is more, no one felt the need for them.[8] Not only is this no longer true today, but as far as the small businessman is concerned, the liberty of the individual to stand on his own feet and prove himself on his own terms has been replaced by the corroding influences of paternalism and protection. His feelings are similar to those of Jefferson in another day who, along with John Taylor, could oppose pension plans or any taxation schemes designed to distribute income more equitably because it was felt such paternalizing would corrupt men's souls by making them more dependent on others and less enthusiastic about the value of hard work. In a later chapter we shall examine more closely the affinity of the Jeffersonian dislike of cities and commercialism with the small businessman's contemporary attitudes toward industrialism and urbanization. For the present it need only be said that he does

[7] Mills: op. cit., pp. 36–7. Mills has observed that it is ironic that this "natural monopoly" was broken in large part by precisely those agencies of mass distribution which the small businessman now denounces as "unfair competitors." The other side of the problem is reflected in the kind of control which any large industry holds over a town to the point where the economy of the whole area is dependent upon it. Detroit is a good example of a large city whose general economic health depends on the welfare of the automobile industry.

[8] "It is often said that [the enterprising individual] 'overthrew mercantilism,' and this is true in the narrower meaning of the term. He did throw off a king and enthrone in his place the free market. This market did not reign without support or without the exercise of political authority, but economic authority was dominant, and it was automatic, largely unseen, and, in fact, seldom experienced as authority at all. Political authority, the traditional mode of social integration, became a loose framework of protection rather than a centralized engine of domination; it was largely unseen and for long periods very slight. The legal framework guaranteed and encouraged the order of small property, but the government was the guardian, not the manager, of this order." Ibid., p. 10.

not always have a high regard for the more mechanized and centralized society of the twentieth century, where one's individual liberty has been lost because of a pernicious "concentration on security" which, he feels, "is perhaps the greatest enemy this country faces." [9]

2

The virtual demise of the independent farmer in America has led to a growing interest in the small businessman, his entrepreneurial aspirations, and the general life and hard times of individual enterprise. He is heralded as being its last representative.

Much ink, more paper, and rather astounding amounts of both private and Congressional energy have been expended in arguments over the proper place of small business in the American economy. Regardless of their eloquence and even importance, however, such arguments are meaningless without reference to a picture of what the role of small business actually is. How is it holding up both absolutely and in relation to the past? What are its problems and just how acute are they?

The first step in painting any portrait is to locate the subject—in this case, an exceptionally elusive one. When the average person talks about small business he is likely to have in mind any kind of business that is locally owned and operated and in which the owner is the "boss": a grocery store with a few employees, the corner bank in the small city or town, or even perhaps a machine shop or manufacturing plant with twelve or fifteen employees. Someone from a big city who is accustomed to large department stores and factories would probably include somewhat larger enterprises in his conception of

[9] William Benton: "Young Man, Be Your Own Boss," *Reader's Digest* (September 1944), p. 31.

small business. In Chicago a factory with seventy-five or even a hundred employees might be regarded as small business, but in a town of two or three thousand people it might easily be looked upon as big business.

No generally accepted definition of small business exists, and it is quite obvious that the same criteria cannot be used in different segments of the economy. Whatever set of criteria may be chosen, the resulting numbers are to a certain degree arbitrary; the resulting delineation of the universe is neither sharp nor unequivocal.[1]

It is not surprising that the term "small business" is sometimes used as a slogan rather than as a description of an area of enterprise—in the words of Senator Murray, as "the way for ambitious but poor men to climb the ladder from day labor to business ownership." It is looked upon not only as a form of business activity but as a "veritable way of life." [2]

[1] See *Small Business—Its Role and Its Problems* (Washington, D.C.: Economic Research Department, Chamber of Commerce of the United States; 1953).

[2] Rudolph L. Weissman: *Small Business and Venture Capital* (New York: Harper & Brothers; 1945), p. 160. In pointing out that small business, to most Americans, is a "way of life" as much as anything else, Weissman recalls that in the catalogue of values traced by the Lynds in their classic *Middletown in Transition* (New York: Harcourt, Brace; 1937) "these thought patterns were found conspicuous: 'That American business will always lead the world. Here in the United States, as nowhere in the world, the little business and the big business exist side by side and are a testimonial to the soundness of the American way of life. . . . That the small businessman is the backbone of American business. . . . In no country in the world are there so many opportunities open to the little fellow as in the United States.' According to the Lynds," comments Weissman, "most Middletown business people think of their city as a community of small business and regard the idea as a virtue. If this and similar evidence is accepted, it means that the roots of small business are deep. . . ." Ibid. In the prose of the politician this feeling is sometimes dressed up with more than a little gaudiness. "It is this American business, so largely made up of small and independent enterprises," stated Senator Murray, "which makes its great appeal to our fighting men in camps and on the battle lines. This is the America they

Notwithstanding such difficulties, myriad definitions have been put forth. Qualitatively, they have included local ownership, absence or near-absence of paid labor, and a limited expansion motive. In quantitative terms, the Senate Small Business Committee has defined a small business as one with fewer than 250 employees, $500,000 in total assets, and $1,000,000 in business volume. The Small Business Administration is somewhat more explicit:

> For business loan purposes, the SBA defines a small business as one that is independently owned and operated and non-dominant in its field, and that meets more detailed standards developed by the Agency. These generally are as follows:
> A manufacturing concern is considered small if its average employment in the preceding four calendar quarters was 250 or fewer persons, including employees of affiliates, and is considered large if its average employment in this period was more than 1,000 persons. If its average employment was more than 250 but not more than 1,000 persons, it may be considered either small or large, depending on the employment size which the SBA has developed for its particular industry.
> A wholesale concern is classified as small if its yearly sales are $5,000,000 or less.
> Most retail and service trades concerns are considered small if their yearly sales or receipts are $1,000,000 or less. The maximum for those selling general merchandise, motor vehicles or groceries with fresh meats is $2,000,000.
> A hotel, power laundry, or trucking and warehousing concern is small if its annual receipts are $2,000,000 or less, and a concern primarily engaged in construction is small if its average receipts for the preceding 3 years are $5,000,000 or less.[3]

---

are fighting for, a land of opportunity to which they yearn eagerly to return when they have defeated the foe." (79th Congress, Report No. 47.) Ibid.

[3] *Small Business Administration: What It Is, What It Does* (Washington, D.C.: Office of Information, Small Business Administration; June 1959), pp. 10–11.

The SBA and Senate definitions give some indication of the number of yardsticks available for measuring small business. When an attempt is made actually to apply these yardsticks throughout the economy, it becomes apparent that there are great gaps in the calibration.

> Probably the most serious handicap to developing thoughtful and appropriate definitions of "small" business is that the requisite information is not available (it has not been collected, will not be collected or cannot be collected). Analysts who are careful to indicate what they mean by "small" business may simply be recording whatever definition they have found it necessary to accept.[4]

The difficulty becomes even worse in cross-analysis. Most of the information is collected on a yearly basis, and without going back to the raw data (also unavailable), the researcher finds the years do not match on the various measurements. Furthermore, the bases of enumeration appear to be different. One man's "finance, real estate, and insurance" is another's dual category of "real estate" and "finance," with the numerical totals bearing no resemblance to each other. The list of such problems is virtually interminable. Nonetheless, almost all information can make some contribution toward defining and describing that hazy phenomenon known as "small business."

During the 1950's business in this country grew quite rapidly, despite recession periods in 1953–4 and 1957–8. The number of firms in operation rose from 4,067,300 in 1951 to 4,589,200 in 1959. (See Table 1.[5]) The average growth rate was 12.8 per cent, with contract construction and finance, real

[4] *Financing Small Business,* A Report to the Committees on Banking and Currency and the Select Committees on Small Business, U.S. Congress, by the Federal Reserve System (April 11, 1958), p. 151.

[5] The tables referred to in this section are in the Appendix, pp. 279–88.

estate, and insurance showing the greatest gains, and mining and quarrying, transportation, and service slightly above average. The lowest increases were registered in retail trade and manufacturing, with the latter losing in absolute numbers between 1953 and 1955—331,000 to 326,100—and again from 1958 to 1959. In retail trade, increases in the number of filling stations and motor-vehicle and accessory dealers offset a decrease in general merchandise and food concerns. The average gain of 65,000 firms a year offset population growth to keep the number of firms per 1,000 population steady at about 26½.[6]

Of the 4,589,200 business firms in this country, the great majority may be called "small." The retail and service trades are the strongholds of little business. But in any category (including manufacturing, where concentration in large units is greatest) and by almost any standard the entrepreneur is numerically superior.

Figures on employment are probably the most complete and reliable for use as a definition of small business. The Office of Business Economics of the Department of Commerce compiles fairly extensive statistics, which have been published and analyzed over a period of years in the *Survey of Current Business*.[7] Each legal entity in the private sector of the economy (which accounts for about 85 per cent of income and employment) is counted once by its primary activity, and the totals are broken down by industry division to show the number of firms employing less than four, four to seven, eight to nineteen persons, and so on up to 1,000 or more. Proprietors and unpaid family workers are not counted, which somewhat distorts employment percentages.

[6] Betty C. Churchill: "Rise in the Business Population," *Survey of Current Business*, XXXIX (May 1959), p. 16.

[7] At the time of this writing, the latest figures available are for 1956.

Three-fourths of all American businesses had fewer than four employees in 1956, and 40 per cent had no paid employees at all. Only 5 per cent employed twenty or more persons, and only .9 per cent, 100 or more. (See Appendix, Table 2.) Into the smallest (0–3) classification fell not only the majority of total business firms, but also at least 60 per cent of all firms in every industry division except manufacturing. Among twenty-one non-manufacturing subdivisions, only lumber and building materials (in the retail-trade category) and motion pictures (in the service category) listed a majority of concerns in the four-or-more employee groups.[8]

Despite changes for various industry divisions, the percentage of total businesses within each employment classification remained about the same from 1951 to 1956. Application of the 1956 figures to total firms in 1959 is therefore a rough but not particularly dangerous procedure. By this calculation, it would seem that out of 4,589,200 businesses in 1959, about 3,456,000 employed fewer than four persons. Only 229,000 firms topped a twenty-man employment level, with 9,200 reaching 500 or more. And although the data are not broken down in this particular category, it can be estimated that an absolute minimum of 4,500,000 businesses are eligible, in terms of number of employees, for Small Business Administration loans.

Service, finance, and retail business show the greatest proportion of firms in the 0–3 classification; in fact, nearly half of all business in 1956 was composed of small retail or service firms with fewer than four employees. The greatest employment concentration was shown in manufacturing and mining and quarrying. Contract construction and transportation, communication and public utilities had above average percent-

[8] Churchill: "Size of Business Firms," *Survey of Current Business,* XXXIX (September 1959), p. 19.

ages in the smallest size grouping. The latter category, however, also showed comparatively high percentages in the 100-or-over class, reflecting the inclusion of large utility companies on the one hand and small truck and taxi firms on the other.

Although analysis by organizational form can be helpful, particularly in estimating financial status, data are quite scanty and often contradictory. Again, the most reliable figures appear to be located in the business population series in *Survey of Current Business,* although the most detailed information is available only for 1947, with additional bits through 1952. *Statistics of Income,* published annually by the Treasury Department, has some usable figures for corporate business. Its material on sole proprietorships and partnerships is virtually worthless, however, because no limitation is made as to farmers or professional persons, and neither employment nor an established place of business is required for qualification as a sole proprietorship.

Survey of Current Business figures for 1952 show a total of 526,000 corporations and 3,595,000 unincorporated businesses; no division is made for that year between proprietorships and partnerships. As is shown in Table 3 (see Appendix) 87.2 per cent of all businesses in 1952 were unincorporated, compared with 88.7 per cent in 1947.

Statistics of Income data for the same year record 615,-698 corporations. Eliminating 7,700 agriculture, forestry, and fishing firms not counted as such in the business population figures, and an excess of about 72,700 financial firms evidently due to different bases of enumeration, the figure of 535,-300 corporations emerges, which is close enough to use for rough approximations. An extension of this process to the 1957–8 *Statistics of Income* gives a figure between 700,000 and 725,000 as the number of corporations operating during that fiscal year. As 15.7 to 16.2 per cent of total firms, it correlates fairly well with the rising number of incorporations since World War II.

Taken by itself, incorporation is not a very reliable evidence of size, but combined with employment figures it shows the concentration of small business by legal form of organization. In 1947 proprietorships comprised 79.6 per cent of all firms within the 0–3 employment size classification, with corporations only 3.7 per cent. (See Appendix, Table 4.) At the other extreme, proprietorships accounted for only 3.1 per cent of firms employing more than 100 persons, compared with 82.6 per cent for the corporations. Partnerships fell into the middle on all counts.

Despite the preponderance of proprietorships in the small size groups, a fourth of all corporations employed fewer than four persons, and only about a third had more than twenty paid employees. This figure is quite low, contrasted with 84 per cent and 1 per cent respectively for proprietorships, or 66 per cent and 6 per cent for partnerships. Nonetheless, it does serve to indicate that small business is numerically dominant in the corporate as well as the non-corporate world.

Incorporation is also consistent with employment size by industry division. Unincorporated businesses dominate the retail and service trades to the greatest extent, with contract construction a close third. Lowest, again, is manufacturing, but still nearly two-thirds of all firms in that division are unincorporated. The only category showing a major discrepancy between percentage of unincorporated businesses and percentage of firms in the 0–3 classification is finance, insurance, and real estate.

In the main, small business means unincorporated business and, more particularly, individual proprietorships. By legal form of organization, as well as by employment, it dominates every industry division. This is not to say that incorporation necessarily means big business, for as shown in Table 4 most corporations also fall within the realm of small business.

Theoretically, asset size is almost as good a base for classifying business by size as is employment. Practically, it is exceedingly difficult to get reliable information concerning assets which tallies with other forms of measurement. No reliable breakdown by asset size alone exists for both incorporated and unincorporated business, although *Statistics of Income,* taken with a grain of salt, gives some notions about corporate assets. There appears to be no information correlating asset size with employment size. *Statistics of Income* for 1957 shows corporations by industry division broken down into asset sizes of less than $25,000, more than $25,000 but less than $50,000, and so on up to more than $250,000,000. Eliminating the entire finance, insurance, and real estate section because of great numerical discrepancy, about three-fourths of all United States corporations had assets of less than $250,000. (See Appendix, Table 5.) Only 5 per cent fell into the $1,000,000 or more category.

Manufacturing and mining and quarrying showed the greatest percentages of firms over $1,000,000 and the least under $250,000. The reverse was true of retail and service corporations, with construction also showing more than four-fifths of firms under $250,000 and less than 5 per cent more than $1,000,000. Public utilities and wholesale concerns were close to average. These are corporate figures only. Since the vast majority of unincorporated business tends to be of considerably smaller size than the corporations, it would be safe to say that at least 90 per cent, and probably more, of all businesses have assets of less than $250,000.

Data regarding sales by size classification are difficult to obtain for all industry divisions, but are available for retail, merchant wholesale, and selected service firms in the business census. The total number of retail establishments listed for 1954 was 1,721,650. Of these, 18,969 or 1.1 per cent had sales of more than $1,000,000, while 18.7 per cent reached more than $100,000 in sales. About 39.9 per cent of all retail trade establishments sold less than $30,000. (For complete figures on number of firms and total sales, see Appendix, Table 9.)

Within the major subdivisions of retail trade, the greatest concentration by number of firms with sales of $1,000,000 or more occurs in food stores, general merchandise firms—especially department stores—automotive dealers, and lumber and building materials firms. By employment, general merchandise stores, automotive dealers, eating and drinking places, and apparel and accessories stores showed the highest number of firms in the over-100 category.[9] Listing of wholesale firms, with classifications of sales from less than $50,000 to more than $10,000,000, shows 165,153 merchant wholesalers in operation during 1954. Reflecting the comparatively larger size of wholesale firms, 1.5 per cent had sales of over $5,000,000, and 12.7 per cent over $1,000,000. On the other hand, nearly a third had sales of less than $100,000. (Complete figures in Table 10.) The 785,589 service firms listed were smallest by sales size. Only 1.1 per cent reached $300,000 or more, while 9 per cent had more than $50,000 in receipts. Some 56 per cent sold less than $10,000 worth. (Additional data in Table 11.)

Data by sales size, then, confirms the numerical superiority of small business as defined by almost any standard, particularly in the realm of retail and service trades. Of all the retail, service, and wholesale firms listed in the 1954 business census, less than a fifth would fail to fit the sales size definition of the SBA.

The geographical distribution of the business population is

[9] *Census of Business, 1954,* Vol. I, *Retail Trade—Summary Statistics,* p. 18.

highly correlated with the distribution of human population and income. As small business constitutes the vast majority of firms, it might be expected to match population and income across the nation; rough estimates confirm this. The areas in which small business is particularly predominant are precisely those to be expected: the agricultural, unindustrialized, thinly populated parts of the United States. Numerically, small business gives the appearance of overwhelming the economy—another "nation of shopkeepers." In real economic terms, however, almost the opposite is true. The same standards—employment, assets, and sales—show that the moans of expiring entrepreneurs have some justification.

Some 40,667,000 persons were listed as paid employees for 1956. Of these 17,661,000, or 43.4 per cent, were concentrated in the nation's 327,300 manufacturing establishments. (See Appendix, Tables 1 and 6.) About a fourth were employed by 2,692,800 retail and service firms. As divided by employment size classification, only 6.5 per cent worked for firms with fewer than four employees. Comparing Table 7 with Table 2, it can be seen that more than three-fourths of the nation's firms accounted for less than a tenth of its employment. Businesses hiring twenty or more, while constituting only 5 per cent numerically, employed more than three-fourths of the paid labor force, while the .9 per cent of businesses with 100 or more employees had nearly 60 per cent of the employment. The major businesses of the country, those with 500 employees or more, accounted for only .2 per cent of the total number of firms, but 43.7 per cent of total employment.

It is not surprising that percentages of employment by size classification should be the reverse of percentages of firms in each employment-size category. Manufacturing showed the least percentage of employment in the 0–3 classification, and retail and service the most, with the finance and contract construction divisions also ranking very high, and mining and quarrying very low. The previously mentioned split in the public utilities division shows again in the low percentage of employment in the 0–3 group.

What is somewhat startling is the extent of the employment disparity. At one end the retail and service firms in the 0–3 group—nearly half the businesses in the country—employ only 4 per cent of the labor force. At the opposite pole the large manufacturing concerns (over 500 employees) by themselves account for more than a fourth of total employment. Table 8 shows even more clearly the domination of the large business in employment. While several of the classifications, particularly retail and service, include firms that would not normally fall into the category of large business, none of the classifications shows less than 30 per cent of employment within the largest 1 per cent of firms. Though the 1956 figures are the latest detailed ones available, averages for all industries—though not necessarily for each division— remain quite constant from 1945 through 1956. The over-all percentages therefore are probably much the same today.

The economic inferiority of small business is shown again in data by organization form. In 1952 the corporate world, constituting an eighth of all business, originated 74.7 per cent of the national income for non-farm ordinary business. Five years later it originated 75.5 per cent of the income and accounted for 66.2 per cent of the national labor force.

Almost nothing is published on the assets of unincorporated business, but they were estimated at a total of $127,000,-000,000 for 1955 by the National Bureau of Economic Research. According to *Statistics of Income,* corporate assets for that year reached $888,621,270,000—a ratio of about 7 to 1. By size classes, 1957 *Statistics of Income* data indicate that only about 5 per cent of corporate assets are held by firms in the less-than-$250,000 classes, while nearly 90 per cent lie with those having more than $1,000,000 in assets.[1]

Like another chorus of the same old tune, selected industry figures on sales reiterate the fact that all the "littles" put together are still not as important as the few "bigs." In Tables 9, 10, and 11 are located the detailed breakdowns of establishments and sales by size classes. Table 12 gives an indication of the relative numerical and economic importance of top and bottom size classes. It is interesting to note that service firms have the highest concentration of sales in the top 1 per cent. This is fairly consistent with the 40 per cent of total employment held by the top 8,000 service establishments shown in Table 8. Furthermore, it illustrates the pitfalls of data in absolute classifications. Service and retail industries tend to be small, but markedly so only in comparison with other divisions. Within their own divisions, analyzed by relative percentiles, they display a high degree of concentration.

At least one other measure of the place of small business in the economy is worth discussing. Since 1951 the business population has been growing at the rate of about 75,000 per year—the difference between the some 415,000 businesses established annually and the 340,000 discontinued. Nearly all of these fall into the category of small business. Out of 431,200 businesses newly established in 1956, about 382,700, or 88.5 per cent, had fewer than four employees. Only .5 per cent employed more than twenty, and .2 per cent more than fifty.[2] Discontinuances, however, reached 341,700 that year. This is not to say that these discontinuances are for the same firms. Nonetheless, a

[1] *Corporation Income Tax Returns, Statistics of Income, 1957–58* (Washington, D.C.: U.S. Treasury Department; 1958), p. 3. These figures include the finance category, eliminated in determining assets in earlier figures, and may be somewhat distorted. Nonetheless, the general outlines are obvious.

[2] Churchill: "Size of Business Firms," p. 18.

third of all businesses do die out within the first year, and about half fail to reach the two-year operational mark.[3] Assuming that not enough expansion is likely to take place within two years to take a business out of the "small" employment class, at least half the discontinuances are accounted for in one blow. But the share of small business in discontinuances is greater than that; figures for 1948, for example, show that 86 per cent of all discontinuing firms employed fewer than four persons.[4] While it must be remembered that most discontinuances are not business failures, discontinuances do serve to illustrate that economically small business is insecure as well as inferior.

It is apparent, then, that even in its totality small business is the poor relation of the American economy. The real question is whether as a whole it is going up in the world, holding its own, or heading for the poorhouse. Because of the lack of precision in defining and describing small business, and also because of the ideological aura about entrepreneurial enterprise, this question has become a fertile area of political haymaking. If nothing else, it has proven that figures, judiciously arranged, can and do lie. But when the maximum possible amount of fog has been cleared away, it would appear that while small business has been holding its own or even gaining slightly in absolute terms, relatively it has fallen noticeably behind in certain areas.

Though it is frequently said that the average business size has increased since the war, employment figures both by number of firms and percentage of employment have remained quite stable. After the first rush of postwar business growth, which lowered concentration levels considerably, there has been

---

[3] Churchill: "Age and Life Expectancy of Business Firms," *Survey of Current Business*, XXXV (December 1955), p. 18.

[4] Churchill: "Survival Patterns of the Postwar Business Population," *Survey of Current Business*, XXXII (December 1952), p. 12.

very little change. If anything, the employment concentration lessened slightly in the years from 1948 to 1956.[5] Within industry divisions, however, definite shifts had taken place during the eight years. Manufacturing and finance, insurance, and real estate clearly increased in concentration, with the larger classifications gaining in both numbers and percentage of employment at the expense of the smaller ones. On the other hand, mining and quarrying, contract construction, and wholesale (especially the latter) moved toward smaller firms. In retailing, the 0–3 classification gained, but at the expense of the other under-thirty classes. The same occurred in public utilities and the service trades, with the difference that the big business classifications increased their percentage of employment too.[6]

As mentioned before, the percentage of corporations in the economy has increased, probably because of the limited financial liability they are required to carry. In 1950 corporation-originated share of the national income was 74.2 per cent. It had gained .5 per cent by 1952 and was up to 75.5 per cent by 1957.[7] Within this time, however, the number of corporations had increased far more than their income gain, leaving unincorporated business somewhat ahead. Of course, it may be argued that this merely reflects the transfer of small and not particularly productive businesses from one legal category to another; there are no figures for income within the corporate division. But making allowances for distortion, it would appear by this admittedly only partial measurement that small business is not doing any worse than before.

[5] Churchill: "Size of Business Firms," p. 15.

[6] Ibid., p. 16. See also Churchill and Murray F. Ross: "The Size Distribution of the Postwar Business Population," *Survey of Current Business*, XXX (May 1950), p. 13.

[7] Jeannette Fitzwilliams: "Employment in Corporate and Non-Corporate Production," *Survey of Current Business*, XXXIX (November 1959), p. 22.

However, the defense must rest there temporarily; other data tell another story. The share of personal income held by business and professional proprietorships, for instance, had shrunk from 10.4 per cent in 1947 to 9 per cent in 1959.[8] The portion of total net sales made by businesses with assets of less than $1,000,000 dropped steadily from 18.9 per cent in 1947 to 13 per cent in 1955; since then it has fluctuated between 13.5 and 14.5 per cent.[9] The rate of earning after taxes—as a per cent of stockholders' equity—by manufacturers holding less than $1,000,000 in assets follows much the same pattern when compared with those holding more than $1,000,000. (See Appendix, Table 13.) The differential was greatest in 1955; after decreasing in 1956, it had risen again by 1958.

Another measure of what has been happening to small business of late is its share in the defense expenditures which comprise a fifth of the national budget. With the advent of the Eisenhower administration and lowered military expenditures, small business improved its position. It received 25 per cent of the $11.6 billion in military expenditures in 1954, as compared with 16.2 per cent the year before. Since then, however, the percentage dropped to 16.6 in 1959, although in absolute dollar value it has remained constant or even increased. (See Appendix, Table 14.) A similar drop took place in amounts spent for research and development, with small business's share at 5.7 per cent in 1956 and only 3.5 per cent in 1959.[1]

The drop in the awarding of prime defense contracts is

[8] "National Income and Product in 1959," *Survey of Current Business,* XL (July 1960), pp. 10–11.

[9] "How Healthy Is Small Business?" *Congressional Quarterly Weekly Report,* XIV (May 25, 1956), p. 592; *Fourteenth Semiannual Report* (Washington, D.C.: Small Business Administration; 1960), p. 16.

[1] *Small Business Administration—1960,* Hearings before a Subcommittee of the Select Committee on Small Business, U.S. Senate, 86th Congress, Second Session, Part I (March 22, 1960), p. 4.

fairly well explained by the fact that the government has come to rely more and more on industries to do research and development as well as production for defense. Such a policy swings the major portion of military expenditures to the companies who have facilities for large-scale operations. True, the Small Business Administration has set aside for small business $4.6 billion in prime contracts since 1953,[2] but the 100 largest prime contractors received 68.4 per cent of all prime defense contract dollars in 1957 and 74.1 per cent in 1958.

Small business is dependent on subcontracting for the defense dollar. The Department of Defense promulgated in the middle 1950's what was essentially a request for the major companies to adopt voluntarily a meaningful subcontract program. Liaison officials were appointed to represent the interests of small subcontractors at "make or buy" decision meetings. The success of the program is a matter of some debate. At a 1959 hearing of a subcommittee of the Senate Select Committee on Small Business it was charged that the prime contractors, having no knowledge of or contact with the SBA, ignored even the liaison officers. They tended to deal with only a limited number of companies whose reputations they acknowledged, refused to rotate lists of bidders, did not allow small companies time to prepare subcontract bids, and more often than not subcontracted to other large companies.[3]

The hearings and accompanying documents provide a rather fascinating example of the sort of battle waged in the name of small business Attacking were the majority of Senators on the subcommittee, headed by New Jersey's Harrison Williams, Jr. Definitely on the defensive were representatives of the prime contractors—Boeing, General Motors, Chrysler, Douglas. Each

[2] Ibid., p. 3.

[3] *Small Business Participation in Defense Subcontracting,* Hearings before a Subcommittee of the Select Committee on Small Business, U.S. Senate, 86th Congress, First Session (April 22–4, 1959), pp. 3–4.

company had been asked to prepare a statement of the total amount awarded in federal defense contracts, the amount subcontracted, and the percentages awarded not only to small business but to a specified list of other major companies. The gist of the companies' attitudes appeared to be that while the principle of subcontracting to small business was a worthy one, it was not to be followed at the cost of poor quality or inconvenience. Prime contractors had schedules to meet and often maintained facilities which with slight change or expansion could handle the development of certain items. Why subcontract simply for the sake of subcontracting? Nonetheless, the companies declared, a substantial amount of the awards they did make went to small business. Boeing was low with 18.6 per cent; Douglas, Chrysler, and General Motors declared for about a third; General Dynamics listed over 40 per cent.

Whatever the practice of individual companies, small business received only 21.5 per cent of defense subcontract dollars in 1956, and by 1958 was down to 17.4 per cent.[4] Certainly this is not much of a share, particularly since it concerns subcontracting rather than prime awards. But the testimony of the company representatives points up a basic factor in the dilemma of small business. The little firm is in many areas at a disadvantage precisely because of its nature—the fact that it *is* small. Where speed, advanced technology, standardization, and wide selection are the keys to the marketplace, the small-time, "half-industrialized" organization finds it hard to keep the pace. More and more the rich markets are cut off, and the small firm is left to compete with others of its kind for the less profitable business. The evidence indicates that this is what has happened since the end of World War II. In definitive terms the little men of the business world are holding their own; only in general merchandise and food retailing has the

[4] Ibid., p. 2.

number of firms actually decreased. As was indicated above, numbers by size classification have remained steady; employment across the boards has also stayed the same, though certain industries have increased employment concentration while others have decreased. Such worsening of the position of small business as has occurred is located, then, in terms of gaining what is after all the ultimate business goal—the dollar. The "poor relations" are not advancing their position, nor are they about to take up the beggar's bowl. They seem to be looking a little shabbier, a bit seedier; but this, like many an exercise in discerning subtleties, is open to debate.

A difference exists, however, between problems inherent in the nature of small business and those arising as the result of a stacked deck. Primarily it is the drawing of this distinction that has occupied those concerning themselves with small business. If the entrepreneur has difficulties because he cannot meet market standards, it may be argued that special treatment merely preserves an artificial, uneconomical structure. If, on the other hand, he has been the victim of thoughtless or even malicious policies, his case is more solidly founded. The discussions of defense contracting and subcontracting practices illustrate arguments resulting from attempts at such delineation. A more classic area in which the small businessman feels he meets discrimination is financing. Here, as in defense contracts, two sets of questions must be considered: the weakness or strength of the small business position and the reasons behind whatever discrepancies exist.

First of all, who wants financing? Within industry divisions, little doubt exists that manufacturers lead the search for loans. They accounted for a third of all business loan applications received through 1959 by SBA, though retail establishments contributed 28.5 per cent.[5] Another measure, found in a 1955

[5] *Small Business Administration—1960,* Part II, p. 88.

Survey of Current Business article by Loughlin McHugh and Jack Ciaccio, is based on replies to a questionnaire sent to business firms. When results were tabulated by employment size, industry division, and age of the business, it was found that manufacturing firms led in desire for credit, with 49.2 per cent stating that they had wanted outside funds during the previous year. Wholesale establishments, which filed only 8 per cent of the SBA loan applications, were close behind with 49.1 per cent, followed by construction at 48.1 per cent and retail at 40.3 per cent. On the whole, 53 per cent of newer firms (those established after 1951) desired financing, as compared with 43 per cent for their elder counterparts. By employment size, larger business evinced more interest in financing than small establishments—64 per cent in the over-100 category, but only 39 per cent of those with fewer than four employees.

But of those businesses which did want outside funds, the smaller ones met with the least success. Table 15 shows the proportions of those that did get all the funds they desired—from 49 per cent for the smallest size classification to 68 per cent for the largest—and those that could get no financing at all. Established firms had a much easier time with financing than the newer firms, which are more likely to be small.

Though the McHugh-Ciaccio survey indicated that industry divisions had about equal luck in getting the amount of funds desired, other data show that manufacturers and mining firms receive the greatest percentage of business loans. The dollar share has decreased somewhat since 1946—from 43 per cent to 37 per cent in 1955. A similar decline took place in combined retail and wholesale trade loans, from 30 per cent in 1946 to 21 per cent nine years later. The loss in these areas was offset by a rise in the loans made to public utility, service, and construction firms.[6] Nonetheless, manufacturers still received a

[6] *Financing Small Business*, p. 30.

third of the total number of SBA loans through December 1959, with retailers just slightly less and service firms in third place.[7]

The type of financing wanted is an important qualification to statements about the success of small business in gaining funds. Short-term credit is apparently not too difficult to obtain from commercial banks and other financial institutions. (It might be noted that there is some disagreement even about this. A survey by Standard Factors Corporation in March 1956 reported that while the percentage of firms with net worth of $500,000 or more that regularly borrowed from commercial banks had stayed virtually constant over the previous year, the percentage for firms of $5,000 to $25,000 net worth had dropped from 53 to 18, and 82 to 44 for establishments with $25,000 to $100,000 net worth.) [8]

But most of the dissatisfaction with small business financing lies in the unavailability of long-term credit. Manufacturing in particular feels the pinch because retail, service, and other industry divisions are less likely to need long-term loans. For purposes of expansion, the equity capital markets are almost completely closed to the small businessman. About 55.4 per cent of the funds needed by even small corporations between 1946 and 1955 came from internal financing, compared with 62.8 per cent for large corporations.[9] The portions in the noncorporate world are undoubtedly considerably lower. Thus the small businessman is often forced to interbusiness financing and bank or non-bank financial institution loans rather than the long-term capital market. Heavy reliance, almost in direct proportion to smallness, is placed on trade payables, that is, the absence of immediate payment to the seller. Sometimes big companies will lend cash to smaller ones, especially suppliers;

[7] *Small Business Administration—1960,* Part II, p. 88.
[8] "How Healthy Is Small Business?" p. 593.
[9] *Financing Small Business,* p. 23.

failing this, they will often lend or finance equipment and supplies.[1] So persuasively have the advocates of small business
argued their case that a major activity of the Small Business
Administration is the granting of business loans. Besides setting
aside defense contracts, issuing certificates of competency, and
providing managerial and technical aids, the SBA makes funds
available to sound businesses who cannot get credit elsewhere
on reasonable terms. The SBA tries to co-operate with private
lending institutions and will not grant a direct loan unless local
participation is absolutely unavailable.

Despite this special treatment in public policy, the howls of
the non-financed have not abated. It has been pointed out
that between 1900 and 1955 the total assets of financial inter-
mediaries increased by a factor of 35, but the share of those
which are important lenders to small business decreased from
53 per cent to 34 per cent.[2] Even the SBA got embroiled in
controversy because of its cautious lending policy. *Small
Business at the Crossroads,* a study made by Wilfred Lumer for
the Public Affairs Institute, vigorously castigates the agency.
Restrictive monetary policies, Lumer argues, hit small business
harder than big business because the former is so dependent on
external funds. Such policies cut off not only commercial bank
lines, but also alternative sources; commercial finance companies, for instance, cannot expand their lending in the face of
tightening bank credit because they are dependent on banks for
a good part of their resources.[3] So the small businessman looks
to SBA and finds precious little comfort there.

That the SBA did not fulfill the role that Congress
intended it to was indicated by the Senate Small Business
Committee by the following:

[1] Ibid., p. 26.
[2] Ibid., p. 39.
[3] Wilfred Lumer: *Small Business at the Crossroads* (Washington, D.C.: Public Affairs Institute; 1956), p. 17.

"At a hearing before your Committee in March, the (SBA) Administrator was cautioned that the members of this Committee, as sponsors of the legislation, had given the Small Business Administration a broad mandate to assist small business in the financial field. While SBA was to protect the interests of the public in assessing the loan applications, it was also expected to be courageous enough to make loans which private institutions had declined. In essence your Committee warned SBA against too narrow an interpretation of the phrase, 'all loans made shall be of such sound value or so secured as reasonably to assure payment.' "

Congressional criticism of SBA's overly restrictive policy and the sensitivity of the Administration to the rising chorus of small business complaints led SBA to liberalize somewhat its credit assistance to small business in 1956. During the first eight months of 1956 SBA claimed it had approved 59 per cent of all loan applications compared to 39 per cent approved during 1955. However, tight credit conditions for small business were not alleviated.[4]

There is always another side to the coin. Philip McCallum, the SBA administrator, said in 1960 that there was evidence commercial banks made more term loans than five years previously.[5] Other sources point to the increased volume of equity for small business (though not gained through the capital markets) and the growing volume of small business credit.[6] Nevertheless, the weight of the evidence appears to be on the side of inadequate financing for small business, particularly in comparison with larger firms. But why? Why should 53.5 per cent of older firms pay less than 6 per cent interest on loans, as compared with only 40 per cent of newer businesses?[7] What is the

[4] Ibid., p. 22.
[5] *Small Business Administration—1960*, Part II, p. 83.
[6] *Financing Small Business*, p. 148.
[7] Loughlin McHugh and Jack Ciaccio: "External Financing of Small and Medium-Size Business," *Survey of Current Business*, XXXV (October 1955), p. 18.

reason the average 1957 bank interest rate was 5.5 per cent for loans of less than $10,000 but only 4.5 per cent for loans of more than $200,000? [8]

The answer is fairly obvious. In addition to constant administrative costs, which are proportionately higher for smaller loans, almost all data show that loans to small business firms encounter greater losses per dollar than do those to big companies.[9] Consequently the stated interest rate on loans to small business rises. This may have the effect of either discouraging the would-be borrower or frightening the potential lender, with the result that no funds are granted at all.[1] Financial institutions are notorious for their caution and desire to protect investor interests; as a general practice, and especially when money is tight, the little man is least likely to be served. That the Small Business Administration, created solely to help small business, should also follow a slow-and-low lending policy with public funds indicates how comparatively poor a risk the small businessman appears to financial institutions. Unfortunately, a vicious circle spins into operation at this point. When the small businessman cannot get funds, he may do poorly as a consequence. His record enters the statistics by which small business is adjudged an unhealthy risk, thus making financing even more difficult to obtain.

Related to the problem of gaining funds from external sources is that of preserving enough profits after taxes to expand. High taxes work definite hardships on the individual who hopes to save money for expansion, yet even on the corporate level small businessmen cry for tax relief. The most obvious complaint concerns the failure to graduate corporate income taxes, putting the small firm at a disadvantage. Normal tax rate

[8] *Financing Small Business*, p. 142.
[9] Ibid., p. 50.
[1] Ibid., p. 14.

52

is 30 per cent for up to $25,000 taxable income, with surtax a flat 22 per cent for anything above $25,000. In addition, it is charged that such tax revision as has taken place favors big business far more than small and consequently accentuates its unequal market position. Elimination of the excess profits tax in 1953, for example, cut only $1,000,000 in liability for firms with net incomes under $25,000 out of $1,600,000,000 for all corporations.[2] Liberalized depreciation under the Internal Revenue Code for 1954 permits more rapid depreciation of new machinery, but not of the used machinery which small businesses tend to buy. Big corporations are better able to use restricted stock option plans to supplement the after-taxes pay of top management, and the same holds true of pension plans. Permission to write off advertising as a business expense favors the huge corporations who buy space and time across the nation, thus enabling them to build up sales at a lower cost per unit than smaller business.[3]

But underlying any discussion of financing, tax structures, defense contracts, or personnel is that wondrous idol-bugaboo, competition. Is free competition really the small businessman's motto? What exactly does he mean when he says it? The answer to the first question, one fears, must be no. The answer to the second is that he means what C. Wright Mills calls "the rationing out of the main chance." His definition of fair competition is pragmatic, judged by concrete results in dollars rather than across-the-boards competition. As has already been shown, free competition has not proven especially beneficial to small businessmen. Some, in fact, "thrive on protected markets; others co-operate with and therefore are frequently financed by large concerns striving for market domination."[4]

[2] Lumer: op. cit., p. 27.
[3] Ibid., pp. 29–30.
[4] *Financing Small Business,* p. 10.

Small businessmen are understandably disturbed about the level of business failures, which has risen from 14 per 10,000 businesses in operation in 1947, to 33 in 1953, to 52 in 1959,[5] to a still newer high in 1961. To quote financial columnist Sylvia Porter, the fundamental reason for the skyrocketing number of business deaths is that

> . . . our economy has entered the toughest, roughest phase of competition in modern times—and in this era the businessman who doesn't recognize what he is facing or know how to fight competition successfully is going under.
>
> He can't bail himself out by price hikes as he could in the first postwar years and through most of the 50's. He can't get by with shoddy merchandise, shabby service, sloppy salesmanship. We are into a real buyer's market—and the seller who can't sell simply won't survive.[6]

A good idea of how the small businessman views the competitive situation was offered by J. Gordon Buss of the Thomson Company, a small apparel manufacturing outfit, in Senate subcommittee hearings on the impact of imports on American small business. Declared Buss: "In his competition with other domestic apparel manufacturers, the domestic manufacturer is assured of certain conditions which hold for his competitors as well as himself." [7] He added that taxes, fabric prices, machinery, market and transport costs, and pay and working conditions were the same for American companies but considerably different for European firms.

The rising volume of imported products has definitely hurt many small businesses in this country. As the gap in tech-

[5] "How Healthy Is Small Business?" p. 592; *Fourteenth Semiannual Report,* p. 8.

[6] Sylvia Porter: "Your Money's Worth," *San Francisco Chronicle,* February 22, 1961, p. 43.

[7] *Impact of Imports on American Small Business,* Hearings before a Subcommittee of the Select Committee on Small Business, U.S. Senate, 86th Congress, Second Session (June 16, 1960), p. 20.

nology closes, foreign goods are not only cheaper but as well made. In the area of "flash goods"—those which sell to a fad market—import copies often take a large share of sales during the time patents are pending. In steadier market fields, small concerns have more difficulty in competition with imports than many large firms because they make only a few products. For instance, many small steel mills depend heavily on simple rods, wire, or fencing because they cannot turn out a full line of products. When undersold by foreign producers, they lose a major part of their business, while the large steel mills, for whom these items constitute only a small percentage of business, remain relatively unaffected. Of course, other small businesses benefit from buying the cheaper imports; a great number, especially in retail and service, are not hurt because they handle a variety of products, many of which have no imported counterparts. But where imports do hit, they tend to hit the small businessman harder.[8]

Admittedly, the particular definition of unfair competition mentioned above is not used solely by small business; big corporations also use it vigorously as a weapon in their battle against business abroad. But it is interesting to observe that the little entrepreneur, in addition, is not satisfied with mere equality of production conditions at home. He does not, as stated before, view approximately equal corporate taxes as at all just. He howls regularly about the attempts of unions to force industry-wide pay scales which cut his profit ratio, sometimes almost to the bone. Where he would draw the line between "fair and free" competition and "unfair" competition seems to depend on precisely where his ox is being gored.

This is not to say that all entrepreneurial complaints about unfair competition and practices are unjustified—far from it. The difficulty lies in setting up a meaningful and reasonably

[8] Ibid., p. 211.

permanent definition. Some practices are a matter of debate; others are more clearly discriminatory. As an example of the latter, one might turn to the Senate subcommittee hearings on the practices of allocating space in shopping centers to small business. The move from the central city has been cited as a trend favorable for small business, but the testimony given at these hearings implies that even in suburbia all is not heaven. The most comprehensive statement of the problem was made by Senator Williams in introducing the topic of the day:

> "During recent years, numerous small, independent businessmen have registered complaints with their trade associations and the Senate Small Business Committee to the effect that they are unable to get into proposed shopping centers because they lack the type of national credit rating required by the financing institutions which underwrite the centers. On behalf of the financing institutions it is argued that since these are long-term loans and they cannot speculate with their policyholders' money, it is necessary for them (1) to insist on the types of tenants which best assure full payment of their lease for the full term; and (2) to preclude the possibility of large chainstores or supermarkets opening in the same area. As a result, the independent businessman in certain retail fields is finding it more and more difficult to obtain space in shopping centers even though he may have the capital, experience, existing market and respect of the community." [9]

Independent merchants do get space in the centers, provided they are not in the food or variety business. But, even so, they are discriminated against in other ways. Sol G. Atlas, a New York developer, testified at length before the subcommittee. The thesis of his statements was that the big department stores and chains are essential to financing a shopping

---

[9] *Shopping Centers—1959: On Alleged Discriminatory Practices against Small Business Concerns in Suburban Shopping Centers,* Hearings before a Subcommittee of the Select Committee on Small Business, U.S. Senate, 86th Congress, First Session (April 28–9, 1959), p. 1.

center, for the reasons stated above. They can take the choice locations with extremely low rentals because they are aware of their position of strength. The independent businessmen, in order to make up the difference, have to pay three or four times as much for secondary locations. Atlas also pointed out, though, that the independents were highly reluctant to sign up for a center until the big quarry had already been landed—a tribute to the relative drawing power of large organizations.[1]

But big business itself also indulges in some practices which make the very existence of small business rather difficult. More Senate hearings, this time on automotive tire distribution, illustrate the sort of competition that goes somewhat beyond bounds. The independent tire dealers—that is, those outlets not controlled by manufacturers—complained bitterly about a form of dual distribution by which manufacturers also competed on the retail level. W. W. Marsh, speaking as executive secretary of the National Tire Dealers and Retreaders Association, Inc., declared that sale and service of replacement tires and tubes was the backbone of the independent tire dealer's business. Between 1946 and 1958, however, their share of the replacement business had dropped from 52 per cent to 33 per cent. Three types of selling practices by the big companies were, he asserted, responsible for this drop. The first was the growth of some 2,000 stores owned by Goodrich, Goodyear, Firestone, and U.S. Rubber. By helping their own dealers in the establishment and equipment of new locations, they could set up impressive shops in growing areas long before those areas could support independent dealers with comparable facilities. These company stores accounted for about 10 per cent of the replacement business.

A second selling practice resented by independent tire dealers was that of selling directly to local accounts by field repre-

[1] Ibid., pp. 2–16.

sentatives. The manufacturers had for years made direct sales to national accounts, Marsh admitted, but going into the local area was an innovation. In effect, it put the manufacturer in competition with retail outlets. As an alternative, sales might be made to local users through dealers but at prices set by the manufacturer, with special discounts or maintenance guaranteed.[2]

Representatives of the manufacturers concerned retorted that the special considerations cited were exaggerations. Such instances as did occur were often necessary to meet the prices offered by low-cost competitors. Nonetheless, the damage done to small dealers by this kind of selling method is fairly obvious. Numerous examples also exist of favors given large distributors by manufacturers; for instance, chain organizations and department stores often get volume discounts and advertising allowances which help lower their prices compared to those of the smaller store.

What happens to the little man in the face of this sort of competition? Sometimes he manages reasonably well, depending on the market conditions in his particular area. In other fields—notably in food retailing—he ceases to exist as a businessman. In 1951 some 492,400 food and liquor retailers were operating in this country; by 1959 the number had sunk to 422,300. (General merchandise stores also suffered a decline during this period, from 74,200 to 67,200.) [3]

Food stores have been especially susceptible to the inroads of chain operations. From 1948 to 1958 chain groceries increased their sales 118 per cent, compared with 60 per cent for all food stores and 53 per cent for non-chain and specialty

---

[2] *Dual Distribution in the Automotive Tire Industry—1959,* Hearings before a Subcommittee of the Select Committee on Small Business, U.S. Senate, 86th Congress, First Session (June 17–19, 1959), p. 8.

[3] Churchill: "Rise in the Business Population," p. 18.

stores. Their portion of total food sales moved from 29 per cent to 38 per cent, and of all grocery sales, from 35 per cent to 43 per cent. Only a fifth of this was accounted for by increases in the sales of already-established stores. The rest resulted from expansion—one-fifth from the acquisition of other stores and three-fifths from opening new stores.[4] Nor are grocery establishments the only ones to feel the hot breath of the chains. Penetration has been heightened in lumber and building materials, drugs, furniture, and home appliances. Over-all the chain stores have tended to better their position in those lines where they account for a significant portion of the market. Their sales have fallen less than those of single-unit stores in times of recession, such as 1958, and have risen faster during the boom periods.[5]

If it does not go under, the small business may assume a subservient relationship to large concerns. Sometimes, as with gas stations, the owner is "little more than an agent of the firm whose product or service he sells . . . [His] compensation is derived from a fixed gross margin on sales rather than from salary." [6] Other businesses turn into satellites, "deriving much or all of their business from subcontracting or performing services for a few large firms." [7] Many of the interbusiness financing practices discussed earlier—equipment lease or rent, outright loans—are symptomatic of such relationships. Some writers contend that the over-all level of both concentration and vertical integration has remained almost horizontal since the turn of the century. They admit, however, that in older industries with final product lines, such as steel, autos, and

[4] *Food Marketing—Report of the Federal Trade Commission,* Hearings before a Subcommittee of the Select Committee on Small Business, U.S. Senate, 86th Congress, Second Session (June 22, 1960), p. 3.

[5] "Production and Distribution," *Survey of Current Business,* XXXIX (February 1959), p. 20.

[6] *Financing Small Business,* p. 2.

[7] Ibid., p. 7.

textiles, concentration and integration have increased.[8] As the market finds settled patterns, the innate economic power of the large concern becomes apparent in its increasing control of not only the market but often of the small organization as well.

This attempt to clarify the position of small business today and the changes it has undergone in recent years is by no means entirely satisfactory. Too much is missing, in terms of unavailable or conflicting data, to construct a complete floor plan of the economy with size as the basic criterion. Furthermore, figures are useful only insofar as they can be related to the human situation, and the human situation is even more contradictory than the statistics. Nevertheless, tables and testimony give a somewhat better idea of what the often-used term, "the plight of small business," actually means. Despite its numerical preponderance from the Bronx to Chula Vista, small business is not looking particularly healthy these days. It is weak, though not abysmally so; essentially it seems to be hanging on. True, the position of entrepreneurs is rather insecure. Being at the bottom of the business heap, they expire far more frequently than their big brothers. Yet with each year, more are spawned. One reason is clear: the small businessman values very highly the upgraded social position that comes from being his own boss, so much so that he will give up hope of attaining success only when it is financially impossible for him to continue. For the same reason the immediate prospect and likelihood of meager profits and great uncertainty will not deter new aspirants; they too have a high regard for the prestige and independence that accompany this new social status. In addition to certain social advantages, the position of entrepreneurial independence has the more immediate economic advantage of permitting the small businessman to be his own employer, perhaps the employer of his family. This par-

[8] Ibid., p. 202.

ticular factor gains special importance during times of depression when there is unemployment among wage earners. The small entrepreneur will then be all the more determined to stick to his business, and a certain number of new entrants will appear simply as a consequence of general unemployment. Indeed, self-employed small entrepreneurs are in a position to reduce their remuneration in real terms to any amount, whereas if they were unemployed wage earners they would not be able to get employment simply by offering themselves at a lower rate.[9]

Notwithstanding the declarations of alarm issuing from Washington and all points west, small business is not in the throes of a fatal crisis—yet. In some industries the little man is doing fairly well because of the nature of his services or location. In others he clearly is losing out. Generally he is dissatisfied with his lot in the business world because that lot is marginality and the disadvantages and insecurity that go with it. The climate of public opinion has been extremely favorable to small business, as witnessed in the creation of the Small Business Administration. But it might also be said that public action in the form of buying is not nearly so munificent. The principle of free enterprise, of the little entrepreneur rising to the top, has long been cherished in this country. Now it is conflicting with reality. Small business has problems, of which a few are caused by actions of malice. These can be corrected in the name of justice without much misgiving. The major problems, however, are frankly inherent in the nature of an economy geared to mass production and speed. A small enterprise, working slowly and producing less, is clearly in a bind.

[9] Joseph Steindl: *Small and Big Business* (Oxford: Basil Blackwell; 1947), p. 61. "It is therefore likely," says Steindl, "that high unemployment (especially of a secular character) contributed considerably to the determined 'holding on' of small firms as a group. This factor probably played a certain role in the United States depression in the 1930's."

Because, if left alone, reality almost invariably comes out on top, those who would save a principle that conflicts with reality must be prepared to ransom it. Will the price for small business strength be paid? Since there is no plainly visible crisis, no clear-cut demand has been made as yet. But in the years since World War II business failures, profits, financing, and selling methods gradually have been formulating an answer: *"Caveat venditor"*—let the seller beware.

3

In the present day of modern industrialism it is no secret that big business has many advantages over small business, of which perhaps the most important is organization. In the economic sphere alone technological changes and innovations in the past half century have resulted in striking corporate developments in all sectors of the economy, to the point where today small enterprise, in spite of its persistence, is severely handicapped. Of equal importance has been the political organization of big business into a variety of power groups, some more effective than others but all reflecting in one way or another the political needs and resources of big business. Among the many organizations through which business managers seek to further their objectives in politics and government, trade associations are the greatest in number—some 12,200 in 1956, according to the Department of Commerce, of which about 1,700 were national and 10,500 local or state. Big business manages to present its point of view politically through such organizations as the National Association of Manufacturers, which was organized in 1894 to consider "questions of national interest to manufacturers" and, although one will find no mention of it in its own records, to fight labor. These leaders of business and industry decided that the time had come when to be unorganized was to be defenseless against the aggressions which might be made against their own interests. In 1912, with the help of the NAM, the Chamber of Commerce was founded and organized geographically into "the largest and most conspicuous spokesman for business."[1] In his presidential address to the NAM convention in May 1913, John Kirby announced that "Great results are anticipated from this new organization. . . . It can and will be a strong factor in . . . guiding the country along conservative and safe lines, and in checking the socialistic tendencies of the times." Clearly, if this is an age of organization, then big business has played a leading part in the "organizational revolution."

In many ways, as Louis Hacker has observed, the American Revolution of 1776 was the small businessman's revolution, ushering in as it did the ideal society of many small and independent units linked together in a free-market economy in which political relationships were minimal and scattered. Today, however, with the development of a new and energetic role for the federal government and the assumption of considerable leadership—in some periods almost dominant control—by private big business, this society has been largely destroyed. Political relationships are no longer minimal and scattered. The result is that the present-day pattern of living is viewed with a good deal of hostility by small businessmen, who feel that the power and authority of big business "does not sit comfortably with the American ideal."[2]

The need for organization has not been discovered and recognized by big business alone. Farm groups such as the American Farm Bureau, the Grange, and the Farmer's

[1] Key: op. cit., p. 126.
[2] Kenneth E. Boulding: *The Organizational Revolution* (New York: Harper & Brothers; 1953), p. 138.

Union have long been involved in social, commercial, and legislative activities, and since the days of the depression in the early thirties have been primarily engaged, in their economic efforts at least, in a " 'revolt against the market'—a determination to control the conditions of exchange for the product of the group." [3] Today there are not only large and bureaucratic labor unions on the industrial scene, but there is a strong labor movement whose organized activity has made it a potent force in political affairs. The moral seems plain enough: few aspects of modern society have been untouched by organization. "Not only are there many more organizations, and many more kinds of organizations, than a century previous," comments Boulding, "but the organizations themselves are larger, better organized, more closely knit, more efficient in the arts of attracting members and funds and in pursuing their multitudinous ends." [4]

It has only been in the last twenty-five years or so, however, that small business organizations have appeared on a national scale. In fact, it would not be an exaggeration to say there has been an "organizational lag" of about fifty years between small business and big business. Nevertheless, in spite of the fact that the group consciousness of the small businessman has never been developed to the same degree as that of the farmer or the workingman, the many economic pressures of the last two decades have necessitated, as far as many small businessmen are concerned, some consideration of the merits to be gained from joining forces. [5] While the small businessman has been slower than some of his big business contemporaries in grasping the full meaning of political and economic events since

[3] Ibid., p. 109.
[4] Ibid., p. 4.
[5] "Habit, inertia, and an unwillingness to cooperate freely," writes Weissman, are handicaps which have still to be removed from the ranks of small business. Weissman: op. cit., p. 150.

the early thirties, he has not been unaware of the overwhelming tendency in our industrial social order toward complex organizations and of their power to influence our society. He has seen government grow at a rapid pace and he has watched labor organize itself on the premise that a businessman is an employer, no matter what his size or efficiency. It can hardly be surprising, then, that many small businessmen have concluded "now is the time for all good men, regardless of party, to come to the aid of small business." [6]

It would be difficult to say at what moment small businessmen, or at least some of them, became convinced there might be some strength for their cause in organized numbers, but there were distinct stirrings along these lines in the middle of the thirties. In June 1935 a National Federation of Small Business was organized in New Jersey to consider the problem of long-term credit and the necessity for federal assistance. In November 1937 DeWitt Emery founded the National Small Business Men's Association, using the irresistible battlecry: "The Sheriff is about to get my business. How are you doing?" [7] During the next few years a variety of other small business groups sprouted in mushroom fashion all over the country, making extravagant claims as to membership and representation and each presenting a particular set of grievances and a platform to match. A number of small business associations were formed after the close of President Roosevelt's Washington Conference in 1938, riding the wave of enthusiasm which sprang from the meetings and hopeful of becoming in time a strong and important force in the body politic. Yet most of these organizational efforts by small businessmen were short-lived. Concern for small business, however, increased through-

[6] Loc. cit.
[7] Quoted in Oliver Garceau: "Can Little Business Organize?" *Public Opinion Quarterly* (July 1938), p. 471.

out the country after the findings of the Temporary National Economic Committee were made public in 1938, and as the Second World War approached, numerous governmental agencies were formed "to represent the public interest" in an attempt to offset "the trend towards greater concentration." [8] In 1940 the Senate Small Business Committee was created,[9] and in the middle of the following year the House of Representatives organized a similar committee.[1] A Small Business Division was set up in the Department of Commerce, with its activities directed to a common purpose—"that of re-enforcing the position of small enterprise and retarding the trend toward concentration." [2]

In spite of all this activity the House Committee on Small Business announced in 1946 that it is

an accepted fact that small business is the only important segment of the economy which is still unorganized. It is true that there are numerous organizations . . . claiming many thousands of members, which address Congress and the executive branch with respect to the alleged problems of small business, but the total number of small business-

[8] David Lynch: *The Concentration of Economic Power* (New York: Columbia University Press; 1946), p. 5.

[9] The Special Committee To Study and Survey the Problems of Small Business Enterprises, created by S.R. 298, 76th Congress.

[1] The Select Committee To Conduct a Study and Investigation of the National Defense Program in Its Relation to Small Business in the United States, created by H.R. 294, 77th Congress.

[2] Lynch: op. cit., p. 5. These agencies "have undertaken to hold hearings and to suggest remedial legislation, to engage in research with respect to the problems of small business, to effect a wider distribution of war contracts, to encourage subcontracting by the large corporations among smaller firms, to render financial assistance to small enterprises, to offer counsel and to provide services to small business in order to enhance its capacity for survival, to maintain effective vigilance over monopolistic and unfair trade practices particularly harmful to small business and to plan for an orderly conversion to a peacetime economy least harmful to small enterprise and least conducive to monopoly." Ibid.

men belonging to such organizations is but a handful compared with the 3,000,000 small firms now in existence in this country.[3]

In 1941 the president of the Illinois Small Business Men's Association was one of many witnesses called to Washington to testify before the Small Business Committee of the Senate. His testimony, given largely in conversation with Senator Mead of New York, was significant because it revealed again the nature and urgency of some of the organizational difficulties of small business as they were seen from both inside and outside Congress.

SEN. MEAD: . . . we have a great many organizations and institutes pleading the cause of small business.

MR. VIRKUS: That is right.

SEN. MEAD: And they all seem to be working alone.

MR. VIRKUS: Yes.

SEN. MEAD: What about coordinating that energy and direction?

MR. VIRKUS: That would be fine. If out of a meeting of that kind, if this committee were to call a group of that kind together, and ask them to sit down and determine a program they would like to see adopted, and then submit it to this committee, it would be the most constructive step that could be taken at this time, in my opinion.

SEN. MEAD: What about having the various groups of organizations in the field get together now? . . . The National Manufacturers, you know, have just the one group.

MR. VIRKUS: Yes. The trouble with that is that there is a good deal of feeling on the part of a good many organizations, as you may know, that they want to play a lone wolf. Now, it is difficult to break that down. But I believe that if this committee were to call representatives of

[3] House Committee on Small Business, 79th Congress: *Report No. 26* (July 1946), p. 2.

the various industries and general groups together, they would respond to that. And if they were locked in a room and told they could not come out until they had formulated a policy, they would formulate one. . . .

SEN. MEAD: It occurs to me it is more the business of the small and intermediate businessmen of the country to get together in one cooperative movement, and then to formulate their policy, and bring their policy to the attention of the committee. As I understand it, we have half a dozen groups in the country.

MR. VIRKUS: That is right. . . .

SEN. MEAD: . . . if you will take the advice of a lone member of this committee, you will exert your energies to the end that small business, now divided in several groups, get together in one organization. . . . The U.S. Chamber of Commerce is a voice, a very profound voice, a very powerful voice for businessmen. But unfortunately many small businessmen are not able to join the Chamber of Commerce. The National Association of Manufacturers is in effect a single voice for the manufacturers of the country.

It occurs to me that small business in looking out for its own program—in view of the fact it is more or less an "orphan in the storm," a "refugee" as it were, or a consignee in a concentration camp—

MR. VIRKUS: Yes; there isn't any question about that.

SEN. MEAD: Under present conditions—you ought to organize into one national organization and formulate your own unified program, and not come here in divers tongues and advocating divers programs.

MR. VIRKUS: Yes.

SEN. MEAD: It is very important, I think, that small business unite into one national organization, because of the precarious position of small business today and tomorrow. . . . There is a shadow hanging over it . . .

MR. VIRKUS: I agree with you thoroughly, sir. We know this, that labor was one time in the same position that small business is. Today it is united.

SEN. MEAD: Today it is not as united as it should be.

MR. VIRKUS: That is right, but it has got only two [AFL and CIO].

Senator Mead expressed the hope that the then separate AFL and CIO would get together and have "just one big labor organization. Harmony is necessary in all these elements of our national existence." The Senator concluded his remarks by saying: "So, Mr. Chairman, whether or not the committee can advise them to do it, I will be very glad to advise them to." [4]

Shortly after his appearance before this Special Committee of the Senate, Mr. Virkus called a meeting in Washington of several other small businessmen who had appeared at one time or another before various Congressional committees, and this group unanimously agreed on the desirability of such a national conference and elected temporary officers and an executive committee for organization purposes. The first National Small Business Conference was held on March 16, 17, and 18, 1942, at the Stevens Hotel in Chicago, and a few months later its title was changed to the Conference of American Small Business Organizations. The Conference was an active national organization in behalf of small business for some twelve years before it closed up shop. Today the National Federation of Independent Business, Inc., is perhaps the largest of the small business pressure groups and is certainly one of the most vigorous spokesmen for the interests of small businessmen.

[4] Senate Small Business Committee, 77th Congress, *1st Session Hearings, December 18, 1941,* Part I, pp. 184–90. It should be stressed that Senator Mead's plea for "harmony" was made on December 18, 1941, less than two weeks after the attack on Pearl Harbor, when he was justifiably concerned with achieving national unity in time of war. Nevertheless, his remarks about the lack of organization in the ranks of small business are valid—in peace or in war.

The National Federation of Independent Business was founded by Mr. C. Wilson Harder in 1943 in a small town on the Peninsula south of San Francisco. A former manager of an automobile agency and member of the United States Chamber of Commerce, Mr. Harder understood the difficulties of unorganized small businessmen struggling for survival in a highly organized society and felt the need for a national association operating solely in their behalf. From its beginning the purpose of the Federation has been "to promote and protect our system of private business, with equal rights for all" and to give small business "a greater voice in laws governing business and our nation." [5] It was hoped that a national organization of independent business and professional people might be able to maintain direct lines of communication and build a better understanding between the "folks at home" and their representatives in Washington. The call went out to people whose stores, offices, warehouses, and manufacturing plants dot the Main Streets and industrial areas in the thousands of towns and cities across the country, from the mom-and-pop grocery outlets to the drug wholesaler, from the country doctor to the medium-sized aircraft parts manufacturer. In the early days of the Federation the only employees were Harder, his wife, and two children. Using the den of their home as an office, they took care of the mailing and kept the books. Today, as it has been since 1947 when it was incorporated under California law as a non-profit corporation, the Federation is run by the original proprietor, President Harder.

By 1945 the Federation, now quartered in a single-room office, had grown to a membership of about 8,000, each member paying annual dues of about ten dollars. A year later the

[5] *The Federation* (Burlingame, Calif.: National Federation of Independent Business; 1957), p. 6.

membership grew to 40,000 and has steadily increased to its present size of over 100,000. Today Mr. Harder has a spacious and comfortable office in the Federation's own building in Burlingame, with some twenty-five people in his employ. In addition, he has hired fifteen other men to work out of the Cincinnati, New York, and Washington offices, plus 150 salesmen located throughout the United States. The Federation has a Public Relations Division in Cincinnati, a full-time lobbyist in the nation's capital, and a legislative researcher who prepares the *Mandate,* a tear-off, self-mailer ballot that is the cornerstone of its activities. From a shoestring operation when it first began to a going concern today, the Federation epitomizes the same entrepreneurial, shoulder-to-the-wheel philosophy it espouses.

Unlike the system of hierarchy and bureaucratic procedures which characterizes large business organizations, the internal structure of the Federation has no rigid pattern. Mr. Harder is responsible to a ten-man board of directors of which he is the permanent chairman. It meets once a year, usually in June, when it reviews the activities of the past year and discusses Mr. Harder's ideas for the coming twelve months. There is no strict budget or tightly planned program since Mr. Harder feels the Federation must be able to respond immediately to problems as they arise. Thus the control of the Federation's funds is in the hands of one man. He can seek approval for any proposal he has in mind by simply calling together a quorum (5) of the board, something he can easily arrange since four of them live in the immediate area and the fifth can be quickly reached by telephone. Having founded the Federation himself, Mr. Harder has made certain that the authority and responsibility for its direction have remained in his hands. None of the board members objects, many of them serving only because they are personal friends of Harder and sympathize with his feelings about small business. They recognize that he is a dedicated man and that the Federation is still his show.

Membership in the Federation is limited to small businessmen who own and operate an independent business that is not dominant in its areas of operation. There is no limit as to size, which means both the corner merchant and Armstrong Tire (whose sales exceed $60,000,000) may belong. This definition gives the Federation a degree of flexibility regarding membership which some definitions of "small business" would not permit.[6] The type of membership is widely diversified: one random district includes doctors, lawyers, accountants, garages, gas stations, banks, insurance companies, electric appliance stores, grocers, and drugstores. Gas stations appear to be the only form of business which constitutes a distinguishable percentage of the total membership; on a regional basis, a significant percentage of members are bankers or owners of independent oil companies who have come from Texas.

In order to build its membership the Federation operates a sales department, with a small group of district sales chairmen and approximately 150 salesmen. Paid on a strict commission basis, the salesmen recruit new members by trying to make a certain number of "sales" a week. The art of salesmanship, so important in a wide variety of small business ventures, is put to careful use in building up first the "customer's" goodwill and then his faith and confidence in the "seller"—the Federation. In much the same way that any salesman learns how to deliver the "pitch" which hopefully will sell his product, the Federation's salesman uses an approach on the prospective member that follows a time-tested formula. There are seven basic steps: (1) the salesman tells the businessman that he is

[6] The Small Business Administration, for example, limits small business to firms whose yearly sales do not exceed $1,000,000 for retail stores, $5,000,000 for wholesale operations, and manufacturing firms not dominant in their areas.

interested in getting his personal opinion on five separate public issues; (2) he then encourages him to vote on the issues and promises to send the ballot to his Congressman; (3) he proceeds to explain the purposes and program of the Federation; (4) he shows him some statements of Senators and Congressmen which are favorable to the activities of the Federation and points out that the national vote of the Federation's membership has been quoted on the floor of the Senate and the House; (5) the salesman then goes on to deliver the first part of his "clincher":

> All of this proves one thing: that Congress will listen to you businessmen providing you can shake just as big a fist as your labor unions, farm groups, big chains and other pressure groups that are working day and night because they have an axe to grind at your expense—and I believe you will agree this is the only way we can hope to get this reduction in business taxes, reduce all of this paper work forced on us . . .

(6) Here the salesman interrupts himself long enough to mention some of the local businessmen who are supporting the Federation and then continues:

> If we each vote on the laws of our land in a concerted action every month, we can put our country back on a firm foundation. This does show that regardless of party or politics or types of business that small business is no longer just standing on the side lines but is taking some very definite action and doing something about it. These men realize like you do that it's only by taking action that independent business can have decent take home profits and can build a sound national economy.[7]

(7) In closing the deal he informs the small businessman that it will cost him between a minimum of twelve dollars and a maximum of $100 a year to become a Federation member and

---

[7] Interview with Kenneth Corkhill, an officer of the National Federation of Independent Business, Inc., February 2, 1958.

goes out of his way to explain that the limit is justified because the Federation refuses to be controlled by any single financial group or power. Usually the salesman tells the story of how Joseph Howard Valentine, who died in 1955, willed the Federation 10,000 shares of stock in his refinery in Salt Lake City, which then had a par value of $.25 per share and one year later rose to $45, only to have Mr. Harder refuse the offer of stock because of the $100 limit on contributions. The entire sales pitch is supported by a variety of visual aids, including elaborate reference to the *Mandate,* a chart showing the district chairman depositing the member's ballot in a pipeline which runs directly to the Capitol, and a picture of the Federation's lobbyist reading the results of their national poll to a Congressional committee.

The general entrepreneurial outlook of small business is clearly the guiding philosophy of the Federation in its approach to new members and, for that matter, in all of its activities. The appeal is made on a face-to-face basis, and the individual businessman, whether laundry operator or local banker, is given the feeling that his support of the Federation is a personal act of real importance. One thing is certain: there is nothing that smacks of the confidence and finesse of a big business organization. The whole philosophy behind the sales technique, as the following paper sent to the district sales representative makes clear, is strictly Main Street, not Wall Street:

> In about eight cases out of ten your new salesmen will not understand that, in order to successfully sell a Federation membership, the appeal MUST be made to the EMOTIONS of the prospect—and that there is nothing unethical or wrong in so doing. Our interview time is short, and no salesman could present, or any prospect understand more than a tiny part of the underlying economic principles which create the necessity for the Federation and its program— *nor is it desirable that either completely so understand it.*

. . . . You must in all your training and retraining continually stress the need to "pour the sales talk into the prospect's own place of business." [8]

One of the assumptions implicit in the statement above is that the independent businessman is fully aware of his own problems and position in our industrial society. For this reason the Federation does not concern itself with selling the "idea," but rather sells a tool of action. Mr. Harder firmly believes that if independent businessmen are brought together at a convention to establish a policy and program, they will succeed only in producing chaos and conflict. They would never be able to agree on anything. Take them aside individually, however, and ask them for their own opinion on any issue—this tactic will lead to a high degree of unanimity.

The Federation reached a plateau in 1951 when the membership was between 75,000 and 100,000. In the last ten years the number of members has fluctuated around this figure or increased slightly, but the over-all growth rate has declined sharply. In 1957, for example, the Federation took in some 24,000 new members but renewed only 70 per cent of the ones who were contacted, thereby resulting in a loss of membership of approximately 5,000. The problem of renewals is important to the Federation and has been receiving increasing emphasis over the years. There has been a steady turnover in the sales force since 1951, necessitating the constant training of new salesmen which, in turn, has reduced sales efficiency. Some seventy salesmen, or about 50 per cent of the total sales force, devote full time to renewals. Experience has shown that 40 to 50 per cent of the renewals are automatic; the other 20 or 25 per cent are retained through the strenuous art of salesman-

---

[8] Deone Hughson: *Suggestions and Ideas about Bringing Through New Men To Become Successful Federation Representatives* (Burlingame, Calif.: National Federation of Independent Business), p. 3.

ship. A businessman is not removed from the membership or mailing list until he has been contacted by a salesman who cancels the renewal. Placing great stress on stabilizing and expanding the sales force, the Federation would ultimately like to have a salesman in each Congressional district. Like all sales campaigns where the individual with the highest totals is rewarded, the Federation has its own incentive program as well as an internal publication called the *Spotlight,* which gives recognition to the fifteen leading salesmen each week. The *Spotlight* also includes hints for better sales techniques and provides the salesman with fresh arguments to be used against big business or big government.

To Mr. Harder the activity perhaps most vital to sales success and the future expansion of the Federation is a vigorous program of public relations. Again the contrast with big business organizations, which are more likely to turn to Madison Avenue for the newest in promotional schemes, is striking. The Federation has one man, its vice president, Edward Wimmer, who devotes his time and energy to selling the public on the virtues of small business and in boosting the work of the Federation. He is, in effect, the idealist who gives his life to the Federation because he believes wholeheartedly in its purposes. His is a thirty-year crusade for the small businessman, whose plight he feels personally.

> I was engaged in candy manufacturing in 1932, when the depression wiped out so many. I launched an educational program designed to awaken the people to the values of the family farm, the independent business enterprise, and the local bank; to point out as well as could be done at that time, the disastrous effects of economic power in the hands of the few—one of those effects being the crash of 1929.[9]

In 1932 Mr. Wimmer founded the Forward America Publishing Guild, Inc., in Cincinnati, Ohio, and for sixteen years

[9] Letter from Edward Wimmer, dated February 14, 1958.

published and distributed papers, booklets, and circulars. In the latter part of 1946 he joined the Federation, taking on a number of duties designed to promote the work of the Federation and the cause of small business. He has lectured throughout the United States, has appeared on radio and television, and for many years has written a weekly column for the *Cincinnati Enquirer.* He is also a frequent guest speaker at national and local conventions of various trade associations such as the Retail Druggists, Automotive Wholesalers, and Independent Bankers. His mission is constant and clear:

> On Main Street America, newsboys, farm hands and low-wage earners rose from rags to riches; bankers rubbed elbows with fruit and vegetable wagon operators; merchant princes, statesmen, editors and clerks won fame and fortune. The real name of this Main Street was Freedom of Opportunity and not until the "Father & Son" signs start going up again on the Main Streets of America will Freedom of Opportunity in this country be assured.[1]

The "public relations" activities of the Federation are carried on by Mr. Wimmer with a zeal that saturates all of its advertising and propaganda. Mr. Wimmer's role, as he sees it, is to awaken the people to what is happening in this country, to stir up concern and excitement about the "chisel age" in which we live, when Main Street has become Chain Street. Calling himself a radical, Mr. Wimmer observes that "a radical is a man who intellectually goes to the bottom of all problems. Dante said, 2000 years ago"—a slight error—" 'The hottest places in hell are reserved for those who in a period of crisis maintain their neutrality.' "[2] Far from being a neutral observer, Mr. Wimmer is a passionate and angry critic of the contemporary American scene.

[1] May Dearness: "Enquirer Interviews Wimmer on Capitalism," *Dayton Press,* February 14, 1952.

[2] Edward Wimmer: *Now or Never, Mr. Independent Banker* (Burlingame, Calif.: National Federation of Independent Business), p. 10.

The key to the Federation's activities is the *Mandate,* a special device for polling the members to learn their opinions on a variety of domestic and international issues. In order to determine which issues should be placed before the membership, the Federation's Washington representative informs the home office about the bills currently before Congress which pertain to small business. Five issues are selected for the *Mandate,* each of which is accompanied by a supporting and an opposing argument. The *Mandate* is then printed and mailed to all of the members, who in turn vote on the separate issues and send the ballot to the Federation's district chairman.[3] He counts their votes for his district and sends the ballot, plus one copy of the tabulation, to his Congressman, with a carbon copy also going to the Federation's home office in California. Mr. Harder and his staff proceed to tabulate the national result based on the returns from the 2,500 or so district chairmen, and the national total is then forwarded to each member of the House and Senate, plus selected members of the executive branch of the government. Congressmen are also sent the results of the vote within their own district, thereby saving them the trouble of doing the counting. Actually the Congressmen and Senators are only given percentage figures—that is, the per cent voting For, Against, or No Vote—and thus there exists considerable discrepancy between the Federation's claim that it represents 100,000 independent businessmen and the fact that only about 25 per cent of the members participate in the balloting. The Federation leaders are sensitive to this situation and therefore are not eager to make public the percentage of returns of each *Mandate.* An administrative assistant to a prominent Senator has written that as far as his office is concerned the

[3] The district chairman resides in a central location and is usually a civic leader who has been recommended by some of the members to the Federation's salesmen.

Federation has been "of no importance" and that "their national polls have absolutely no influence at all on decisions either for or against legislation." He pointed out that the Senator for whom he worked has "no way of determining the Federation's qualifications with respect to any specific bill, or whether the views it may express really do reflect those of its members." He went on to say, in a candid manner often more characteristic of administrative assistants than Senators themselves: "I hope you will believe that the foregoing represents an attempt at a frank statement and not simply a protestation of virtue." [4]

The most important member of the Federation politically is its Washington lobbyist and vice president, George Burger, Sr. Like others who have gone to work for the Federation, Mr. Burger has come up "through the ranks" of small business. With only a grammar school education and some work experience as a traveling bill collector for United States Motor Company (which later became the Chrysler Corporation) he established his own business in New York in 1911, retailing automobile tires and accessories. Ten years later he became first president of the Greater New York Tire Dealers Association and then president of the National Association. In 1929 he was one of the founding members of the United Tire Stores of America, an organization designed to give "tire independents" the benefit of mass purchasing power to help them meet the competition from Sears, Roebuck's arrangement with the Goodyear Tire and Rubber Company. Mr. Burger began his

[4] There are, of course, comments more flattering to the Federation, although they sometimes have the air of a public testimonial rather than a private appraisal. Congressman Abraham J. Multer, for example, wrote that the Federation and its lobbyist "are among the most effective national groups working in Washington. They are on the job all the time, trying to improve the conditions of the small businessman. Not only do they sponsor and urge the enactment of legislation that is helpful to the small businessman, but they also work against legislation that is bad for that important segment of our economy." Letter dated February 19, 1958.

own consultant service for independent tire dealers in 1941, acting as a lobbyist in their behalf. In 1946 he became a member of the board of directors of the Federation and in two years was elected vice president in charge of the Federation's legislative activities.

As a lobbyist Mr. Burger's major objective has been the preservation of small business through consistent and vigorous enforcement of the antitrust laws. This concentration of purpose, however, has not prevented the Federation from being concerned with all phases of government policy. Among Mr. Burger's claims for his twenty years of lobbying is the establishment of the Senate Small Business Committee as a permanent committee in 1950. It is difficult for any organization to lay claim to the sole responsibility for the passage of important legislation, but it is not unusual for its representatives to try, if for no other reason than to promote their own special group and salute themselves. Mr. Burger is no exception.

> . . . as far as trade association activity, it was probably our exclusive handiwork that brought about the acceptance of Congress in the creation of the Small Business Administration, which agency as you know, its main function is to make loans to small business. And, the recent action of the House in proposing this Agency be made a permanent agency, it may be found that in the First Session of the present Congress, we played no minor part, and I repeat no minor part in having the House vote this legislation 393 for and 2 against. We are striving right at this moment to have concurrent action taken by the Senate.
>
> In 1947, the writer, then a few months later joined in by the National Federation of Independent Business, by our exclusive handiwork was able to bring about action under the Robinson-Patman Act invoking a section of that law as applied to the rubber tire industry, namely the Quantity Discount, for the sale of rubber tires. This case is not concluded as yet and if finally validated, it will act as a guinea pig for all other industries to follow where

monopoly or concentration is rampant within a particular industry.[5]

The Federation also takes credit for helping to repeal the Basing Point Bill and the passing of the Celler-O'Mahoney-Kefauver Act of 1949, which plugged up a loophole in the anti-merger laws by amending Section 7 of the Clayton Act.

Mr. Burger's techniques as a lobbyist reflect the general attitude of many small businessmen in their own dealings as independent proprietors. The art of selling is given the same importance in influencing legislators as it is in persuading customers.

> Lobbying is no different than salesmanship. In other words, it is my belief that in salesmanship a good salesman is successful for himself or in his own business only after he builds up in the first instance the customers' goodwill, faith and confidence in the seller. . . . Carrying out this principle to the fullest degree, you gain the respect and confidence of members of Congress and Federal agencies. This does not mean that they will always concur but they will respect your sincerity for an honest objective.[6]

The activities of a lobbyist are multifarious. In giving the position of the Federation Mr. Burger spends a good part of his time testifying before Congressional committees. A typical presentation by Mr. Burger would proceed along the following lines:

[5] Letter from George J. Burger, dated February 17, 1958. It is worth noting that the style, grammar, and tone of this letter is, to repeat a similar point made previously, very much in the down-to-earth tradition of Main Street. This particular letter, written to a graduate assistant of mine who helped with the research on the Federation, was four single-spaced pages in length typed by Mr. Burger himself. It is chatty and biographical throughout. "In the first part of your letter," he writes at one point, "you put the question 'Why you joined the Federation.' A good question, my boy." This is not the kind of communication one would be likely to receive from a business executive on either Wall Street or Madison Avenue.

[6] Ibid.

I am George J. Burger, Vice-President in charge of legislative activities of the National Federation of Independent Business. . . . Our national headquarters are located in Burlingame, California. We also maintain division offices at New York, Cincinnati, and Chicago.

Mr. Chairman, no officer or group of officers is permitted to speak for the Federation prior to the direct nationwide vote of our entire membership. I make this statement so that I will qualify under the mandate of our nationwide membership.[7]

Mr. Burger will go on to show that the Federation's membership is above 100,000 and will offer an explanation of the *Mandate* and how it operates. Frequently he will invoke the results of past or present Federation polls to support his testimony and will often have the arguments on both sides of a specific issue read into the *Congressional Record* to impress the Congressmen with his fair-mindedness. Occasionally he feels called upon to talk about his own experiences and difficulties in his "40 years as an independent tire dealer." He usually concludes his remarks by thanking the members of the committee, pointing out that his association with the Federation has endured for so many years because it has never failed to live up to its professed goals, and, finally, making a plea for the "little guy" in our country.

For their own part the members of the committee first inquire about the over-all operation of the Federation in order to establish its basic integrity as a pressure group and then turn to the more immediate issues under consideration. More often than not the committee is concerned with solutions to antitrust measures, the operation of the Anti-Trust Division or perhaps the Federal Trade Commission, and questions arising

[7] *Price Discrimination,* Hearings on H.R. 114, U.S. House Select Committee on Small Business, 84th Congress, 1st Session (Washington, D.C.: 1955), p. 203.

over the many problems of monopolistic practices in the economy. Because of Mr. Burger's knowledge of the tire industry, his opinions in this area are especially sought. In 1953 the Senate Select Committee on Small Business prepared a report which drew heavily on Mr. Burger's own Tire Consultant Service for information which later became the basis of its recommendations. Mr. Burger has been particularly effective and articulate in his defense of the independent tire dealer, and it is not surprising that the Federation itself has a special interest in the independent gas and tire dealers among its members.

Another political function of Mr. Burger is to appear before the platform committees of both major parties prior to their national conventions and present the demands of small business. In 1956, according to one Federation publication, Mr. Burger and Mr. Harder were the only representatives of small business to appear at the platform-drafting hearings of both the Democrats and the Republicans. The Federation has repeatedly asked both parties to commit themselves to vigorous enforcement of the antitrust laws, tax reduction for incorporated and unincorporated smaller firms, higher tariff laws, measures to protect small business from labor unions, withdrawal of commercial activities on the part of the government which compete with small business, a reduction in the federal paperwork burden on independent businessmen, and continuation of the Small Business Administration with its responsibility fixed solely to Congress.[8]

Although the Federation has not been directly responsible for a good deal of Congressional legislation, it has nonetheless met the requirements of an active interest group seeking to pro-

[8] *Report on Activities of the National Federation of Independent Business Pertaining to Small Business Planks Adopted at Democratic and Republican Conventions 1956* (Burlingame, Calif.: National Federation of Independent Business; 1957).

mote the welfare of small businessmen.[9] It has a sizable membership, its financial condition is healthy, and it conducts a conscientious operation in its *Mandate*. Its lobbyist in Washington is vigorous and hard-working. Unlike the associations which speak the professional language of big business, the Federation is without polish in its dealings with people and issues. But what it lacks in sophistication as an organization it more than makes up in dedication to its chosen mission of representing the hard-pressed small businessman. More important than anything else, however, the Federation is run much like a small business, with its original and only proprietor, Mr. Harder, still minding the store.

But neither a small business organization nor the political perspective of small businessmen can be adequately examined without first considering the ideology of small business itself. The relationship of ideology to politics is no less close and pertinent in the small business arena than it is in that of labor or big business. In order to understand some of the actions and reactions of small businessmen today, it is necessary to give some thought not only to the economic privations resulting from their position in the economy but to the set of beliefs, arguments, and symbols which have helped to form their general outlook on life. Something of the small businessman's heritage and the folklore that has followed him throughout most of our history is already known. Almost any Congressional committee report on small business makes it clear that every

[9] There are many small business pressure groups but most represent a particular type of small business. The Federation has one other important competitor, the National Small Business Men's Association. In 1957 the expenditures of the Federation amounted to $32,161.97 as over against $27,268.31 for the NSBMA. The Federation ranked 22nd in total expenditures out of a total of 133 business lobbies and was among the top five lobbying groups concerned with small business. See the *Congressional Quarterly Weekly Report*, XVI, No. 6 (Washington, D.C.: 1958), p. 151.

community is traditionally stamped for good or for ill by its small businessmen—in fact, the town is said to take its character from their enterprise and civic-mindedness. When a man makes his way into small business ownership, his perseverance is hailed as a "practical application of our highly prized ideal of equal opportunity under the American flag." As a Senate report says, his struggle

> has been a great motive force among our people. It stimulates expression of the fundamental virtues of thrift, industry, intelligence, schooling, home ties, and family pride—in short, those fireside virtues which have counted for so much in developing our strength and character." [1]

The preservation of small business, therefore, is urgent and vital in furthering the American ideal, "a goal which transcends economic and political forms and processes as such, and remains fundamentally concerned with the character of the men and women who comprise the nation." [2] In short, it is doubtful if the virtues and values of any individual have been so consistently and unanimously proclaimed as those of the small businessman. However, when the ideology of small business is viewed against the backdrop of our modern industrial society, it may become necessary to revise the popular image of the American small businessman.

[1] *U.S. Senate Small Business Committee—Its Record and Outlook,* Progress Report of the Special Committee To Study Problems of American Small Business, 89th Congress, First Session, Report No. 47 (February 12, 1945), pp. 2–3.

[2] Weissman: op. cit., p. 164.

The General Ideology
of American
Small Business

<u>1</u>   The small businessman has so
often been taken for granted as being an essential pillar of our
democratic society that it frequently comes as something of a
discovery to realize that in actuality we know very little about
his ideas, beliefs, or values. In many respects we know more
about small *business* than we do about small businessmen. The
old independent entrepreneur, who grew up under the liberal
capitalism of small property holdings, has seen the economy
shift to a system of corporate capitalism, until today he lives
"on a small island in a big new world." In the language of the
lawyer, the small businessman is being "absorbed, merged, and
acquired" to the point where he is described as one of the
vanishing Americans of the twentieth century. Nonetheless, he
has endured with considerable tenacity as an important force in
present-day society.

The survival of the small businessman, while significant as
an economic reality, is even more noteworthy as an ideological

phenomenon. In the past half century American society has witnessed the growth and spread of industrialism on the largest scale imaginable. At the same time, the ideology that was once suited to a society of small capitalists has persisted almost as if it were the economic law of the land. Political candidates of both parties never tire of announcing that the continued life of the small businessman makes the free enterprise system free and that if he succumbs it will die with him. Only the existence of a healthy, militant small business community, we are repeatedly told, can prevent the erosion of our democratic way of life by the organization and power of big business. In a broadcast before the Second World War a well-known radio commentator expressed the familiar feeling toward the small businessman:

> When we speak of business we must not think solely of large capital, huge industries and famous names. These do not comprise American Business. If one should attend an annual convention of the American Bankers Association, for example, one would see around 5,000 bankers in session, but of these 4,950 are men and women who head country banks. They are the small bankers who carry the bulk of the business for the bulk of the people. . . . Small business is a vast network of communications which sends depressive or tonic influence to the country. We are more dependent on the small businessman than we realize— more than he realizes. The community takes its reading of the national economic temperature from the thermometer of the small businessman's countenance.
> This is a small-town and small-business country. . . .[1]

It is as if the small-propertied world of the small independent businessman was still a going concern, and the ideology which

---

[1] W. J. Cameron: "The Small Businessman." Talk given on the Ford Sunday Evening Hour, No. 20 of the 1939–40 series of broadcasts over the Columbia Broadcasting System from Detroit, Michigan. Quoted in Kelley and Lawyer: op. cit., pp. 6–7.

enforces this picture is so little changed "that in the minds of many it seems the very latest model of reality." [2]

Mills has pointed out that in the nineteenth-century world of the small entrepreneur power was so much more decentralized and anonymous that it did not require "ideological cement." Conversely, he claims it is in the new managed society, where power is centralized and only anonymous when it is manipulative, that it has been necessary to formulate new ideological justifications for the power of the modern corporation, a power which is "not easily justifiable in terms of the simple democratic theory of sovereignty inherited from the eighteenth and nineteenth centuries." The new managers or "vested interests," he maintains, need an "ideology" in the sense of wanting a comfortable set of self-interested rationalizations under cover of which they can conduct their business and perpetuate their power, while at the same time justifying their practices and policies to the public and, perhaps, to themselves as well.

> The whole growth of ideological work is based on the need for the vested interests lodged in the new power centers to be softened, whitened, blurred, misinterpreted to those who serve the interests of the bureaucracies inside, and to those in its sphere outside.[3]

This emphasis on "ideological justification," however, does not convey the full sense and meaning in which the term "ideology" will be principally understood and used here. The "ideological demand" Mills is talking about is for new and compelling "myths" about the corporations and about the men who run them, so that public opinion can more easily be

---

[2] Mills: op. cit., p. 34. Mills says that the small businessman "has become the man through whom the ideology of utopian capitalism is still attractively presented to many of our contemporaries."

[3] Ibid., p. 154.

converted into goodwill which, in turn, must be "continually managed and sustained." Few will dispute the importance of this particular problem, and any difference of interpretation with Mills is not one of disagreement regarding the manipulatory potentialities of big business. Nevertheless Mills's approach to the problem of ideology is more narrowly conceived than our own and for this reason is not very useful in our present endeavor. To take but a single example, Mills is not entirely clear as to the question of *intent* on the part of the "vested interests"—that is to say, is their demand for ideological justification "self-delusion" or is it "design" or "conspiracy"? One easily gains the impression that Mills looks upon ideology as simply the reflection of the economic self-interest of whatever particular group or "interest" he may be describing. In this sense ideology becomes almost exclusively an attempt to "manipulate symbols and marshal arguments which will persuade others to take actions from which the ideologist stands to profit financially." Viewed in this way the ideologist may or may not actually believe the things he says. If he does happen to believe them, "it is only because he has succeeded by wishful thinking in convincing himself that truth and self-interest coincide." [4] Sutton and his associates have shown that the relationship between specific ideologies and economic interest is not always as clear as some would make out. They point out that because a businessman gives "passionate support" to the principle of a balanced federal budget does not mean that he has arrived at this position by meticulously weighing all the econometric factors or by carefully calculating the effects balanced and unbalanced budgets will have on his profit prospects.

[4] Francis X. Sutton, Seymour E. Harris, Carl Kaysen, and James Tobin: *The American Business Creed* (Cambridge, Mass.: Harvard University Press; 1956), p. 12.

It is true that with sufficient ingenuity one can construct a chain which reconciles practically any ideological position to the economic interest of its holder. Or one can make the task easier by attributing to the ideologist a mistaken or unduly certain conception of his own interest. One can make the task still easier by widening the notion of self-interest to encompass psychological satisfactions other than economic returns. But these expedients are really the end of the theory they are designed to salvage. They reduce it to a tautology: "Men act in their own interests" becomes "Men act as they are motivated to act." [5]

For our purposes the ideology of small business will be examined in terms of some of its ideas, attitudes, and values. In particular, these will be viewed as part of a major tradition in American political history that has not lost its force in our modern industrial society. The ideology of small business partakes of many attitudes that were prevalent in the United States prior to the rise of industry and has much in common with those values which are usually associated with a pre-industrial society. By placing the ideology of the small businessman in the context of what will be called the "agrarian spirit" it is hoped it will be possible to develop a better and richer understanding of small business. What is even more important, against this ideological backdrop it will be possible to show that the small businessman is a contemporary advocate of the agrarian spirit.

At the same time it should be made clear what is *not* implied. There is no implication that he wishes to return to the Jeffersonian era or that he is a farmer at heart. No claim is being made that in literal terms there is a *total* commitment on the part of the small businessman to a pre-industrial society or that *all* small businessmen would prefer to live in such a society. Nor is it to be inferred that the agrarian spirit repre-

[5] Ibid., p. 13.

90

sents an ideology peculiar *only* to small businessmen. The ideology of pre-industrialism in America is looked upon here as an "ideal type," in the belief that it is profitable to discuss the ideology of small business within the context of those values usually identified with a pre-industrial way of life. If it is reasonable to suggest that present-day industrialists are committed to industrialism and its values, then by creating in turn an ideal agrarian ideology of pre-industrialism it will be possible to detect some of the ideological differences between big and small business. Our concern is not so much with the economic factors which lead the small businessman to hold the particular views he does but rather with identifying his views and attitudes and *locating* them on some political spectrum.

In spite of the triumph of industrialism in the last 150 years the ideologies of anti-industrialism have won a victory of their own in the battle of ideas. Reinhard Bendix has pointed out that industrialization in the Western World has continuously been accompanied by a variety of protests and attacks on the dehumanization of men as a result of the effects of industry. This is not to say that the industrial way of life has been lacking in its own intellectual supporters and defenders, but simply that in retrospect it would appear that the ideologies of anti-industrialism have reigned supreme during a period in which industrialists have organized the greatest technical and economic progress known to history.[6] In the United States the earliest spokesman in behalf of the ideology of anti-industrialism was Thomas Jefferson, whose ideas about manufacturing and industry were never concealed. Jefferson felt strongly that America, unlike Europe, was blessed with a

[6] I am indebted to Reinhard Bendix for much of the discussion on the ideas of pre-industrialism. Many of the points that are touched upon here are more fully and capably explored in his brilliant study of managerial ideologies, *Work and Authority in Industry* (New York: John Wiley & Sons; 1956).

surplus of land and therefore we should "never wish to see our citizens occupied at a workbench, or twirling a distaff . . . let our workshops remain in Europe." [7] The Jeffersonian doctrine of agrarianism was rooted in the experience of a rural America, and it is not surprising that to this day appeals to this tradition strike a responsive chord in many people.

In the South the early advocacy of agrarianism as the foundation of a democratic society was conceived as a weapon in the struggle against the forces of industrialism rising in the North. It was an anti-industrial position whose central argument was that industrialization was the moral and physical corrupter of the owner of property as well as the working man. The conflict, symbolized in part in the struggle between Jefferson and Hamilton, has deep roots in the political and economic development of America. As fortunate as this country has been in not experiencing a succession of embittered political battles such as have marked the history of many European nations, there nevertheless have been in American political history antagonistic traditions which have caused bitter conflict.[8] Sometimes this conflict has been called, depending on the particular circumstances, a North-South split. At other times it has been characterized as a struggle between labor and capital. On still other occasions it has been viewed as an agricultural-industrial conflict. No doubt each of these descriptions contains more than a little truth, especially when it is related to an immediate political or economic problem. However, none of these explanations entirely succeeds in accounting for all of the elements present in the continuing antagonism. For this reason there is an advantage in regarding

[7] Thomas Jefferson: "Notes on Virginia," in *Life and Selected Writings* (New York: Modern Library; 1944), p. 280.

[8] Many of the observations on the importance of America's political traditions have come from extended conversations with Norman Jacobson.

this traditional antagonism as a conflict between the heritage of the pre-industrial age (in our broad terms, the agrarian spirit) on the one hand and the cosmopolitan spirit on the other. The former represents the broad tradition of John Taylor, Calhoun, Henry George, and Robert LaFollette, incorporating therein the Southern agrarianism of Jefferson and Fitzhugh with the entrepreneurial spirit of Adam Smith and the Yankee temper of the North and Midwest; the latter embodies the tradition that links such men as Hamilton, Webster, and the two Roosevelts. Against the background of these two divergent traditions one can view in a clearer perspective lesser but nevertheless significant conflicts, such as that between ruralism and urbanism. Much of the bitterness and emotional fervor that does exist in American politics arises from the fact that some people are committed, albeit implicitly, to one tradition and some to the other. It is true that up to now this agrarian-cosmopolitan conflict has not severely disrupted our political system, which is merely to say that neither of the two major parties has a complete monopoly on any one tradition. The Democratic Party embraces both Southern agrarians *and* Northern and Western urban groups, while in the Republican Party Midwestern businessmen and farmers represent one school of thought in opposition to Eastern and Western industrialists. Our purpose is to show that the small businessman is a contemporary spokesman for the agrarian spirit and shares many of the values and ideas which are usually identified with it. These pre-industrial values serve as an ideological framework within which one can see not only those things in which the small businessman believes, but also what kind of person the small businessman is.

2

One hundred years ago George Fitzhugh expressed his views on the evils of industrialism, and so bitter was his condemnation of the relationship between employer and employee in the industrial North that he could exalt the institution of slavery as a happy alternative. Slavery, he believed, was the sole remaining guardian of Christian virtue, and only by preserving this system of paternalism and affection could the disastrous effects of industry be avoided.

At the slaveholding South all is peace, quiet, plenty and contentment. We have no mobs, no trade unions, no strikes for higher wages, no armed resistance to the law, but little jealousy of the rich by the poor. . . . We have enough for the present, and no Malthusian spectres frightening us for the future. Wealth is more equally distributed than at the North, where a few millionaires own most of the property of the country. (These millionaires are men of cold hearts and weak minds; they know how to make money, but not how to use it, either for the benefit of themselves or of others.) High intellectual and moral attainments, refinement of head and heart, give standing to a man in the South, however poor he may be. Money is, with few exceptions, the only thing that enobles at the North.[9]

In this one passage can be found many of the elements which are at the core of the agrarian spirit. Not only is the basic hostility to industrialism made clear, but in contrast many of the rural values and folkways of the South are affirmed as the epitome of the good life. Where there are mobs, labor difficulties, and lawlessness in the industrial North, serenity,

[9] George Fitzhugh: *Sociology for the South* (Richmond, Va : A. Morris Publisher; 1854), pp. 253–4.

peace, and harmony prevail in the agricultural South.[1] While conflict rages in the North because of the cruel division of labor, in the South there is intellectual, moral, and economic stability. Property, the bedrock of Southern living and the possession of virtuous men, is nothing but a blunt-edged weapon in the hands of Northern industrialists, who use it to rob the working man of his individuality and spirit. Fitzhugh's choice of words might be considered somewhat extreme today; certainly his defense of slavery would not be held in high regard. But his remarks have a rural ring and flavor to them that still serve as a reminder of conditions that prevailed before the industrialization and commercialization of America.

It is not an overstatement to say that the tradition and thought of pre-industrial America have persisted longer in the rural sections of the country than in the urban. It has often been pointed out that rural America tends to be Protestant and even Fundamentalist, and that it is hostile to and distrustful of the large metropolitan areas where innovation and experimentation are the rule rather than the exception. It is in the rural areas that the Women's Christian Temperance Union has had its strongest support, and in the South at least, the rural sections have consistently been the main strength of the Ku Klux Klan. Laski was only one of many to have understood that "Xenophobia is endemic in rural America." [2]

If the rural person views the big city with suspicion and thinks no more highly of the people who live there, it is equally true that he himself has "a more developed attitude of nationalism, in the sense of love of his own country or region,

---

[1] Jefferson of course had remarked many years earlier that "the mobs of great cities add just so much to the support of pure government, as sores do to the strength of the human body." Jefferson: op. cit., p. 280.

[2] Harold Laski: op. cit. p. 157.

than the bulk of the urban population." [3] There is no question that the rural population is more homogeneous, if for no other reason than that the largest number of immigrants have settled in the cities. The rural sections of the country have always contained only a small number of outsiders, and it follows that the people who live there have much less contact with foreigners. At the same time mobility in rural areas is much more limited, inasmuch as "country folk" usually die in the place where they were born. "It is evident," comments Carl Friedrich, "that all these factors produce a more pronounced group sentiment. In its modern form, this sentiment is known as nationalism." [4] The fact that ruralism has never been sympathetic to the work of the melting pot in America goes a long way toward explaining its general hostility both to minority groups and to alien philosophies and ideologies as well. In this connection one can detect more than a little similarity between a deep-seated agrarian mistrust of the mingling of ideas and cultures in the large metropolitan areas on the one hand and Jefferson's dislike of the city, Calhoun's fear of industry, and LaFollette's antipathy to Wall Street on the other.

The heritage of pre-industrialism embraces many diversified elements. Jefferson's farmer and Adam Smith's small capitalist share many of the same values and are in fact mutually replenishing. Equally important in its contributions to the range of pre-industrial values has been the frontier experience in America, which not only profoundly influenced Washington and Jefferson but left its permanent imprint on the great

[3] P. Sorokin and C. C. Zimmermann: *Principles of Rural-Urban Sociology* (New York: Henry Holt; 1929), p. 407.
[4] Carl J. Friedrich: "The Agricultural Basis of Emotional Nationalism," *Public Opinion Quarterly* (April 1937), pp. 50–1.

Western adventure. Both the farmers and the early business-men, those who worked the land as well as the shopkeepers and merchants, were affected by the triumph of the frontier, and to this day the legacy lingers and permeates every aspect of American life. There was nothing conservative on the front line of the West. With buoyant self-confidence and self-assertion the frontiersmen were building a new order of society, and the energy they poured into this venture became a rich new American resource. Self-reliance, inventiveness, decisive action—these were the qualities necessary for survival on the moving frontier. But more than anything else there was the feeling of freedom, and if the teeming cities never became the haven or symbol of free men, it was because they imposed a pattern of living that violated all of early America's cherished ideals. On the frontier a man was free because he was independent; in the city he was a cipher because, at bottom, he was a dependent man. It is a conviction that has endured in spite of the technological displacement of the frontier, and as a tradition it pervades the feelings of many in our own day who, like the small businessman, see themselves as little men in a big world yet still strive to preserve individuality and independence.

In many respects the small businessman is almost always looking for or longing for a frontier. It is as if he has fastened onto a goal which is no longer available in the form in which he seeks it. For example, an increasing number of small businessmen, including butchers, bakers, television repairmen, garage operators, grocers, and the like move out of this country each year seeking a frontier economic climate for free enterprise. In 1959 the Canadian government opened two new immigration offices—in Minneapolis and Los Angeles—with the avowed mission of persuading small American tradesmen to go North. While many hundreds may make such a trek,

they are of course still a minority. Nevertheless, those who remain seem to share a large part of this motivation and desire
to find a new frontier in the great North or somewhere else
away from the crowded cities. It is merely another indication
that the spirit of the frontier is not yet dead in the soul of the
individual who goes into small business.

If the morality of the frontier has become in so many
ways the morality of America, among other reasons it is because it has been able to blend a simplistic faith with a
righteous attitude. Sin and virtue, evil and good—these are
still the only choices for many people today as they pass
judgment on what is right and wrong in this country and
abroad. They are inherited ways of looking at things that can
be traced largely to the frontier. Little wonder, then, that the
frontier experience, which for Turner was what distinguished
this country so sharply from the nations of Europe, should
have also helped give expression to American nationalism. It
was the frontier that had given America its uniqueness, and
Americans were quick to develop the sense of pride and accomplishment that comes from being different. In his *Innocents
Abroad* and *A Connecticut Yankee at King Arthur's Court*
Mark Twain captured the nativist mood as he poked fun at
the aristocratic institutions and foppish ways of European
cultures. The psychological necessity for renouncing Europe
had its counterpart in the intense self-respect which had already become an important dimension of the American Way.
The frontier exuberance of the nineteenth century combined
a full consciousness of nationality with a vibrant democratic
impulse, and when to all of this is added what has been called
the most vaunted and celebrated of American attitudes—
namely, a dynamic individualism—one can easily see what
the frontier has meant for this country's development. Its importance as a theory of American exceptionalism has been

frequently exaggerated and even distorted, but when this has been said it remains nevertheless a powerful tradition in American life. For a nation of urban dwellers the frontier and its code of agrarian values still evoke nostalgia, testimony enough that those who live in our crowded cities can still identify themselves with the romantic figure of the backwoodsman as they yearn after Crabtree Corners.

In a series of articles on "soap operas" that appeared a number of years ago in *The New Yorker,* James Thurber succeeded in describing with extraordinary skill some of the rural feelings and attitudes which constitute an important part of the agrarian spirit.[5] His comments are especially pertinent because they capture a state of mind and a general outlook that are endemic to the small-town scheme of values. In much the same way that many novelists are able to write a more human record of war than social scientists can reveal through masses of data, so Thurber's account of "Ivorytown, Rinsoville, Anacinburg and Crisco Corners" is a telling portrayal of rural habits and sentiments.

The daytime serials, Thurber reported, perpetuate the ancient American myth of the small town, idealized in novels, comedies, and melodramas at the turn of the century and before. The heavy predominance of "small towns in Soapland is a continued and often-emphasized victory for good, clean little communities over cold, cruel metropolitan centers." The differences between "small-town people" and "big-city people" coincide easily with the traditional concepts of good and evil, distinctions between the two being made in the "old-fashioned terms of the moral town and the immoral city." As Thurber so neatly put it:

[5] James Thurber: "Soapland," Part II, *The New Yorker* (May 29, 1948). Mr. Thurber's articles comprise a series of four delightful accounts of the soap opera in America which *The New Yorker* featured under the title: "Onward and Upward with the Arts."

Almost all the villains in the small-town daytime serials are émigrés from the cities—gangsters, white-collar criminals, designing women, unnatural mothers, cold wives, and selfish, ruthless and just plain cussed rich men. They always come up against a shrewdness that outwits them or destroys them, or a kindliness that wins them over to the good way of life.

Neither Jefferson nor Calhoun in his own day would have quarreled with such a characterization.

In Soapland the agrarian spirit provides the setting and background for a world comfortably at rest. One serial writer told Thurber that "the word 'republic' has been slyly suggested as preferable to 'democracy,' apparently because 'democracy' has become a provocative flaming torch of a word in our time." Soapland, if nothing else, is a peaceful world, "a political and economic Utopia, free of international unrest, the menace of fission, the threat of inflation, depression, general unemployment, the infiltration of Communists, and the problem of racism." [6]

The traditional "Western" movie is often a melodramatic expression of a similar sentiment and morality. Here one finds the wide-open spaces of the range representing Good, where the beneficence of nature and simplicity of living impel the cowhand to lead a decent, clean, and honest life. He sits tall in the saddle and stands straight in his boots. He works hard to provide for his family, cares deeply about his home and property, and is ready to protect the "women folk" from all

---

[6] "Except for a maid or two," Thurber says, "there are no colored people in the World of Soap. Papa David, in 'Life Can Be Beautiful,' is the only Jew I have run into on the daytime air since 'The Goldbergs' was discontinued. . . . Lynn Stone and Addy Richton, who have written several serials, were once told by a sponsor's representative to eliminate a Jewish woman from one of their shows. 'We don't want to antagonize the anti-Semites,' the gentleman casually explained. They had to take out the character." Ibid.

danger. It is the "slicker" from the East who symbolizes what is Bad. Wearing a black hat, a thin black tie, and a mustache, he walks with an alien, self-assured swagger that shows contempt for the plain and simple life of the West. His manner is suspicious and he cannot look a man square in the eye. More often than not he represents the cruel and cunning moneyed interests of the syndicate from back East out to do the little folk in. He knows his way around, can handle people with a smooth suavity, and yet it is only a question of time—about an hour and a half—until he falls before the forces of law and justice.

There is exaggeration here just as there is a facile playing with words. Yet the folklore of the small town and the small community is very much alive today. In its modern dress it represents a compelling ideal to which the rugged individualist can be determinedly faithful amidst the insecurity and impersonality of our industrial sprawl. Robert Wood has been struck by the "fragments of small town culture" persisting in the suburb of today, where the hope is cherished that the development and extension of such fragments will help resurrect our small-town heritage and thereby provide at least a partial answer to the onrush of bigness and organization. It would be a reassuring sign that a great nation has not completely abandoned its fundamental principles. The problem, Wood writes, "is not one of fact but of values, and it is concerned primarily with examining the benefits which the small town supposedly bestows." Although the suburb tries to fuse the political ideology of small government with the social mores of the small community, the problem is not limited to the present suburb and the present generation.

It extends to Tocqueville's Northwest town and Jefferson's ward, to the English parish and the European village before

America. The question is universal and timeless, and, simply put, it is: why believe that the small community produces the best life, and more especially, the best government? [7]

The agrarian spirit of the frontier nourishes many deep-seated suspicions, but the cosmopolitan spirit does not, or at least not of the same things. It is more tolerant of ideas emanating from foreign shores; the mingling of many cultures and races in such cities as New York and San Francisco is a vital and important part of the life there. Tensions and conflicts are inherent in the very nature of the urban community, and the "high mobility" of urban groups "makes the situation of multiple contacts part and parcel of the daily life of city people." [8] Anti-urban feelings reflect a moralism based on a rural model of the good life. Urban disorganization is disparaged, while an overadmiration for "roots" and "ties" is displayed with approval. As Riesman has pointed out, it is a moralism that sees the city "through the eyes of a folkish ideology of consensus, hard workmanship, and a simplistic view of the integrated, well-adjusted homey individual." Riesman is further moved to observe that those who share such feelings have failed to recognize that what they have

admired about rural or small-town life has been less its pleasures than its pieties—pieties often only possible because of the "export" of adventure to the cities, pieties

[7] Robert Wood: *Suburbia: Its People and Their Politics* (Boston: Houghton Mifflin; 1959), p. 260. See also pp. 11–19. For a particularly able discussion of the importance of the small community in America, see Arthur E. Morgan: *The Small Community* (New York: Harper & Brothers; 1942); see also Granville Hicks: *Small Town* (New York: Macmillan; 1946).

[8] Jitsuichi Masuoka: "The City and Racial Adjustment," *Social Forces* (October 1948), p. 38.

102

often exaggerated by the nostalgias in the mind of an observer unfamiliar with the forms rural deviance takes.[9]

It is a truism that since the turn of the century America has been transformed in economic terms from a rural nation into an urban one. Not only has there been a large migration from the country to the city, but those who have remained in the country have themselves been increasingly influenced if not dominated by the values, manners, and recreational conveniences of the city, which are only a few of the urban effects that have rubbed off onto the hinterland. Census figures show that approximately half of the people who live on farms in some states are earning their wages in such typically urban occupations as salesmen, clerks, and bookkeepers. Where over 90 per cent of the working force in 1820 was engaged in agriculture, today only about 10 per cent is made up of farm owners and tenants. To the small businessman as much as to the farmer this rapid development has meant the loss of personal security, a kind of security which could only survive and have meaning in a system where the individual lived out his life rooted to the land or worked in an enterprise that was stamped indelibly with his own personality. His way of life had been secure because the social world in which he lived was as isolated as it was peaceful. More than anything else, the independence he had prized as a businessman was what he also had valued for himself as a family man and as a member of the local community. He had controlled his own fate and had been captain of his own ship. It is something he cannot claim for himself today.

[9] David Riesman: "The Study of the City," *City Lights* (quarterly magazine formerly published in San Francisco). Riesman's article was developed from a paper presented at a conference on "The Urban Person: A Program for Research" at the Fourth Annual Symposium of the Committee on Human Development, University of Chicago, January 31, 1953.

Many of the values of the frontier which have thus far been associated with the agrarian spirit can be easily seen as those with which the small businessman is generally quite familiar. He has long appreciated the value of owning not only his own home but the "tools" with which he has worked. If he was concerned with politics, he liked the idea that he had some direct control over the local problems at hand. In his secluded world "social action did not ramify out in unanticipated ways to produce incalculable results. There was an obvious and close relationship between social cause and effect, reward and punishment." There was real comfort in knowing that if a man set out to do something, nothing but his own self could prevent him from realizing his goal. "As one moved from childhood into adolescence, courtship, and marriage, and the assumption of adult responsibilities, the blueprint for behavior was stable, consistent, unquestioned." [1]

The growing powerlessness of the small businessman today to direct and control his life chances has not been a development he has watched with dispassion. His hostility to much of what he has seen grow up around him has manifested itself in a number of ways. He has had to make grudging adjustments to the modern secular society, a society in which personal relationships are more likely to be scattered and partial than close and complete. Not only has he seen his business prospects become entangled in a maze of bureaucratic confusion over which he himself has little influence, but even his role and function as a parent have so changed that his own children learn more about life outside of the home, from people he does not know and has never seen, than they do from him. Perhaps the most important change upsetting his equilibrium is the unmistakable trend toward centralization of power and

[1] Arnold W. Green: "Why Americans Feel Insecure," *Commentary* (July 1948), p. 19.

control. Today economic reality no longer means family employment or family holdings. It means employment in vast industrial, business, and governmental structures. At the same time there has been an increasing concentration of wealth and power in the hands of an industrial élite. Instead of the individual entrepreneur minding and managing his own economic affairs, he finds himself in a world, as Paul Meadows has described it, where there is a growing *rapprochement* between big business and big government and where atomized individuals are hired to serve as little pegs to fill predetermined bureaucratic holes.

Nor is the small businessman accustomed to a way of life where common interests are few and where "the differential sharing" and participation in social life have become so great that "the human being in industrialism is pushed first one way and then another on a gridiron of claims and counter-claims." He would far prefer a pre-industrial pattern of living that was "smooth, personal, simple, concrete, and homogeneous." As it is, however, his life is qualified and conditioned by a network of formal institutions that are dominated by pecuniary considerations. "The continuity of existence with the historic past and the unquestioning dependability of a personalized society belong to other days, happy in retrospect." [2]

The jarring life of the big city, in addition to being sharply different from the peace and quiet of rural living, also has

[2] Paul Meadows: *The Culture of Industrial Man* (Lincoln, Nebr.: University of Nebraska Press; 1950), p. 24. It should be noted that the danger of drawing an exaggerated picture of the "historic past" of the small businessman is a real one. In attempting to accentuate some important differences between a pre-industrial society and modern industrialism the temptation is great to talk simply in terms of black and white, overlooking entirely any shadings of gray. Actually one could ask if the society the small businessman looks back upon really did exist. Some of the people who write about this period seem totally unaware of this possibility; in fact, they often sound like romantics dreaming of the Middle Ages or afraid of the perils of modern living.

symbolic significance as a way of life and a set of values to which the agrarian-spirited individual is deeply antagonistic. The cosmopolitan spirit is in many respects a conglomeration of ideas and people with no deep historical roots in the rural tradition of the country. The agrarian spirit, on the other hand, is extolled as the touchstone of the virtuous life, and just as "small town" people represent all that is good and decent, so the "city folk" are seen as exemplars of evil and cunning. Thus the agrarian spirit tends toward a provincialism and an isolationism that are in marked contrast to the internationalism of the cosmopolitan spirit. Those who are committed to the values and outlook of the former generally have a narrower range of interests than the cosmopolitan type. They are primarily interested in the problems of the local community because it is the only world they know or care about. As frequent observers have noted, their orientation to the community close at hand involves such a parochial preoccupation that it virtually excludes any real concern for international and sometimes even national affairs. On the other hand, as Robert Merton has shown, the cosmopolitan individual is oriented significantly to the outside world and regards himself as an integral part of the Great Society. He seldom even cares about his own city, preferring instead to discuss and think about national and international problems. In an important sense this explains the power and control of the political machine in the city and the general problem of apathy in city politics. The interests of the cosmopolitan individual, "far from being parochial, are ecumenical." In discussing the network of personal relations between the "local influentials" and the cosmopolitan, Merton says the

cosmopolitan influentials have notably little interest in meeting *as many* people as possible. They are more selective in their choice of friends and acquaintances. They typically stress the importance of confining themselves to friends with whom "they can really talk," with whom they can "exchange ideas."

The point is pertinent because one of the virtues of the small town, consistently glorified, is that everyone there has all kinds of friends and is known by everybody. "If the local influentials are quantitativists, the cosmopolitans are 'qualitativists' in this regard. It is not *how many* people they know but the *kind of people* they know that counts." [3] In commenting on the same theme, Riesman referred several years ago to the remarks of a columnist in the *Chicago Daily News* who had complained that there was no true community in Chicago, that he never saw his friends in Evanston unless he met them in New York or Pasadena, and that "we really ought to live in the country where we could see our friends every day."

> I observed to [him] that it was because he had the base of Chicago that he could be cosmopolitan, that he could see his friends in such pleasant settings elsewhere, and that if he lived in the country as a country-man he would be most unlikely to have friends; he would have neighbors, from whose gossip and from whose limitations he would long to flee to the city. I know perfectly well that for myself my long summer residence and occasional winter residence on a Vermont farm is only made possible by city earnings, and hospitable by city friends and values.[4]

As Thurber has already indicated, people living in the small town look upon those who reside in the urban centers as alien to everything they themselves treasure in the rural folklore of American history. They distrust the city because they do not understand it. They associate it and its residents with

[3] Robert K. Merton: "Patterns of Influence: A Study of Inter-Personal Influence and of Communication Behavior in a Local Community," in *Communication Research,* edited by Paul F. Lazarsfeld and Frank N. Stanton (New York: Harper & Brothers; 1949), p. 194.

[4] Riesman: op. cit.

all of the difficulties and anxieties of the modern industrial
era. The comfortable stability which they once knew and to
which they were emotionally suited has been overturned, and
in the attempt to protect themselves from the uncertainties and
upheavals of a soulless world they seek a kind of scapegoat onto
which they can fasten their fears and hostilities. Arnold Rose
has shown that feelings of anti-Semitism are in many ways
an expression of hatred against the economic success or perhaps the political radicalism historically connected with life
in the city. To those who view the city in this way, the Jews
are the "urban people par excellence," a striking reflection of
the city. "In much of America, 'New York' and 'Jew' are almost
interchangeable epithets. It is not simply that the Jew adapts
to city life and makes a success of it. The Jew is willing to submit to the repression of the 'free instincts' which is required
by the city." The Jew is thought of as "rootless, as unattached
to the 'community' with its meaningful values. The Jew is
mysterious; he might be the manipulator of all those forces
which seem to control the life of the little man in the big city." [5]
The agrarian spirit, in a word, is intolerant of foreigners and
"un-American ideas"; it prefers the rural simplicity of an
"Americanism" it can understand and glorify. Its antipathy
to the Jews and other "aliens" who exemplify the urban industrial world arises from a strong antagonism to the city—
to its impersonality, its sharpness, its weakness, "to the pushi-
ness, the cliquishness, the 'capitalism' and the 'communism'
which it creates." [6]

[5] Arnold Rose: "Anti-Semitism's Root in City Hatred," *Commentary*
(October 1948), p. 376. It is interesting to recall that the great national-
ists in American history were rarely rooted in local communities, but
came from *outside* the country: Tom Paine, Hamilton, James Wilson—
they, unlike Jefferson or Adams, had no *local* attachments. Consider also
the great "unifiers": Napoleon, Hitler, Stalin.

[6] Ibid., p. 377.

The persistence of the agrarian spirit, as typified by the range of feelings of the small businessman, can be seen also in the particular homage paid with insistent regularity to the Constitution of the United States. The Constitution has long played an important role in American thought, and for the conservative especially it has been the foundation of many of his deepest political convictions. While conservative opinion regarding different political and economic issues has varied from one period to another, the conservative mind and temper in America have never really deviated from their basic opposition to innovations or reform. Since America has never had a monarchy, a titled aristocracy, or a national church to symbolize a link with the traditions of the past, conservative theory has turned to a sanctification of the Constitution. This document has embodied—as no other American institution could—the conservative reverence for almost everything that has evolved through time and thereby survived the test of experience. It is in this sense that the Constitution has been at the center of American conservatism.

In keeping with the sentiments of the agrarian spirit the Constitution has been an important rallying cry for some of the most nationalistic and patriotic elements in the country. One of the most striking manifestations of this is seen in the continued controversy over the proper role and function of the government. To the small businessman the best government is the one that has the least to do and say, reflecting again his attachment to the political and economic way of life that flourished before the rise of industry and the effects of urbanization. The Constitution was drawn in a rural, pre-industrial setting, when homogeneity and self-sufficiency were two of the primary features of society and when the liberal tradition in economic thinking was proclaiming that each man acting in his own interest was automatically contributing to the interest of society as a whole. Today the small businessman, apprehensive of the complexities and entanglements of modern living, is concerned with preserving what he feels are the true ideals and guarantees which, through the Constitution, became the basis of our free enterprise system.

The Conference of American Small Business Organizations continually warned in its literature that the small businessman today must fight to save himself from economic starvation "brought on by ever-increasing competition conducted by government under the rules of socialism." The job of offsetting this dangerous development is a big one, the Conference pointed out, made all the more difficult because "a substantial majority of the American electorate has lost its one-time veneration for the principles of economic freedom," and is willing to accept government paternalism and "socialism" instead, at least whenever it sees a selfish advantage in such action.[7] The National Federation of Independent Business, Inc., has also expressed a similar attitude toward the disturbing trends in our present society. Its language in the statement that follows is typical of many testimonials to the fact that America has the highest standard of living in the world and that we should therefore refrain from urging any "change in our form of Government."

Let us all Think American. Let us all Talk American. Let us all Do Business the American Way.

No nation on earth, regardless of its form of government, ever gave to human beings so much liberty and material prosperity as our own Constitutional form of Freedom. We started out as thirteen little States, ridden by poverty and threatened by savages. We were, however,

[7] The Conference of American Small Business Organizations thought so much of an editorial from the *Railway Age,* dated January 29, 1949, in which these and similar statements were made, that it had copies reproduced and sent to all of its members.

blessed by God. We now represent the utmost in individual freedoms and individual prosperity. Compare our United States with any other land on earth. The workingman here is a king compared to the workingman in any other country. Nearly all of us have modern homes—electric lights and power—gas cooking—telephones—automobiles—automatic refrigeration—electric washers and irons—radios—insurance policies. Most of us own bonds and have money in the bank, plus a thousand and one other conveniences and luxuries.

Are we ready to exchange all this for the crazy promises of some foreign crackpot? Isn't it time for us to thank God for America and our many blessings? Isn't it about time that we wake up and do a real job, selling American principles? [8]

The industrial and urban revolution that began to change the face of America in the closing decades of the nineteenth century has also left its mark on the twentieth in the form of many imposing problems of political and economic organization which the framers of the Constitution could never have anticipated. The complex, interdependent character of contemporary life, as Philip Hauser has observed, has imposed many strains on our governmental heritage. Not only has the clash of urban and rural as well as upstate, downstate, and sectional interests cut across our traditional governmental jurisdictions, but technological and social innovations have brought about the growth of governmental responsibilities and, in particular, its centralization. The pleasant consensus and equilibrium of a pre-industrial society have been upset by the

new physical and economic structure produced by the industrial and urban revolutions, the increasing interdependence of the various elements of our economic and

[8] National Federation of Independent Business, Inc., undated circular entitled: "Before Urging Change in Our Form of Government First Make a Few Comparisons."

social order, the breakdown of traditional social controls, and the inability of our inherited social institutions to cope with the new situations and new problems of urban life.[9]

The distance separating the temper and outlook of the agrarian spirit from many of the realities of the contemporary scene can be further seen by the strain to which the traditional concepts of nationalism and sovereignty have been subjected. Over the violent protests of many small businessmen, the continued participation of the United States in international affairs, ranging from financial loans to foreign countries to proposals in the United Nations for international control of atomic energy, has contributed significantly to the undermining of our inherited concept of sovereignty and to the deterioration of our traditional concept of nationalism. In a later chapter the foreign policy to which many small businessmen today are ideologically sympathetic will be more closely examined. For the moment it need only be pointed out that both the domestic and international issues of the present day have their origin in the needs and tensions of an industrialized America. The pre-industrial perspective of the small businessman is often ill-suited to cope with the many problems emerging out of such a society. The agrarian spirit, mirroring the values and aspirations of a small, homogeneous, and predominantly rural society, can be expected to respond with extreme disfavor to the changes in the material and structural features of our social order. Misreading the effect for the cause, the ideological outlook of the small businessman has led him to view the "New Deal" and the "Fair Deal" as a "revolution" of drastic pro-

[9] Philip K. Hauser: "Some Political Influences of Urbanization," an essay originally presented to the Conference on Evaluation of Social Institutions in America at the Princeton University Bicentennial, October 1946, reprinted in part in Paul K. Hatt and Albert J. Reiss: *Reader in Urban Sociology* (Glencoe, Ill.: Free Press; 1951), p. 462.

portions.[1] He has failed to see that the deeper, more urgent revolution of which he too has been a part is a continuing one whose beginnings date from the passing of his own preferred entrepreneurial society. To the small businessman, the "assassination of Adam Smith," along with the "insidious effort to undermine American traditions" by instilling in the minds of Americans "a contempt for the principles of individual independence and achievement, pride of family and country"—all this is symbolic of the destruction of ideals, qualities, and propensities "which some members of an aging generation still fondly regard as characteristic of a great American people." [2]

One of the most important ingredients in the agrarian spirit is a straightforward and at times excessive individualism. It is an individualism marked by a strong dislike of both large-scale organizations and the increasing concentration of political and economic power in our society. In contrast, the cosmopolitan spirit is far more hospitable and sympathetic to the needs and demands of bigness in organization in an age of limitless technology.

The hostility to bigness in America is characteristic of a culture that has traditionally favored the "little man." Like our sys-

---

[1] The election of Franklin Roosevelt in 1932 and his subsequent successful presidential campaigns indicated, among other things, that the people were not unhappy to have a government administered by leaders who were capable of recognizing and dealing with some of the major problems of a troubled industrial order, not the least of which were economic depression and recovery. As Hauser has remarked: "The proliferation of alphabetical agencies in the early days of the 'New Deal' was largely designed to deal with urban problems. . . . Much of the permanent legislation resulting from this period, such as that relating to Social Security, labor organizations, the stock market, the banks, and housing, were aimed directly at the unsolved problems of urbanism. . . ." Hauser: op. cit., p. 467.

[2] From the *Return of Adam Smith,* published by The Caxton Printers, Ltd., Caldwell, Idaho, and distributed by the Conference of American Small Business Organizations.

tem of government, it derives from "the familiar intimacy of the New England town meeting, where people knew each other and all preferences and objections rose easily to public consideration." Master and workman, merchant and competitor, shop and home, writes Lynd, "as envisaged in the traditional symbols and assumptions of the culture, involved no such disparities in power as exist today." [3] Bigness in society, along with large-scale organizations and the concentration of power, is a valuable and useful servant of modern man, just as the integration of industry is an intelligent and efficient way to produce the needed goods of an industrial society. The utility of co-ordinated bigness is an acknowledged mainstay of technological abundance, and "laments of liberals such as Mr. Justice Brandeis against 'the curse of bigness' reflect but a wistful nostalgia for an era that can never return." [4] While the small businessman does not necessarily wish to "return" to the days of the past, he nonetheless looks upon organization and bigness in our present-day society—and this is the important difference—with suspicion and reluctance instead of enthusiasm.

The language of small business in these matters draws on the vocabulary of pre-industrialism. Because of the economic conspiracies and cutthroat competition of the large corporations, the protection of small business has automatically become the rallying cry of many earnest individuals. Trustbusting continues to be "an altar of sacrifice on which an occasional corporate goat is laid to appease a wrathful public." [5] This opposition to bigness usually favors breaking up the large corporations into their component parts in the belief that

[3] Robert S. Lynd: *Knowledge for What?* (Princeton, N.J.: Princeton University Press; 1946), p. 78.

[4] Ibid., p. 210.

[5] Meadows: op. cit., p. 27. For one of the first treatments of this point see T. W. Arnold: *The Folklore of Capitalism* (New Haven, Conn.: Yale University Press; 1937).

it is neither efficient nor in the public interest to have a single corporation, in the words of Charles Noyes, "producing a variety of goods from kitchen utensils to washing machines and generators, or from nylon to munitions and commercial solvents." It represents a position that is entirely consistent with the nineteenth-century philosophy of pre-industrial capitalism, which held that a genuine free-enterprise system with unbridled competition would inevitably bring about the greatest prosperity and the greatest good for the greatest number. One can find the same view clearly outlined in the economic pronouncements of Friedrich A. Hayek, who favors not only drastic curbs on monopoly but a return to uninhibited free competition.[6]

To the small businessman it seems perfectly obvious that democracy cannot survive when society is dominated by what he feels are anonymous economic units. His own ideal society is one populated by men and women who can know, and be known by, one another. To him the anonymous man of modern industrialism is really no man at all. "That is one reason why he tends to become the forgotten man. The man known only by hearsay and distant rumor is a monster."[7] John Crowe Ransom put it simply in his defense of the little man of Main Street against the industrial financier of Wall Street:

> Who, then, runs the Big Businesses? The executives, the officers, the directors, a small company of men, all in the position of trustees for the invisible and putatively brainless owners. Assume that they are honest trustees, as they probably are. What is honesty in a trustee? The virtue of a business executive is like that of a statesman, it consists in getting all he can for his wards.

[6] See Charles E. Noyes: "Is Big Business Bad Business?" *The Nation* (August 6, 1949).

[7] Willis Fisher: "Small Town Middle-Westerner" in *Who Owns America?* edited by Herbert Agar and Allen Tate (Boston: Houghton Mifflin; 1936), p. 228.

Then, in keeping with the agrarian spirit's distrust of international dealings, Ransom expresses with striking clarity and frankness a sentiment with which the small businessman is in full accord:

> The standard of international morality is lower than the standard of personal morality, and the code of Big Business is lower than that of little business. The most charming statesmen are prepared to tell lies and break treaties and wage unjust wars in the name of their country, and amiable gentlemen on becoming business executives proceed to cut the throats of their small competitors and hire labor for the company on terms that sacrifice the dignity and elemental needs of the laborers. We have been informed that the "economic man," who used to be cited by economic theorists as the man who acts strictly in the pursuit of gain and is immune to moral and personal considerations, was an abstraction that never existed. He does not exist in the small businesses, or at least he is hard to find there, but he is the regular thing in Big Business.[8]

The small businessman looks upon the concentration of wealth in the hands of big business today as the modern outcome of the Hamiltonian conception of property. Under the Hamilton philosophy, as one writer put it colorfully: "Dives might throw crumbs to Lazarus and permit his dogs to lick the sores of Lazarus; but that is the end of his obligations." [9] The entrepreneurial outlook of pre-industrialism, however, following the principles of Jeffersonianism, considers the right to own property as the greatest instrument by which it is possible to secure life, liberty, and the pursuit of happiness. But in Jefferson's terms property was not trusts or banks or monopolies; it was land and personal enterprises held or obtainable by any self-respecting individual. A man should not only own his prop-

---

[8] John Crowe Ransom: "What Does the South Want?" in *Who Owns America?* pp. 183–4.

[9] Frank Lawrence Owsley: "The Foundations of Democracy" in *Who Owns America?* p. 65.

erty but should personally manage and control it in order to give him and his family a sense of economic security and independence. Jefferson regarded stocks and bonds as an insecure basis for a truly free and democratic society, and in the eighteenth century directors and presidents of corporations undertook "the art of avoiding the payment of dividends to small stockholders who had no voice in directing the management of the business." As Frank Owsley has said, the insecurity of citizens

> who depended upon such property over which they no longer had control was doubtless a strong factor in the Jeffersonian advocacy of the agrarian State. Perhaps the Jeffersonians believed that city life was not a good life, but the loss of economic independence and security which accompanied this life was what made the great Virginian and his colleagues fear urbanization and look upon land as the best form of private property and the only safe basis of a free State.[1]

For much the same reason the small businessman today feels it is time to turn away from the "frenzy of Big Business," as Ransom calls it, "toward something older, more American, and more profitable."

In 1942 the Conference of American Small Business Organizations urged the appointment of an "Assistant Secretary of Commerce for Small Business." The motivation for this proposal was not simply pride of small business or even its need for special service on government procurement, although the latter was certainly an important wartime consideration. A compelling need, reflecting again the small businessman's attachment to the values of a pre-industrial society, was far deeper. It was devotion to the principle of proprietorship in the American economy, a principle that might well be called the common denominator of small business.

[1] Ibid.

At the turn of the nineteenth century the great majority of Americans possessed property or had opportunities to acquire it.

> The independent men of the soil, small businessmen, small bankers, small commercial producers and traders, constituted a citizenry, correctly conscious of personal interest, exercising personal responsibility, making a natural, dependable security for our democratic institutions.[2]

These men believed that the liberties which they were pledged to preserve could last only if most of the property and businesses in the country remained in the hands of private individuals. The relation of owner and property, be it a piece of land or a small enterprise, was seen as a source of personal identification. The agrarian-minded citizen felt that, in commercialism, the integrity of the individual was undermined when everything he did was subjected to the impersonal considerations of economic pursuits. In the present day the attack on big business by the small businessman follows in the same vein: the weakness of big business, he feels, is not merely that it is big, but that it is a drift away from proprietorship.

The cleavage between large and small business over the issue of proprietorship, or the "area of discretion of management," is frequently profound. From the point of view of the small businessman, managers of big business tend to be hirelings, intent primarily on achieving an equilibrium among the conflicting forces of labor, the government, and the consumer. These men simply respond, over and over again, to the strongest combination of pulls, following the path of least resistance. The small businessman believes that a purely professional management can "go along" with almost everybody, and that it usually does. Mr. R. Harland Shaw, for many years assistant to the chairman of the Conference of American

[2] John C. Rawe: "Agriculture and the Property State" in *Who Owns America?* p. 42.

Small Business Organizations, has given a good deal of thought and attention to this problem. In his view the management of big business

> goes along with big labor, with big government, with fascist and corporative tendencies in the government— with NRA first and then with OPA and OPM and WPB industry committees—anything for harmony and convenience and *job safety for management,* regardless of what happens either to the country or to the other fellow.[3]

Shaw's words echo the sentiments of a large number of small businessmen in their concern over the movement away from proprietorship in modern industrial society. When a few "independents" among big business leaders have themselves hewed to the proprietary line—Ernest Weir, Clarence Randall, the Block family, for example—they have been damned by their associates. As far as the small businessman is concerned, the same is true when "an energetic labor thinker," as Shaw would call him, appeals to management to stand against industry-wide bargaining and "maintain local integrity"—he is met with indifference and even hostility.

The controversy over the issue of industry-wide labor-management contracts is a long-standing one about which many businessmen feel bitter and resentful. The Conference of American Small Business Organizations considered for some time "throwing down the gauntlet to the hired managers of big businesses on the issue . . . which is poison to the small manufacturer as a rule." [4] The small businessman's position

---

[3] R. Harland Shaw: "Small Business in Relation to the American Government and the American Way of Life," April 3, 1953, an unpublished statement outlining the basic position of the Conference of American Small Business Organizations. (Italics in the original.) I was privileged to discuss a number of small business problems with Mr. Shaw during the course of an extensive correspondence, and I am in his debt for many penetrating observations.

[4] Shaw: letter to author.

derives from certain basic premises which, if developed carefully, would most likely make a number of familiar points and
proceed along the following lines:

(1) Two decades ago union leaders were imploring Congress to pass a law compelling each employer to bargain collectively with his employees. Congress passed the Wagner
Labor Law, later amended by the Taft-Hartley Act. Now
these same union leaders consider it. too much trouble to
negotiate separately with each employer, and therefore are
trying to compel employers to agree to industry-wide labor
contracts.

(2) But in any industry-wide labor-industry combine the
worker would be the chief loser. He, individually, and the
local union would lose their identity and independence. Decisions affecting his economic life would be made by a small
group of labor and industrial leaders who would give small
heed to his individual and local needs.

(3) Denied the right to bargain collectively with his local
employer, he becomes merely a voiceless automaton in a vast
labor-industry empire.

(4) Industry-wide labor contracts also adversely affect industry and business because they lead eventually to federal
ownership. When a strike or lockout is of long duration in any
industry or public service, the federal government is forced
to intervene to save the general public from undue suffering
and hardship.

(5) After these governmental seizures occur a few times
and the public becomes fed up, legislation for complete control
of that industry or public service will be a public demand.
When labor leaders have control over the economic life of both
labor and industry through industry-wide labor contracts, they
will control the United States.

(6) The small businessman also takes quite a beating in

an industry-wide labor contract. A labor-management contract is agreed to by leaders of big labor and big industry. The small employer in that industry or public service is presented with the industry-wide master or pattern contract and told to sign or have a strike called against his business. There is no opportunity for him to bargain collectively with his employees. He must obey the dictates of the big labor-industry combine or suffer the consequences.

(7) The general public also loses under industry-wide labor-management contracts. Big Labor sets the wage costs, Big Industry sets the selling costs, and the public must pay the demands of both through increased prices on all goods and services it buys.

(8) Business competition becomes non-existent and the American competitive enterprise system becomes only a memory.

(9) Big Labor and Big Industry become so powerful that only a Big Government can contend with these two immensely strong groups, with the consequent loss of economic and political liberty by all of us.[5]

The "unholy alliance" of big labor, big government, and big business is, to the small businessman, one of the most pernicious and corrupting tendencies in industrial society today. To the managers of big business, industry-wide bargaining may seem to provide an easier opportunity to handle labor with less trouble *to themselves*. The independent entrepreneur, however, looks upon it as an instrument to throttle, both directly and indirectly, a lot of small businesses. He sees it also as a tendency to standardize as well as to stratify society. "It reduces flexibility and increases rigidity in the economy as a

[5] See *The Sure Road to Dictatorship in the USA,* a booklet published by The State Publishing Company, 12 North Third Street, Columbus 15, Ohio.

whole," comments Shaw. "Big business management frequently is strictly hired and lacks the incentive to individuality which results from a large proprietary interest." Therefore, as a very condition of its own survival, "small business is defending a principle of society which, in the opinion of many economists, is valuable to the whole society including some managements who don't like it." [6]

A number of people with a profound faith in the system of free enterprise have urged that steps be taken to prevent corporations from continuing to monopolize the American economic and political system. One of the major proposals leading in this direction, of which Senator O'Mahoney was for years the most active spokesman in the United States Senate, was that of Federal Incorporation. The enactment of such laws would include a limitation upon the total amount of property which any single corporation would own, a limitation designed to preclude the existence in any industry of a single company large enough to dominate the industry, and the incorporation of investment corporations under separate laws designed to preclude their becoming holding companies or agencies of monopoly control. A typical proposal for Federal Incorporation has been outlined by H. C. Simons,[7] and Shaw's forceful denunciation of its provisions is particularly significant because it reveals the fundamental position of small business.

> I resent and repudiate every statement, single and collectively. . . . It is the worst possible set of devices from the standpoint of the *proprietor* that I have seen put together in one place in a long while. I can hardly imagine its endorsement or advocacy by any sincere well-wisher of business. . . . Rather it looks like the concatenation of the devil from a laissez-faire standpoint. Federal incorporation—wholly apart from robbing us of the benefits

[6] Shaw: letter to author.
[7] See H. C. Simons: "A Positive Program for Laissez-Faire," quoted in Weissman: op. cit., pp. 156, 158.

of what Justice Holmes called "48 separate laboratories"—
would mean the heavy hand of the Washington bureaucracy on every detail that it saw fit to regulate. The "high
command" of an army does not seek to regulate all of the
private life of the private—but a) the choice of *what* to
regulate is exclusively that of the high command; b) each
of its regulations is law. All of us small business guys would
be just buck privates under the Washington high command
in that situation. Running down the other details: the one
idea that appears workable—because it is the simplest—
is a simple limitation on maximum size. This would simply
assert that society has determined that it will not have, and
will not tolerate, corporate aggregations (whether directly
or indirectly controlled) in excess of "X" size. Society says
this in its own protection—not because mere size is bad,
but because beyond "X" the problem of administering
fairness and justice gets too burdensome. Therefore, says
the society, "X" is the limit. No vast bureaucracy is necessary to enforce this. Personally I don't agree with this
philosophy—I merely say it is workable. All of the rest of
the details . . . I consider simply foolish and dangerous
limitations on human ingenuity, many of them quite difficult of enforcement, all of them (in my opinion and I
am sure in that of practically every member of this organization) unnecessary or unwise, and the whole phantasma-
goria thought up by some one who never rose by his own
efforts in the ranks of business.[8]

3

J. W. MacIver, field director of the National Small
Business Men's Association, has posed what he calls "an ethic"
for the small businessman and the free-enterprise system, a
system he fervently believes did not develop just by accident.
"The men who conceived the ingredients of our way of life
drew on our western culture. God in his wisdom granted a
franchise of freedom of choice to each individual and ex-
changed the responsibility for the defense of the freedom of

[8] Shaw: letter to author.

every other individual." To MacIver it is an imperishable truth, and having been endowed with a franchise of personal freedom from our Creator, we have a responsibility to fight for it and not sacrifice it:

> Sure, many small businessmen supported Franklin Roosevelt in the thirties, at least in 1932. Most every group in the country did. But had the small businessman had an ethic, they could have prevented what FDR brought about. Of course, the 1930's gave impetus to everything that happened then, but it didn't start there. Teddy Roosevelt was the real villain, really—by busting the trusts and all his talk about conservation and public parks where the Government was to play a big part. This set in motion a type of ethic that made it possible for FDR to follow through and move ahead.[9]

This "ethic," while central to MacIver's own thinking, also provides an additional perspective from which it is possible to view the general outlook of the contemporary small businessman. It is difficult to defend the ethic of our corporate structure, as MacIver points out, because by its very nature it is immoral.

> A truth has to be moral, else what is Heaven for? A corporate structure is a legal fiction. By law it is able to limit responsibility and hence morality. The first error is coupled by the second. Since it is a legal fiction, it can have no heart. And the head is therefore not responsible for the soul since it has no soul.

On this basis our man-made laws, in creating the corporate structure and ultimately the corporate society, have provided an easy avenue for individuals to avoid the dictates of their conscience.

To the small businessman the American Way of Life is a logical product of the ample room and lavish raw materials

---

[9] These comments are drawn from two 3-hour interviews held on June 2 and 4, 1959, at Stanford University. I want to acknowledge here my thanks to Mr. MacIver for his time and courtesy.

which nature provided. Our Constitutional rules of the game were expressly drawn to make it possible for enterprising individuals to translate them into productive usefulness. Yet today, he complains sadly, "whenever the subject of being your own boss comes up, more people seem to be interested in 'security' as projected but never achieved by Karl Marx, Lenin, Henry Wallace and their disciples." [1] He remembers the depression days of the New Deal when it became the gloomy fashion to forget about our pioneer spirit and resign ourselves to living in a "mature" economy. Graduating classes heard a lot about how to get a "secure" job but not much about incentive, initiative, and hard work. While today's industrial giants may be rich, strong, and secure, it is the millions of small businessmen "who believe in free enterprise, and who have the initiative and leadership to try it for themselves— to be their own boss, to add to rather than take from the supply of jobs and productive output of our system"—who give yeoman service to the American heritage and keep the faith.

Thus the small businessman, struggling against the main drift of a new society, remains an important anchor of what many persons are wont to call "the American Way." In spite of the major changes which have been wrought by the triumph of industrialism the agrarian spirit persists, remaining very much alive in the minds of those who still are tied to the past, uncertain of the present, and distrustful of the future. The thinking and temper of the small businessman, as we have seen, indicate a profound ideological attachment to the values of a pre-industrial order. He is deeply suspicious of what is alien to his preferred pattern of living, whether it be the intrusion of foreign ideologies onto the American scene or the upsetting of stability and tradition as a result of the spread of new ideas

[1] *Pulling Together* (Twentieth-anniversary publication of the National Small Business Men's Association, circulated in 1957), p. 8.

and the mingling of different cultures and peoples. Cosmopolitanism, representing an urbanity and sophistication toward which the small businessman feels distinctly aloof if not hostile, embodies also the spirit of experimentation and change which, perhaps more than anything else, has caused the most grief to the independent entrepreneur. Tending toward an agrarian provincialism that is both narrow and rigid, the small businessman is especially antagonistic to the forces abroad in the world which have led us into the complicating involvements of internationalism. His isolationism, in a word, is as strong as his individualism.

The small businessman, lastly, represents the proprietor "who—and who alone—made America." We have fought for the "little fellow," says Shaw,

> because he is little and needs help, but far more because *America Needs Him.* Our loyalty is not a selfish loyalty to the little businessman—it is rather a loyalty to the America that he, and millions who preceded him, built. It is a loyalty to an America that big labor most of the time, big business part of the time, and big government all of the time (whether consciously or not), are willing to sell down the river.

Any move that undermines the position of the proprietor or weakens the principle of private competition "is a move away from a republic and in the direction of empire, or cartelism, of all the things which have twice led to the fall of Rome." [2]

[2] Shaw: letter to author.

CHAPTER IV

Big Business
and the
Spirit of Industrialism

<u>1</u>   If the small businessman is reg-
ularly proclaimed as a cornerstone of American democracy,
the big businessman is just as often regarded as a threat to its
survival. In the unreal world of heroes and villains the colors
are always black and white, never tattletale gray. Ever since
big business emerged as a national issue at the close of the
nineteenth century it has been the center of a controversy that
has succeeded in dividing its defenders and attackers into
seemingly irreconcilable camps, even though the ground be-
neath them both has shifted perceptibly in the last several decades. The themes which pervade our politics today are very
different from those of the thirties, and to miss this point is to
misread the nature of many of our present-day conflicts. Twenty-
five years ago it was possible to use the language of political ex-
tremes: in a very real sense one was either pro-labor or pro-
capital, a liberal or a reactionary. Today such terms as "Left"
and "Right" have lost much of their former meaning and in
many ways have become ambiguous. It is part of a "general

process of compromise, merging, and adjustment that has been going on in the nation since 1936. Our politics, like our milk, are now homogenized." [1] It is against the background of some of the major forces that have helped to reshape the political life of the country that the small businessman and his politics must ultimately be viewed.

And so it is with the big businessman. It is equally important that the ideas, methods, and goals of big business today be re-examined, not for the purpose of presenting an apologia for much of its past performance as a dominant and too often predominant force in the country, but because many descriptions of the contemporary big businessman frequently are little more than shopworn stereotypes that have long since outlived their usefulness. The essential conservatism of American big business is a matter of record. It is only a part of the record, however, and by itself does not tell the complete story of the big business community. In spite of sharing many of the values and assumptions to which the small businessman is committed, the big businessman in many important respects is shaped in a different mold. His conception and understanding of the problems of a modern industrial society set him apart significantly from the small businessman. As a big business leader he is not only more sympathetic to the values of industrialism, but is in a better position to cope with the kinds of issues which

---

[1] "American capitalists compete with liberals in supporting the Bill of Rights—with a few reservations on both sides about national security in wartime. The Left also has become homogenized, or, in the socialists' sometimes useful patter, institutionalized. Today even protests against the social system have become part of that system, just as the avant-garde in culture is now a battalion in the regular army. Picasso gets top prices for his pictures, the Museum of Modern Art deals on terms of perfect equality with the Metropolitan, T. S. Eliot writes a Broadway hit, and the Department of Justice has its Civil Rights Division, which defends the rights of some citizens while the rest of the department is busy taking away the rights of others." Dwight Macdonald: "The Defense of Everybody," *The New Yorker* (July 18, 1953).

arise from a highly complex social order. It would be stretching a point too far to refer to the "new look" in the ranks of big business, but there is little doubt that some of its more enlightened members are giving serious thought to reorienting the philosophy of American conservatism to the needs and demands of a twentieth-century industrial society. Thus, before it is possible to gain a clear perspective of the small businessman and the political implications of his attachment to the values of pre-industrialism, it is necessary to bring the present picture of big business into sharper focus.

At the turn of the century the rising big businessmen were interested in getting rich—and doing so with as few restraints imposed upon them as possible. Reflecting a familiar fear of American conservatives since the Civil War, they were opposed to a strong government because they knew it might well embark upon projects designed to curb the economic freedom of business while at the same time it gained support from an aroused electorate. During the 1950's the Republican administration and many of its leading business spokesmen found it necessary to alter their position on what the role of the government should be in these critical times. The Republican platform prose, as well as some of the Republicans' other political pronunciamentos, especially those emanating from Congress, may not always seem to indicate a real change of heart, but nonetheless many of their actions often speak louder than some of their words. During the Roosevelt and Truman administrations most of the crucial political and economic issues were fought out, as Samuel Lubell has noted, within the Democratic Party. Civil rights, how to balance the interests of the newly emergent labor power against those of the rest of society, the yearning for security against another depression, the hunger for social status of the climbing masses—these had been the pressing problems for the many factions in the Democratic coalition. They were not, however, the issues which had fired the Republican voting elements with great enthusiasm; the latter remained "rooted in business interests, which suffered comparatively less in the depression. Their struggle for social and economic standing was fought out in terms of the agrarian frontier that has now passed." [2] As a result the Grand Old Party, up until 1952, was unable to capture leadership from the Democrats because it had no forward-looking program to offer the American people. It generally opposed and criticized the way things were being handled in Washington and talked wistfully to the voters of a bygone political era. But once the G.O.P. had been restored to power, it had to grapple with the difficult task of formulating a program that would meet the problems of our day.

One of the most important political developments to leave its mark on the United States in the last thirty years has been the "revolt of the city." Certainly a large measure of the success of the New Deal lay in the fact that it awakened urban groups to the enormous political power implicit in their numbers. Although President Roosevelt did not start this revolt,

> he extended to them the warming hand of recognition, through patronage and protective legislation. In the New Deal he supplied the leveling philosophy required by their sheer numbers. . . . In turn, the big-city masses furnished the votes which re-elected Roosevelt again and again— and, in the process, ended the traditional Republican majority in this country.[3]

It is in the context of this "big city generation" that certain developments in the business community need to be considered. Conservatism as a political philosophy has gradually come to recognize that a policy of resisting proposals for reform is not

[2] Samuel Lubell: *The Future of American Politics* (New York: Harper & Brothers; 1951), p. 201.
[3] Ibid., p. 29.

enough; it must be prepared to offer its own program of political action. Many conservatives are willing to admit with Clinton Rossiter that American conservatism, both as a program of action and as a philosophy, has failed the American people. "The fact that American liberalism and progressivism may likewise have failed them does nothing to soften the force of this charge. The conservative has had a certain function to perform in our society: to furnish the nation with farsighted preservative leadership. His performance has at best been uninspired. . . ." [4] The "preservative leadership" of conservatism, however, will succeed in becoming farsighted only if it responds to the demands of the present generation. Many businessmen are aware that Herbert Hoover's philosophy of "rugged individualism," with its yearning for rural self-sufficiency and an affinity for the natural laws of the market-place, is not resilient enough to meet the tensions and discords that spring interminably from the heavily populated industrial centers of the country. The Democratic Party was successful for twenty years because it made its strongest appeal to the millions who lived in the cities, voters who looked to the government not with trepidation but in the expectation that it would guarantee them certain minimum safeguards essential for a decent livelihood. That the Democrats were able to rise to the occasion explains in large part why they became and remained the party of the majority. The Republican Party in the 1960's is faced with no less formidable a challenge.

The big businessman who, in the words of Rossiter, "is or ought to be the core of American conservatism" seems to be increasingly aware that the periodic revival by conservatives of "the cult of Herbert Spencer" is inadequate as a solution to the problems of the present period. There are many indications

[4] Clinton L. Rossiter: "Wanted: An American Conservatism," *Fortune* (March 1950), p. 96.

that he has been attempting to supply some answers to the question of what should be the nature of conservative leadership in an advanced industrial society. Heretofore conservatism has given tacit support to the doctrine of individualism, a major pillar of American democracy, by applying it to its own demands for complete economic freedom, so that the businessman could achieve his short-range goals of money and power. In the process, however, conservatives have found it doubly difficult to build a "preservative philosophy" of their own.

> Conservatism, grounded as it must be on tradition or even traditionalism, has as its normal thesis the primacy of society over the individual. American conservatism, caught up in the reckless surge to material glory of the most dynamic country in all history, has emphasized the primacy of the individual over society. To that extent it has not been conservative at all. A theory of conservatism must be compounded of tenets and institutions that bring order, continuity, stability. The elements of such a theory must in turn be held together by the binding cement of aristocratic responsibility, of *noblesse oblige*. Individualism, however, is not a cement but an explosive charge, constantly sputtering, periodically going off, and generally preventing the coagulation of the ideas and institutions of American conservatism into a harmonious patter.[5]

The big businessman, traditionally, has cared very little for theory or philosophy. As a man of action, he has always prided himself on his extensive practical experience: he has met a payroll and has become wise in the ways of the world. If he has paid little attention to ideas, he has always respected facts—hard, cold facts, plus a little horse sense. The bill of particulars is familiar. It need only be remarked that many big business leaders today no longer completely fit the conventional pattern. If his interest in profits cannot be said to have diminished appreciably, there are signs at least that the

[5] Ibid., p. 104.

big businessman is taking a more active interest in problems that are not exclusively profit-oriented. He is responding affirmatively to David Lilienthal's warning that a moral obligation to engage in public service during a part of every qualified man's best years has become an actual necessity. The revival of *noblesse oblige* in politics and public service is in large part due to the big businessman's increased interest in presenting positive solutions to the important problems of the day. If he has to prove that institutions other than the government can satisfy the tremendous human needs that have spurred the rise of the "welfare state," he knows he must do more than "bid the mighty quest for security be gone by branding it unworkable or un-American." To those needs "he cannot forever say 'no.' His retort must be, 'I have a better answer'; for if, as Senator Taft has written, 'free enterprise cannot take any more government,' free enterprise must aim at making more government unnecessary." [6] One need not claim that big businessmen have developed a brand-new social conscience or are suddenly possessed with far-seeing vision. The point being made here is that the business leaders of today cannot be viewed with the same set of glasses through which the businessman of twenty-five, much less fifty, years ago was seen and judged.

2

Early in 1953 A. A. Berle, Jr., observed:

In the twenty years between the exit of President Hoover and the inauguration of President Eisenhower, American government has come full circle. The new Republican Administration is repeating with surprising fidelity the pattern of President Hoover—a government of big business, manned by big business. From this world, Eisenhower, like Hoover before him, has chosen first-raters. All

[6] Ibid., p. 112.

have outstanding records of honesty and achievement in business; all have records of integrity. But there are solid reasons for believing President Eisenhower's government will not be a repetition of Hoover's—save perhaps in slogans. Striking as are the similarities, there are deep and fundamental differences.[7]

The assertion that big business in 1953 was not the same as big business of the Hoover period carries implications of considerable importance. The comparison of the two is predominantly a study in the evolution of American capitalism. In this connection Berle's comments are of particular interest inasmuch as he has been one of the foremost students and critics of big business power and control in the country.[8] More than twenty-five years ago Berle contended that the new corporate concentration of power was a private oligarchy, rivaling that of the church in the medieval state, and needed to be controlled and checked by the community. His statements, therefore, about the "deep and fundamental differences" which characterized the Republican administration of President Eisenhower are especially noteworthy in that they point up the argument being made here that there have been some important changes in the big business community in the last two decades. It is one thing to be opposed to big business because of a conviction that its interests are fundamentally antithetical to the deeper values and purposes of a democratic society, a view which for many years was the bedrock of much liberal, not to mention socialist, criticism. It is something else, however, to make the erroneous assumption that big businessmen, simply because they *are* big businessmen, are unaware of the significant developments which have taken place in the United States since 1932 and are still operating according to the old

[7] A. A. Berle, Jr.: "Businessmen in Government: The New Administration," *The Reporter* (February 3, 1953), p. 8.

[8] See A. A. Berle, Jr., and Gardner C. Means: *The Modern Corporation and Private Property* (New York: Macmillan; 1933).

rules of the game. To assume that America's industrial and financial leaders of today are little more than carbon copies of the business leaders of a generation or two ago is to overlook the fact that many businessmen learned some hard lessons from the experience of the New Deal and did not emerge from the ordeal unscarred. That they are still dedicated to preserving "free enterprise" is true enough, but this in no way invalidates the statement that there have been some important shifts in the political and economic outlook of American big business.

Many conservative businessmen have long recognized that the capitalist system has been in serious trouble since 1929. They know that many problems have not as yet been satisfactorily met and resolved, and they know that the war itself intensified the pressures. The more alert businessmen, as C. Hartley Grattan has put it, realize that something has got to be done, and that unless they and business can deliver, they are through. The prevailing view among big businessmen in the early thirties —that the depression was the result of individual weaknesses rather than serious faults in the economic system—is rarely, and certainly not publicly, maintained today. When big businessmen were asked in 1930 what aspects of the depression the government could legitimately handle, the answer, in the words of the president of the National Association of Manufacturers, clearly indicated that in their opinion "the overshadowing problem of all problems is crime." [9] But the big business government of President Eisenhower was at least aware that its responsibilities included, at the very minimum, what steps might have to be taken along the lines of a public works program or other more drastic government-sponsored projects to avert a serious economic dislocation. Thirty years ago the concern of big business leaders

[9] John E. Edgerton: "Annual Address of John E. Edgerton, President of the National Association of Manufacturers," *American Industries,* XXXI (October 1930), p. 18.

for the immediate and narrow interests of the economic elite was so overweening that business was blind to the most urgent needs of the public at large. Alarmed for its prestige and profits, the business community—after assuming full credit for prosperity—could generate no meaningful sense of public responsibility in the face of depression.[1]

Business leadership, in effect, had betrayed conservatism, for the latter became the exclusive property of a single social and economic minority—business. Today, however, it seems evident that big business is at least more aware than ever before of its larger social responsibilities and commitments.

Harold Laski, in arguing that in no other country but the United States "does the direct pursuit of money-making wear a more virtuous air," stretched a good point too far by claiming that big businessmen today are so interested in getting rich in the quickest possible way that they do not consider the domain of national politics, in any real sense, to be their concern. Like many other critics of the United States, Laski drew an incomplete if not altogether inaccurate picture of contemporary business leaders as a result of viewing present-day America from the perspective of the 1920's. "It has become so important in the United States to be commercially successful," he wrote, "that it is rare for businessmen to look upon their civic duties as important." Yet today big business is not entirely shirking these responsibilities even though, in the minds of some people, it is misguided in its estimates and analyses of the situation. Many persons for that matter see great danger in the increasing determination of big business to take an active part in as many civic affairs as possible. In another passage Laski declares that the big businessman "has no hesitation in using violence against the men who go on strike," that he knows very little of the history of American labor, "assumes that politics are not his affair," and that "the larger issues of American life are some-

[1] James W. Protho: "Business Ideas and the American Tradition," *Journal of Politics,* Vol. XV, No. 1 (February 1953), p. 82.

thing that he has rarely examined and still more rarely understood." [2] Each of these assertions undoubtedly contains some
truth, but as a composite portrait of the contemporary American big businessman it overlooks many of the important though
perhaps less dramatic developments of the last quarter century.

The big businessmen who worked in the Eisenhower administration unquestionably had much in common with the
business leaders who surrounded Herbert Hoover, but they
were men, as Berle has described them, who had grown in a
different stand of timber.

> In Hoover's time they represented property and ownership.
> Now they represent power and administration. Hoover was
> the owner of large enterprises; Andrew Mellon, his Treas-
> ury Secretary, was the dominant stockholder in the Alu-
> minum Company of America, Gulf Oil Company, and a
> string of related enterprises. Eisenhower's team are not
> owners. They have brilliant records as salaried adminis-
> trators. . . . Like most big businessmen of today, they
> are professional corporate officeholders. In the previous
> era, the businessmen turned Cabinet officers were success-
> ful risk-takers and developers . . . a successful man be-
> came a billionaire. Now he manages a multi-billion-dollar
> corporation at a large salary.[3]

Whereas the businessman of the 1920's was almost solely
preoccupied with efficient utilization of men, equipment, and
materials to produce maximum profits, today's corporate manager takes a much broader view of his responsibilities. He is
concerned with his customers, his employees, the community
in which he is located, and the preservation of the "American
way of life," as well as with his stockholders. He has not, however, betrayed his primary responsibility to the owners of the
business; he realizes that their long-run interests are best represented by following a course of action that insures the perma-

[2] Laski: op. cit., pp. 170–2.
[3] Berle: "Businessmen in Government," p. 8.

nence of their enterprise and the stability of the entire business system.

It is clear that the motivation for increased social responsibility is not purely charitable. Business action has largely consisted of defensive responses to an awesome new formulation of the Tenth Amendment which seems to be hovering just around the corner: "The powers and services not faithfully exercised by the business world will most likely be appropriated by the federal government." The fear of increased government control prevents the big businessman from careless profit-grabbing. He must be sure that everyone is reasonably well fed and happy before he takes his fair share of profit. Although business contributions to the welfare of the society are not manifestations of a new selfless altruism, benefits do accrue to the labor force, the community, and the society at large when considerations other than the maximization of immediate profits influence corporate policy.

The remarks of W. A. Patterson, president of United Air Lines, to a recent business conference are characteristic of many modern business executives who have understood the meaning of events during the past thirty years. It is clear they do not plan to assume the role of passive spectator or steadfast reactionary as big government steadily saps their strength and then voraciously swallows them up.

The time is past when management can close its eyes to the kind of world we live in and blithely buy and sell, hire and fire, expand or contract, and then expect government to maintain full employment, public welfare and political harmony. . . . If American business is to remain faithful to its role as one of the custodians of the "American way of life" it must rise to today's challenge and realize that it is management's responsibility to encourage adoption of a structure which will encourage enterprise rather than penalize success, a structure tailored to the economy of the next decade rather than a carryover from the conditions of World War II.[4]

A further illuminating feature of the more enlightened businessmen of today is the recognition on their part that the principal responsibility of leadership in modern industrial society is to adapt "free enterprise" to the Benthamite principle of fostering the greatest good for the greatest number. They have realized that much of the social and economic base of the New Deal has become a permanent fixture on the American scene, and in spite of their antagonism to many features of the Roosevelt program they are cognizant of the desire of the American people for continued welfare services and recognize that this desire is more than "the irresponsible clamor of the mob for bread and circuses." Welfare is now recognized as "a justifiable demand, consonant with the necessities of social evolution" and in keeping with the American political tradition.[5] As realistic business leaders they are aware of the two major alternatives which are open to them: social welfare must be dispensed either by business or by the government, by "welfare capitalism" or by the "welfare state." To the businessman this is, in effect, no choice at all, for in his view the "welfare state" is the first step toward a total collectivism in which the state becomes all-powerful. In short, if the United States is to have a welfare society it must be firmly grounded, as far as big business is concerned, "in our free enterprise tradition; it must be accomplished under the auspices of competent and efficient business leadership, not under the arbitrary power of wasteful, bureaucratic government."[6]

[4] W. A. Patterson: "Growing Dimensions of Management," *Alumni Bulletin* (Stanford, Calif.: Graduate School of Business, Stanford University; January 1959), pp. 18–19.

[5] Russel W. Davenport: "The Greatest Opportunity on Earth," *Fortune* (October 1949), p. 65.

[6] Alpheus T. Mason: "Business Organized as Power: The New Imperium in Imperio," *American Political Science Review* (June 1950), p. 336.

The philosophy of "welfare capitalism" has perhaps been most clearly and forcefully expressed in the pages of *Fortune* magazine. In February 1951 the editors dedicated the entire issue to a re-examination of "the meaning of America," under the title of "U.S.A.: The Permanent Revolution." The editors stated in their preface:

> Some may think it strange that a magazine dedicated to reporting and analyzing American business should step so far out of its literal field as this issue does. But on many occasions in the past *Fortune* has undertaken major assignments outside the strictly business field, not out of idle experimentation, but because of our awareness of how closely American business is interwoven with American life. The old adage that "business is business" is no longer true—if it ever was. One cannot do business intelligently in America unless one is intelligent about America.[7]

To the editors of *Fortune* there is no better demonstration of the adaptability of the American system than the changes that have taken place as a result of the "transformation of American Capitalism." At the turn of the century American capitalism seemed to be living up to the description and prediction of Karl Marx—what he and the muckrakers pilloried, in the words of the editors, as "the inhuman offspring of greed and irresponsibility, committed by its master, Wall Street, to a long life of monopoly." It seemed to establish irrefutable proof that capitalists must inevitably and inexorably place their insatiable desire for profits ahead of any larger consideration for the welfare of the people. In the opinion of *Fortune* early twentieth-century capitalism was close to the capitalism that Andrei Vishinsky used to denounce so laboriously and humor-

[7] "U.S.A.: The Permanent Revolution," *Fortune* (February 1951), p. 61. The statements of the editors used in the discussion that follows of the "new capitalism" appear in their section entitled "The Transformation of American Capitalism." I have relied primarily on this particular source because it is a most insightful treatment of the general problems under consideration.

lessly, and even some Americans still seem to think of capitalism in this guise.

The transformation is best understood in terms of the changing role and attitude of big business. In the eyes of *Fortune* this has been nothing less than a metamorphosis: the cutthroat, profit-seeking businessman of the past has shown signs of becoming a benevolent business leader with a sensitive awareness that he has an obligation to consider the needs of society in addition to his own immediate desires. It is not necessary here to question the literal accuracy of this picture; what is important is that, even as a generous overstatement, it points up certain important developments which have turned American capitalism into something which neither Karl Marx nor Adam Smith could ever have anticipated. The late nineteenth- and early twentieth-century pictures of American capitalists became stereotypes all over the world:

> Daniel Drew feeding his cattle salt to make them drink heavily the day before market . . . foxy Jay Gould, whom Vanderbilt called the smartest man in America, cornering the national gold-coin supply through his White House connections, and systematically and openly robbing the Erie; gelid old John D. Rockefeller perfecting the trust system and eliminating competitors like clay pigeons.

This, say the editors, was the principle of property ownership carried to its absurd conclusion—"capitalism gone berserk." Popular resentment grew quickly, and with the help of an aroused press there began the transformation of American capitalism.

Reference has already been made to the most important development to take place in the modern industrial enterprise— the separation of ownership and control. As Berle and Means have characterized it, the power in the control of the "active property"—the plant organization and goodwill—has superseded the power inherent in "passive property"—the stocks and bonds.[8] To the philosophers of the "new capitalism" this development has marked the difference between the single pre-occupation of businessmen to make money as quickly as possible and the present realization that the business community, in the person of the professional manager, has an added responsibility to society as a whole. This is not to say that he in any way minimizes his obligations to the stockholder to make a profit for the corporation. As *Fortune* plainly admits, any self-respecting businessman would rightly suspect a colleague who claimed he was not in business to make money. But, the editors maintain,

> the great happy paradox of the profit motive in the American system is that management, precisely because it is in business to make money years on end, cannot concentrate exclusively on making money here and now. To keep on making money years on end, it must, in the words of Frank Abrams, Chairman of the Standard Oil Company of New Jersey, "conduct the affairs of the enterprise in such a way as to maintain an *equitable and working balance* among the claims of the various directly interested groups—stockholders, employees, customers, and the public at large."

The corporation manager is "part of a group that enjoys power only so long as it does not abuse it—in other words, precisely so long as it does not exercise power the way men and groups of men used to."

In the great transformation of the American economy it is no secret that the private-enterprise system, heralded in classical economic theory, has been replaced by the corporate-enterprise system. The private shop, where the same person is typically owner, worker, and manager, bears little resemblance to the modern corporation. In the past half century the corporate form of life has moved from the periphery to the very

[8] Berle and Means: op. cit.

center of our social and economic existence, until today it is an institutional expression of our way of life.

The activities of the modern corporation have gone far beyond the economic sphere of production of goods and services. Corporate power, as Berle has emphasized, is now exercised in relation to certain obligations and responsibilities to the public.[9] The corporation that at one time was concerned only with economic man and the enhancement of the equity of the owners now bears a social responsibility for the whole quality and tone of American life. In this sense, as Professor Rostow suggests with tongue in cheek, even the image of the corporation has changed.

> It is no longer symbolized by a grim and energetic tyrant, single-mindedly driving his staff on to new feats of money-making. Today the presidents of the endocratic corporations wear buttoned-down striped shirts, not stiff collars; tweed jackets and flannels, rather than formal three-piece suits; wrist watches, not great gold repeaters at the end of heavy gold chains. In the public mind and in fact, the great corporation is more often than not a friendly committee of smiling bureaucrats, cheerfully sharing the burdens of the world around them.[1]

The vastly increased complexities of modern business have changed the job of management and in the process have brought about an enlarged appreciation and acceptance of its obligations not only to stockholders but to employees, customers, the government, and the public at large. The deeper social foundations of corporate business today have raised the standards of business leadership and performance and have made its most enlightened leaders fully aware that the success

[9] A. A. Berle, Jr.: *Economic Power and the Free Society* (pamphlet published by the Fund for the Republic, 1957).

[1] Eugene V. Rostow: "To Whom and for What Ends Is Corporate Management Responsible?" in *The Corporation in Modern Society*, edited by Edward S. Mason (Cambridge, Mass.: Harvard University Press; 1959), pp. 60–1.

of the entire system depends upon principles as well as profits. In a book that attempts to examine the philosophy, Richard Eells has stated the problem succinctly:

> Although, as has been frequently pointed out, the strategic decisions of the businessman were once relatively limited in scope and number—what to produce, how to produce, and how to market—the emergence of large-scale enterprise in a dynamic society has forced him to concentrate upon decision areas that have wide social and political dimensions. In addition to the traditional techniques of market operation, he has also to consider such instruments of policy as political action, negotiations of a quasi-diplomatic sort with other organized groups, and communication relationships that demand much beyond limited "public relations" techniques. The community that a business serves, and on which it depends, is regional, national, and even international in scope. Nor can that community be defined adequately in territorial dimensions. The functions of business and the businessman are thus to be seen in the framework of the greater society and not as isolated functions. Their new significance can be understood only by relating these functions to some of the basic ideas and institutions that have endured, and will continue to endure, through the short-run ups-and-downs of social change.[2]

The problem of change is one to which businessmen have traditionally reacted with suspicion and hostility. They have contented themselves with a concern for stability, the protection of business interests, and fiscal responsibility, but little more. They have lacked a willingness to explore—as businessmen—means for dealing with new problems as they arise. Many of the present-day business leaders, however, recognize that what is needed now is a new initiative on their part to help develop

[2] Richard Eells: *The Meaning of Modern Business* (New York: Columbia University Press; 1960), p. 7. See also Roger M. Blough: *Free Man and the Corporation* (New York: McGraw-Hill; 1959) and Theodore V. Houser: *Big Business and Human Values* (New York: McGraw-Hill; 1957) for elaboration of this particular theme.

policies and programs which will deal effectively with these emerging problems. One of the critical failures of the business-man in the past was that he had little sense of history. He stressed the static and paid no attention to the dynamic aspects of both business and society. Now it is becoming increasingly clear to many businessmen that if the economic system is to survive it must continue to change. They have come to under-stand that change is the essence of its being. One of the hard lessons they learned from the 1930's was that business lost out in the struggle for political power because it had been pre-occupied with the past and had been unable to comprehend the social forces at work in society and its own place in the changing scheme of things.

James C. Worthy, vice president in charge of public rela-tions at Sears, Roebuck and Company, has stated that what is needed is for businessmen to join in the support of policies that will contribute to the long-range health of society as a condition for the long-range security and opportunity of business. A case in point is the status of the Negro. Worthy believes that busi-nessmen must take the lead in providing more equal economic opportunity without regard to race. He acknowledges there are many aspects to the problem: education, housing, accultu-ration, prejudice in all its forms and manifestations. But the economic aspect is fundamental, and this the businessmen can do something about. Worthy recognizes, too, the richer promise of an industrial climate.

> An industrial economy provides a better atmosphere for working out the problems of relations between the races than a nonindustrial. This is clearly seen, for example, in the handling of school integration problems in the South. It is significant that where business groups are powerful, as in North Carolina and Florida, businessmen tend to caution moderation on the part of political leaders and to keep in check some of the more rabid forms of racial

demagoguery. Because industry needs stability, new southern industries tend to locate in areas where there is the best promise of avoiding severe racial tensions. In both the South and the North it is likely that in the long run industry will provide the framework within which can be worked out some reasonably satisfactory solutions for the most intractable single problem of American society, the relations between the races.[3]

Worthy is not happy with the application of "conservative" to everything with which the businessman is identified. He recognizes that the businessman has helped to bring about this association because he has usually thought of himself as conservative and people generally expect him to be. "In the past the businessman was a man of property and the conservative attitude came to him naturally. The modern businessman," Worthy points out, "has inherited the attitude but not the property. He is likely to be a professional manager with only a relatively small ownership interest in the business he manages." [4] Today the businessman plays a central role in that his business actions induce social changes which, in turn, require him to promote social policies that will facilitate the needed social adjustments.

The necessity for the businessman to look beyond his own immediate economic self-interest is viewed today as the necessary condition for the preservation of the corporate-enterprise system. To this end the enlightened big businessman has made a number of important discoveries. For example, he has found that a strong trade union movement tends to strengthen the business system by increasing public confidence in its over-all justice, by assuring workers that they do not stand alone and

[3] James C. Worthy: *Big Business and Free Men* (New York: Harper & Brothers; 1959), p. 187. This point is of particular interest because it bears directly on the discussion in the previous chapter about the cluster of values and beliefs which constitutes the pre-industrial outlook.

[4] Ibid., p. 182.

unprotected, and by showing there are powerful forces in the society which are explicitly dedicated to the welfare of workers. Paul St. Sure, president of the Pacific Maritime Association and the employer with whom Harry Bridges and his union must deal, recognizes that there are two broad avenues open to businessmen in the search for industrial peace: one is by trying to curb, if not outlaw, the right of association along trade union lines; the other is the encouragement of association or the conscious use of balance of power as the strategy of industrial peace. For this reason, among others, he has opposed (as a businessman and a Republican) so-called "right-to-work" laws because he believes their passage would not bring peace on the waterfront or any place else where business and labor confront each other. His feeling is that if responsibility in labor-management relations is the overriding objective, it will not be achieved by attacking the institutional structure of unionism.[5] Businessmen should not be devoting their time and energies to contesting the union for the loyalty of the worker. In 1914 the National Association of Manufacturers declared that "the real and ideal union is the one between employer and employee." Businessmen like St. Sure reject this approach and philosophy. They agree with Professor Lloyd Fisher that the essential issue is whether the function of an employer shall be confined to that of managing his industrial enterprise or whether he must, by the exercise of this function, be a *boss* as well.[6] The small business-

[5] These ideas and many others of a similar nature were expressed by Mr. St. Sure at Stanford University in a lecture he delivered to my undergraduate course in Public Policy. Of particular interest at the time was the fact that the Pacific Maritime Association had joined with Bridges's International Longshoreman's and Warehouseman's Union in a mutual effort to study the complex problems of automation in the shipping industry. Mr. St. Sure was emphatic in pointing out that the problem on the West Coast waterfront was not to destroy or carry on continuous warfare with Bridges's militant union but to work out a plan which would accommodate the interests of both parties.

[6] Lloyd Fisher: *The Price of Union Responsibility* (Berkeley, Calif.: Institute of Industrial Relations, University of California; 1948).

man likes and expects to be boss; the big businessman, however, cannot afford the price.

It should be emphasized that a growing number of big business leaders today do not look upon these matters merely as questions of abstruse social philosophy. They see them as highly practical considerations, reflecting once again a different mood than that of the small entrepreneur. Worthy goes so far as to say that the cloak of conservatism fits the big businessman poorly.

> On all counts liberalism is a more suitable philosophy for business than is conservatism. It fits the businessman's innovating role and emphasizes, as conservatism does not, the need for promoting social policies that will preserve and strengthen that role. The humanitarian aspect of liberalism underscores—again, as conservatism does not— the need for constant concern for the human impact of business actions and the obligation of business to serve the long-range public interest. The liberal viewpoint is more likely to encourage the exercise of initiative in recognizing and dealing with problems than is the conservative. Liberalism implies a much stronger faith in the capacities of men and women than does conservatism with its more skeptical bias, and this, too, conforms more closely with the outlook of many businessmen. Not least important, the philosophy of liberalism provides a much more useful framework within which to relate business to the rest of society and to maintain confidence in the integrity and basic good will of business leadership.[7]

There is much of the pious platitude here, and certainly one cannot conclude from these high-sounding words that the leaders of big business are all similarly inclined. They are not. What is important in the viewpoint expressed above is that it is much more likely to come from a high-ranking business executive who commands some measure of power and influence in our industrial society than, say, from the small shopkeeper who at

[7] Worthy: op. cit., p. 193.

the very outset distrusts the corporate business community for both its pronouncements and practices.

Underlying this outlook of big business is the basic assumption that capitalism has been chopped down to a manageable size as a result of various reforms and controls undertaken by the government, and it is therefore up to business to exercise the moral leadership in society. The corporation as a unit of experimentation should be substituted for the old federalism; businessmen, in other words, should assume the positive functions of decision-making within the corporation, unfettered by the federal government. The corporation has exhibited a sense of responsibility to its employees not only, as *Fortune* says, to prevent or anticipate the demands of labor unions "but for the simple, obvious, and honest reason that a satisfied, loyal group of employees is at least as much a capital asset as a modern plant or a vital piece of machinery." Elton Mayo long ago pointed out, to the satisfaction of many businessmen, that job satisfaction on the part of employees—the feeling of having done a good job and of having it recognized by people who know what a good job is—is often more important than being preoccupied with material benefits.[8] The tremendous growth of public relations activities is another indication that the corporation is aware of its social responsibilities, although the degree to which it fulfills those responsibilities may be something else again. More and more corporation managers understand that "good business public relations," as *Fortune* has defined it, "is good performance publicly appreciated, because adequately communicated."

The editors of *Fortune,* in stressing the new responsibilities of the business community today, do not claim that "business is already rolling us down the six-lane, high-speed highway to

[8] Elton Mayo: *The Human Problems of an Industrial Civilization* (New York: Macmillan; 1933).

economic paradise." They are frank to say that big business still has a good deal to answer for. In their opinion, however, what is important is that "the business leaders *are* setting the pace, and *are* being followed. What counts is that the old concept that the owner had a right to use his property just the way he pleased has evolved into the belief that ownership carries social obligations, and that a manager is a trustee not only for the owner but for society as a whole."

David Lilienthal has recently expressed the same conviction about the new sense of social awareness felt today in the ranks of big business. In his opinion it represents "a proud and fruitful achievement of the American people as a whole," for big business is much more than an efficient way to produce and distribute basic commodities; it is also a social institution that promotes human freedom and individualism.

> This change is more than a negative matter, the virtual disappearance of the tycoon and the capitalist, of the newspaper cartoons so familiar in the years prior to the Great Depression. There is an *affirmative fact,* highly relevant to any consideration of Big Business and of a new appraisal of the validity and relevance of the old fears of Bigness. There is a decided trend—trend is perhaps not a strong enough word to describe it—to a new kind of "top boss" of large business undertakings. He is a man with a strong and practical sense of responsibility to the public, and an awareness of the ethics of present-day business competition. Coupled with this trend, is the great increase in top managers who have been trained, as professional men, in the now numerous and seasoned graduate schools of business administration. Then, too, there are the newer type of executives who have come to management posts with a background of technical training and experience, as chemists, chemical engineers, physicists, mechanical or civil engineers, or have been promoted from specialized technical posts, such as experts in the technology of textiles or glass or petroleum.
>
> These men represent graphically, in their persons and in

their outlook and function, the coming age of Big Business.[9]

3

In 1888 Lord Bryce made the observation that "public opinion stands out, in the United States, as the great source of power, the master of servants who tremble before it." Whether this was a completely true reading of the political situation at the time or not, public opinion in the nineteenth century was little more than a spontaneous assemblage of individual opinions. Public relations men and public opinion polls were still to be discovered as useful tools on a national scale, and our vocabulary had yet to be enriched by such terms as "captive audience." At the turn of the century big business was essentially uninterested in "public opinion." It was concerned with other more pressing problems, and its attention was fixed on other battlefields where the real struggle between property interests and State regulation was being fought. The law courts were ruling that the efforts of the States to control corporations constituted the taking of property without "due process of law." Business lobbyists were active in the legislative chambers in what has been called "open corruption openly arrived at," and in some legislatures votes were being bought and sold with ease. It was a time when business enterprise was able to carry on many of its activities without the knowledge of the public and with considerable protection from both politics and the law.

In the past fifty years, however, business power has had to retreat to new positions in the face of various reforms that have made corruption at least more difficult and "bossism" less strong. As David Riesman and others have pointed out, power groups today, and especially organized big business, have been

[9] David E. Lilienthal: *Big Business: A New Era* (New York: Harper & Brothers; 1952), pp. 26–7.

forced to learn new techniques of manipulation and persuasion; they know that the central issue of property rights and democracy, or "interests" versus "numbers," will be decided in part at the grass roots. Ideas, like commodities, cannot be left entirely to the "free play of the market."

But whatever else can be said of big businessmen today, they can no longer be charged with being disinterested in public opinion. The "public be damned" attitude of the past is ill suited to the political climate of the present; for that matter, big business, through promotional activities and educational campaigns, is continuously trying to win new friends and influence more people. The mere fact that business has grown so big and has become so powerful means that its leaders must of necessity be concerned with many of the societal problems which are a direct outgrowth of this development—unemployment, foreign aid, rising prices, social security, and all of the other public matters in which the stake of big business is so large.

The great price-rigging conspiracy in the electrical equipment industry, which resulted in jail sentences for several top-level executives of General Electric and Westinghouse early in 1961, is a case in point. Leading officers of this giant industry, publicly pledged to the concept of competition, had privately conspired to rig prices to the detriment of their customers on a staggering scale. In the words of the Federal District judge who presided over this court drama, the cases were "a shocking indictment of a vast section of our economy."

Reaction to the convictions ran the gamut from severe condemnation of all businessmen to sympathy for the executives who had performed their duties.[1] Yet both those who condoned

[1] F. F. Loock, president of the Allen-Bradley Company which was fined $40,000 in the antitrust proceedings, euphemized a widely shared way of thinking among modern businessmen who learned long ago that they must band together to protect themselves, remarking that "no one attending the gatherings was so stupid he didn't know they were in viola-

and those who condemned price-fixing were unanimous in their concern about the attitude of the general public. The diverse reactions to the case give some support to Berle's contention that the power of big business today is partially curbed by the force of public opinion. The dirty wash was hanging on the line for everyone to see, but the total disregard for the public's feeling which characterized another era's business leaders was replaced by expressions of concern that public confidence toward the world of big business had suffered a serious setback. The shame of the sorry episode cannot be exaggerated. However, the reactions of leading businessmen were not those of "grasping, greedy, cutthroat competitors" who had fleeced everybody in sight and did not give a damn about the consequences. The difference is that many did care about public opinion. Today's leaders have long since learned that corporations which exercise power affecting many millions of lives must find their "claim of legitimacy" through a record of responsibility and accountability. They are cognizant of the fact that obligations arise with power. Moreover, they know that responsible actions which help to build public confidence are in their own best interest.

Henry Ford II, chairman of the board of the Ford Motor

tion of the law. But it is the only way a business can be run. It is free enterprise." *Time* magazine (February 17, 1961), p. 85. Other businessmen did not subscribe to Loock's definition of free enterprise. Malcolm Forbes, editor of *Forbes,* summed up this feeling: "For the seven responsible businessmen who drew thirty-day jail sentences on criminal charges of price-fixing and bid-rigging, the judge's firm action was a personal tragedy. Nevertheless, as firm believers in the capitalistic system, the editors of this magazine feel strongly that such 'informal' price-fixing and monopolistic agreements endanger the whole free enterprise system. Such acts by businessmen are as damaging as excessive government regulation or trade union abuse of power. . . . If, as a result of the publicity and punishment involved in the electrical case, other U.S. businessmen put their houses in order in this respect, then the case will turn out to be a good thing for free enterprise." Article entitled "Monopoly *vs.* Freedom," in *Forbes* (March 1, 1961), p. 9.

Company, spoke out against the men who by their actions would undermine the goodwill of the public. It is doubtful if his father in his day would have felt compelled to talk in the same manner.

> In the past twenty years there has been a material change in the whole outlook of our larger business enter- prises, a change toward far greater social maturity and responsibility. Business today understands well how its actions may impinge not only on the lives of individuals but also upon the goals and the policies of our nation both at home and abroad. . . .
>
> It would indeed be a sad thing, if the good will and confidence that business has laboriously built up over the years should now be washed away at this very critical juncture in our history. . . .
>
> Of one thing I am sure, the confidence and faith of the American people in business—particularly in the big corporations that play so vital a role in our whole life— will not be strengthened by alibis, excuses, or counter- recriminations.
>
> If we are to preserve the good name of our companies, we must be sure that management does everything rea- sonable in prudence and good sense to prevent such things happening, and takes swift and sure corrective action when the occasional misdeed does occur. . . .[2]

One of the major developments in the evolution of Ameri- can capitalism in the last thirty years has been the increasingly closer working relations between government and big business. While it certainly cannot be said to have resulted in complete harmony, it has nevertheless produced an unprecedented sys- tem of government-industry planning on a national scale. To take just one example, Berle points out that the oil industry operates on the basis of a price-stabilization plan that must be periodically approved by Congress. The Interstate Oil Compact provides that the Bureau of Mines determine the consumption

[2] From a speech to the Minneapolis Junior Chamber of Commerce, quoted in *The New York Times,* April 21, 1961.

needs of the country, and the oil-producing States set their production schedules to meet the requirements. In addition, under the federal "Connolly Hot Oil Act" it is a criminal offense to make shipments of unallocated oil. Similar though perhaps less detailed plans have also been worked out for other industries such as steel, sugar, and aluminum, with the result that the government has become the chief customer of certain big businesses and has in addition created and facilitated conditions contributing to business success. All of these arrangements have required continuous contact between businessmen and Washington, with both sides of necessity deeply concerned about public opinion. For the businessman particularly it has been a new and somewhat sobering experience.

> . . . [he] has had to be in Washington, at Chamber of Commerce meetings, or on the air. His public relations staff has been steadily taking a hand in discussions of political theory; appeal from a failure of governmental cooperation (as the businessman saw it) was taken to the public just as politicians appeal an adverse decision of Congress to the grass roots. The successful administrator of a large corporation has been willy-nilly, a type of politician. This is a good introduction to government life.
>
> Such was not the custom of the older generation. The great capitalist-owners of the day of Andrew Mellon or the elder Morgan kept away from the public. The late George F. Baker rejoiced in the fact that in fifty years he had made only two speeches, both of them not more than a couple of sentences long. Contrast this with Benjamin Fairless or Clarence Randall, campaigning in season and out for the position of the steel companies during the steel crisis, or with General Motors, maintaining for years a weekly broadcast over a national network to explain its political philosophy and ideas and to exhort Americans to support the leadership offered by American business [3]

[3] Berle: "Businessmen in Government." Berle has made the additional observation that American businessmen today must be credited with having accepted scientific education. "The abstract scientist is now

All the familiar slogans against government regulation are still in use, but since the days of the New Deal many business-men have reluctantly and tacitly accepted the necessity for positive government. The grudging and tempered acceptance of strong government by many elements in the big business community by no means indicates a reversal of their former hostility to government interference. Many business leaders, confronted with a *fait accompli* in the thirties, found it expedient to shift their immediate point of view to accord with the political realities of the time, but without compromising their future right to oppose or to help in changing governmental policies. At the same time, however, a considerable number of business leaders went much farther than this in accepting ideas sponsored by the Roosevelt regime.

> Their analysis of the economic situation led them away from the individualism of earlier ideologies to the collectivism of modern industrial and commercial practice. Sponsorship of the National Industrial Recovery Act by the national Chamber of Commerce, for instance, represents a policy which does not, at least, deny the extensive positive functions assumed by government in the program and which made less significant the outdated Whig claims for individualism.[4]

---

subsidized in universities by research grants made in volume by the hardest-boiled boards of corporate directors. Socony-Vacuum Oil Company, in endowing a fellowship in petroleum exploration science at Harvard, announced that 'the petroleum industry was founded on the vision and knowledge of educated people.' . . . Many indeed of the great business-men now emerging in government were technically trained themselves, either formally in universities or less formally through training programs of the companies in which they worked. . . . These men are a far cry from the shrewd operators, the students of the stock market who carried the banner in Hoover's day. The wider outlook of the new men will stand them in good stead in government." Ibid.

[4] Thomas Paul Jenkin: *Reactions of Major Groups to Positive Government in the United States, 1930–1940* (Berkeley, Calif.: University of California Press; 1945), p. 398.

The traditional fear of the government on the part of big businessmen reflects in many important respects more of an anti-Populist point of view rather than a strictly antigovernmental one. Businessmen, as we have seen, have not been reluctant to call on the government for assistance of one kind or another whenever it has suited their purpose or when they felt it was necessary. "The conspicuous antigovernmental orientation of the business community," comments Professor Protho, "is itself an incident of the more basic fear that popular control will, through the device of universal suffrage, come to dominate the governmental process." The business leader today is as much aware as the labor leader that the government is "capable of meritorious service in the cause of 'right,' " but he also knows that "politics as it is practiced in the twentieth century offers the constant threat of intruding the mass man's delusion into the social order." [5] If in previous times businessmen could rely on the courts to uphold their policies and activities regardless of what a majority of the people might have felt, they know that today the courts, if they have not completely bowed to the popular will, more often than not give judicial sanction to legislative decisions. The leaders of the business community, therefore, consider one of their principal jobs to be that of convincing the people that big business is vitally concerned with helping to make the present industrial social order a more democratic one. Their task no longer is to oppose the people or even to stand aloof from them, but rather to demonstrate that as businessmen they can be trusted to carry out their responsibilities as "the new ruling group of our society"—to use Peter Drucker's phrase. Or, as Professor Alpheus T. Mason has said, the people —Hamilton's "pure, original fountain of all legitimate authority"—need to be brought in line with the contemporary ideology of big business.

Speaking before the annual convention of the United States

[5] Protho: op. cit., pp. 71–2.

Chamber of Commerce in 1951, Secretary of Commerce Charles Sawyer indicated what he believed was the most important challenge facing America's business leaders. He asked them to join him in a campaign to teach Americans "that our prosperity and even our very existence depends on a profitable and a constantly growing business community." He went on to stress that the biggest sales job now confronting business was to sell itself to its employees and to the public and that businessmen should make a concerted effort to explain and emphasize the contributions of business to the nation's welfare. Businessmen have "a sale to make and the sale has not been closed," Mr. Sawyer declared. He made it clear that the Department of Commerce would welcome the opportunity to help in such an effort "and I suggest the United States Chamber of Commerce as the organization which should initiate it." [6]

A growing number of today's business leaders realize that an industrial society cannot survive if the purposes and goals to which the business community is committed contradict the beliefs and values which society professes. They remember all too well the conflict which resulted from the clashes between business and the rest of society a short generation or so ago and are anxious to avoid its repetition. They not only have learned that the people expect business leaders to fulfill the promises on which society rests but are fully aware that society itself will lose its rationality and cohesion if business denies these social beliefs or if it fails to give them adequate fulfillment. They have come to understand what perhaps was not possible thirty years ago, that "either the beliefs themselves will become meaningless or society will become a failure and will lose the allegiance of its citizens." [7] Believing, as Drucker has said, that both the state and business "have to be organized on the same basic be-

    [6] *The New York Times,* May 2, 1951.
    [7] Peter F. Drucker: *The New Society* (New York: Harper & Brothers; 1949), pp. 36–7.

liefs and principles," the contemporary leader of big business is more sensitive to public opinion than he ever has been in the past and is equally determined that nothing shall be done to upset the relatively favorable image of big business now shared by a large number of the American people.[8]

It is not necessary to deny that a strong undercurrent of hostility toward big business still exists in order to demonstrate that its reputation has improved in recent years. Big business has been devoting its energies to bringing about just this situation. In 1934 the National Association of Manufacturers spent only $36,000 for public relations, but just three years later 55 per cent of its budget or $793,000 was earmarked for propaganda and public education—clear evidence that business leadership has recognized the value of popular support. But it should also be remembered that if big business to some extent has been successful in convincing people that it is working in the service of American ideals and goals, not the least of the reasons is that its leaders believe they have a fairly clear picture of what is wanted today by a great majority of the American people. In this respect the meaning of the New Deal has not been entirely lost.

One of the clearest signposts of the "new responsible business era" is the recent emergence and development of comprehensive curriculums in graduate schools of business. As recently as twenty years ago most business schools were little more than workshops that provided students with basic financial and eco-

[8] See "Big Business from the Viewpoint of the Public," a study of the Public Affairs Group Survey Research Center, Institute for Social Research, University of Michigan, Ann Arbor, 1951, for an illuminating account of the attitudes of the American people toward big business. The report was concerned only with the ways in which people think and feel about big business in the modern economy of today. The survey needs to be studied in its entirety, but it is clear that a larger number of the American people from various walks of life have a more sympathetic attitude toward big business today than was true twenty-five years ago.

nomic skills. Although they probably did little to improve the businessman's ability to relate his own activities to long-range social developments, they were at least partially responsible for introducing the professional methods and skills which have largely replaced "good business sense."

The steady advance of managerial efficiency undoubtedly served to benefit the national economy, and graduate business school curriculums are still geared to equip students with the tools they will need to compete successfully in the "corporate free enterprise" arena. However, the typical course of study today is planned so that the student is made aware of the total environment in which he must make business decisions. Not only are ideas and research which originate in the academic world communicated to the business world via business-school alumni, but the direct influence of the schools, acting as the spokesmen and even the conscience of the business community, has been of considerable importance in changing management policies and practices.

Stanford's Graduate School of Business includes a curriculum element which illustrates the increasing attention given to the social environment:

> *External Environment of Business:* This group consists of a course in the economic system, both national and international; a course in the legal framework of business; and an integrating course in business, government and public policy. It is intended that this sequence of required courses will make the student more aware of the external forces which impinge upon the firm; of the interaction of the firm and its economic, legal, political and social environment; and of the way in which these forces and institutions are changing and evolving through time.[9]

[9] *A Statement of Philosophy, Objectives, and Needs* (Stanford, Calif.: Graduate School of Business, Stanford University; June 15, 1959), pp. 23–4.

A University bulletin describes several courses from the External Environment sequence:

Business 302: Business Activity and Public Welfare: This course deals with . . . aims and social functions of business; capitalism, its evolution, weaknesses, and accomplishments; various contradictory concepts of social welfare; . . . Repeated attention is given to the problem of devising a practical program for *modification of the capitalistic business system so as to maximize its contribution to social welfare* and international betterment. [My italics.]

Business 306: Introduction to Business and Government: . . . includes study of such topics as historical business-government relations, multiplication of contacts with governmental agencies, policies affecting particular industries, government in relations to business organizations such as trade associations, competition between business and government, government aids to and levies upon business, and a survey of new relationships between business and government.[1]

Programs at business schools have been characteristically sensitive to changes in technology, methods, human aspects of organizational behavior, and the general business environment. The separation of ownership from management and the rise of labor unions to power have been particularly important influences on general business policy. The business schools still try to nurture whatever entrepreneurial spirit exists in the hearts of students, but just as they know that a ruthless individual today is not likely to reap the same profits and benefits as did his nineteenth-century counterpart, so they are also well aware that most graduates are destined for professional managerial posts in corporate hierarchies.

The new emphasis on adjustment to the ways of the benevolent corporation has not dulled the traditional profit motive. The monetary goal is essentially the same, but community serv-

[1] *Stanford University Bulletin,* Series 12, No. 18 (April 26, 1960), p. 25.

ices and good labor relations have replaced authoritarian methods, squalid company towns, and sweatshops. "Amid at first heavy overtones of humanitarianism and social responsibility there emerged the hard cold fact that, in the long run, authoritarian methods are relatively ineffective. Knowledge of how to secure more effective action within organizational structures is expanding at an increasing rate." [2]

Business-school administrators and professors are sufficiently distant from the daily turmoil of the marketplace to recognize the dangers which confront a business world that remains static in the face of various social and political forces. The Stanford Business School's "Statement of Philosophy, Objectives, and Needs" makes it clear that the need to adjust business attitudes and practices to changing conditions is paramount. Furthermore, the statement indicates the School is prepared to meet the demands and challenges of continued social change by assuming a large share of the responsibility for insuring the very survival of American business:

> The continued viability of American capitalism will depend on its vigor, which in turn will depend primarily on the flexibility of our business leadership. . . . [The effective manager cannot] look upon the political and legal environment as a massive and passive obstruction to be circumvented or overcome. He must recognize that he will be shaped by his environment just as he will help to shape it.
>
> Business is a dominant social and economic institution of our time. The wisdom with which it is managed and directed may well determine whether freedom of enterprise will survive. In no other area is a flexible professional leadership more vital, for unless managerial and institutional changes keep pace with major social, economic, and technological developments, tensions of such magnitude will be generated as to jeopardize not merely economic and political stability, but national survival. The need for more

[2] Ibid. (A Statement), p. 2.

and better managers is imperative. The challenge to develop such managers has never been greater.[3]

Modern business schools are more than a collection of classrooms and instructors. They are increasingly dynamic and progressive institutions whose functions of preparing men for professional business careers and acting as the intellectual centers of American business are certain to influence the future course of the business world. The continued increase in stature and size of graduate business schools will mean that an increasing number of professional managers with professional codes of ethics and feelings of social responsibility will join the corporate ranks. A top official of the steel industry has confirmed this entire development:

> The quality of business leadership requirements is trending away from the dominant entrepreneur type of earlier decades. This separation of owner and manager roles has had a very forcible impact on the manager's authority, responsibility, and accountability and, therefore, on the type of manager. The corporate form of organization, as opposed to the partnership or individually owned enterprise, has created an increasing demand for professional managers and business specialists. Thus, executive ranks are filling today with an ever-expanding proportion of college graduates and men with graduate professional training.[4]

Professor Norton Long has elaborated on the same point:

> In a short thirty years we have passed from a corporate order whose managerial style derived from the so-called "robber barons," the divine-right Bayers, and the public-be-damned Vanderbilts, to the business-school-trained, public-relations-conscious professional of the highly specialized complex corporate bureaucracy of today. While the latter-day manager may not be as other-directed as Ries-

[3] Ibid., pp. 2–4.

[4] Desmond McCall: "Some Notes on Management Development," *Alumni Bulletin,* Graduate School of Business, Stanford University, Vol. XXV, No. 3 (July 1956). See also James C. Worthy: op. cit., Chapter x, "Education for Business Leadership."

man and William H. Whyte, Jr. suggest as a nonowner and a professional manager, he has a concern for harmony and the avoidance of trouble that sets him apart from his predecessors. His attitude toward striking employees can never quite have the same sense of outraged feudal lordship confronted with a servile revolt that envenoms the Kohler strike. Nor as a nonowner can he have quite the same view of the corporation as his property to do with as he pleased, by God, as seemed so right and fitting to the self-made Calvinists of American industry's heroic stage.[5]

Several years ago a survey of college graduating seniors was conducted for the purpose of learning their plans and aspirations regarding careers in the business world.[6] The results not only provided a striking illustration of the changed nature of American big business as viewed by a large percentage of 150,-000 college men, but confirmed once again that the compelling desire for security has become a national concern of overriding importance. "Bulling about the future, the state of the economy, and their place in it," commented the editors of *Fortune,* "they seem, to a stranger from another generation, somehow curiously old before their time. Above everything else security has become the great goal." These men have turned their backs on what their fathers before them had automatically assumed was the most cherished prerogative of youth—"the desire for venture."

For the graduating senior, security, although it has many diverse meanings, is principally "bound up in people."

Spiritually, it means working for people, in the sense of service, of justifying one's place in the community. Materially, it is, simply, working *under* them. The class of '49 wants to work for somebody else—preferably somebody big. No longer is small business the promised land. As for the idea of going into business for oneself, the idea is so

[5] Norton E. Long: "The Corporation, Its Satellites, and the Local Community," in *The Corporation in Modern Society,* p. 205.

[6] "The Class of '49," *Fortune* (June 1949).

seldom expressed as to seem an anachronism. "I never saw a bunch that so wanted to make their free-enterprise system work," says a professor of business administration, "but they are interested in the system rather than the individual enterprise. They will be technicians—not owners." . . . From the huge metropolitan universities to the small-town campuses the men of '49 everywhere seem haunted by the fear of a recession. "I know A. T. & T. might not be very exciting," explains a senior, with a phraseology that has become almost standard on U.S. campuses, "but there'll always be an A. T. & T." The "always" is a key word, for the principal criterion of the job-seeking senior is now the question of longevity. . . .[7]

The entrepreneurial spirit that characterized previous generations of business aspirants is almost totally lacking in the college graduate looking around today for a job in industry. Money, for one thing, is not necessarily seen as the all-important answer to the problems of the future; the college seniors, *Fortune* points out, "simply will not talk of the future in terms of the dollar. In terms of the Good Life, however, they are most articulate." Nor are they worried because business is both big and organized. Anonymity does not conjure up the same fears it might have thirty years ago, particularly for a group that looks to big business for the security it wants—the opportunity to sink roots and settle down.[8] Most important of all, however,

[7] The growing need for sociability oriented completely around people was one of the major themes in David Riesman's *The Lonely Crowd* (New Haven, Conn.: Yale University Press; 1950), especially in chapters vi and vii. The editors of *Fortune* make the same point: "What kind of job do the seniors ask of Big Business? Merchandising is still the number one choice, but in the last few years a relatively new field, personnel, has been building up to a phenomenal—and illuminating—popularity. The field itself can be discussed in a few words: it is one of the most overcrowded; the work is semi-professional and it is rarely open to new recruits. Why, then, '49's enthusiasm? Wearily, recruiters report an explanation that, from campus to campus, varies by hardly a syllable: 'Because I like people.' " *Fortune* (June 1949), p. 163.

[8] It is interesting to note, in line with the discussion of the agrarian-spirited small businessman in the previous chapter, that the editors of

is the feeling that big business is "the most effective vehicle for community service; in the eyes of the senior the same attribute, efficiency, that makes the large corporation appealing as a sanctuary from depression, also makes it, on a foot-pounds-of-energy basis, by far the best stage for being useful to other people."

In 1913 Brooks Adams expressed the feeling of many people when he stated unequivocally that the "capitalist" cannot be considered a responsible individual because "he is not a trustee for the public. . . . He is too specialized to comprehend a social relation . . . beyond the narrow circle of his private interests." It was because Adams felt the business leader of his day did not exhibit this "preeminent requisite for success in government" that he maintained he was "incapable of feeling his responsibility, as a member of the governing class." [9] Almost half a century later many big businessmen are attempting to prove, with all of the resources at their command, that Adams was wrong.

It is not that today's Titan is any less interested in seeing his own business enterprise return him a handsome profit or even a big fortune, if that were possible. In point of fact, the change in the big businessman has come about because of the emergence of the corporation and its crucial impact on every seg-

---

Fortune report that only in the Southwest is there still a vigorous determination on the part of graduating seniors to go into business for themselves. In other parts of the country, notably in the Northeast and Far West, the majority of college graduates view small business as "small mainly because it doesn't deserve to be large" and because "it suffers from nepotism, shaky finances, and a roll-top-desk philosophy of management." Not so, however, in the Southwest: "to judge from the seniors of two of its universities the region would appear to be the last great reservoir of the gambling spirit. At Texas A. & M. 75% of the senior class want to go into business for themselves." Ibid., pp. 86–7.

[9] Brooks Adams: *The Theory of Social Revolution* (New York: Macmillan; 1914), pp. 208–9.

ment of our industrial society. The swaggering exploits of the Robber Barons ushered in a phase of triumphant capitalism that saw the crushing of competitors, the amassing of personal wealth for a privileged and fortunate few, and the bringing to fruition of qualities of acquisitiveness that were essential to the winning of immense corporate power. But to win this power calls for a talent and temperament far different from what is necessary to insure its consolidation. The big business leader today is confronted with a complex bureaucracy that demands a certain managerial skill and expertise in every phase of the corporation's specialized activities, rather than a colorful capacity for creating new empires. If at one time the adventuresome businessman was in effect the creator of all he surveyed, placing upon the new corporate institution the clear stamp of his own aggressive personality, today he is likely to be dwarfed by its size and its impersonality, not to mention its growing staff of public-relations experts, "human-relations" technicians, survey makers, as well as financial and production specialists. In addition, the businessman today has to contend with the power of a pressing labor movement and at the same time pay close attention to all of the regulatory problems and demands of a welfare state. Galbraith, Lerner, and others have put it well: where the profit motive was at one time the touchstone of almost all of the businessman's decisions and actions, today his primary concern is the holding and administering of the vast aggregates of power at his command.

There should be no misunderstanding of the argument being presented here. The ranks of big business today are full of men who follow the tradition of Sinclair Lewis's Babbitt and would find nothing wrong in pulling a shady deal at the expense of a less fortunate competitor if it would bring them some immediate economic advantage. This, after all, is what they understand the ethics of business to be all about, and our corporations are overflowing with advertising men, sales managers, and run-of-the-mill vice presidents who have long been among the greatest defenders of a severely competitive business system, which they firmly believe has been responsible for making this country what it is. Nonetheless, an important group of enlightened holders of business power exists today, men who need to be viewed in a different light and who require a new personality profile in place of the familiar Titan.[1]

Business leadership in America has traditionally been buttressed by some basic tenets. Bendix points out that the original beliefs were simple: success is virtue, poverty is sin, and both result from the effort or the indolence of the individual. Along with this belief has gone the idea that a man could do with his property whatever he wished—ownership itself was the proof of virtue—and thus no use that was made of it could be regarded as injurious to the social welfare as long as it resulted in an increase of the property. While these ideas still persist among contemporary industrial leaders, especially when they are called upon to justify their behavior or articulate their beliefs in, let us say, a crisis brought about by the insistent demands of a labor union, they are very often expressed in a much more modern form. It is what Alfred P. Sloan had in mind when he wrote that "those charged with great industrial responsibility must become industrial statesmen."

> . . . industrial management must expand its horizon of responsibility. It must recognize that it can no longer confine its activities to the mere production of goods and services. It must consider the impact of its operations on the economy as a whole in relation to the social and economic welfare of the entire community.[2]

[1] See Max Lerner: *America as a Civilization* (New York: Simon and Schuster; 1957), especially Chapter v, for an extended discussion of American capitalism and capitalists.

[2] Alfred P. Sloan: *Adventures of a White-Collar Man* (New York: Doubleday, Doran; 1941), p. 145.

This new type of businessman, several cuts above the old-fashioned, money-grasping buccaneer, is the result of the transformation process of the past sixty years in America. This process has seen the legendary capitalism of a market system of competing small enterprises give way to a still emerging structure of industry and government that has produced a new separation of powers more relevant for America today than the classical separation of governmental powers. Many of those who head the corporate empires of our day have had a part in developing the idea of the welfare state itself or in administering its controls over business or in supervising the American economic aid program abroad. While there is certainly no ideological commitment on their part to the idea of an expanding and powerful government, it is nevertheless true that these big businessmen have had to face squarely many of the problems that have arisen as a result of the new American collectivism. Furthermore, they have discovered that the old catchwords appropriate to a free-market economy are no substitute for the kind of imaginative thinking and creativeness needed to insure the survival of our whole economic system, not to mention their own positions and power. For that matter, they believe that business can be trusted with responsibility for enlightened leadership in a welfare economy and that businessmen are the proper guardians of the public interest. Certainly the theory of trusteeship is not a new one in American life, but to many leaders of big business today it has the particular merit of offering the promise of social and economic accomplishments while concomitantly showing that the government need not be entrusted with such an assignment. The apostles of "welfare capitalism" have not only provided a modern version of "business in the nation's service" but are also convinced they speak for those forces in a position to decide what *constitutes* the public welfare and, what is more, how to promote it.

The Agrarian Spirit
in an
Industrial Age

1

A responsible official of the Democratic Party in California recently made the observation that if the small businessman is not a Democrat in his politics, "someone had better inform National Headquarters because they are counting on his vote." Whether such a remark about the expectations of the Democratic Party leadership is in itself accurate or not is of no immediate concern here. But it is true that in many quarters there is a widespread conviction that the small businessman is basically "liberal" in his political orientation. He is, after all—so the image runs—the classic example today of the "little man" being pushed around by big business; he therefore supports those groups and organizations, among them the Democratic Party, which are opposed to the growing power of economic concentration, and at the same time he favors a forward-looking social program at home and abroad. In light of the rapid growth of corporate monopoly capitalism, according to a familiar argument, only the preservation of an active and dynamic small business community can prevent the total control of society by big business, since the small business-man is a cornerstone of our democracy.

There is reason to challenge the validity of this argument insofar as it relates to the conventional image that is projected. Politically speaking, the small businessman is not easy to categorize. To say that he is simply the younger brother of the big businessman, a capitalist in his own right whose only concern is to make money, is to offer a rigid economic interpretation which not only cannot satisfactorily account for all of the small businessman's political beliefs, but suggests that big business and small business share the same values and are striving for similar goals. Certainly, in an important sense the *economic* problem of small business is, in the end, a family quarrel between the big and the small capitalist over the distribution of available profits.[1] At one level of abstraction this view can be of real value, and if one wanted to depict the small businessman strictly in terms of his economic problems and expediencies such an analysis could be extremely convincing.

There is no doubt that a great many of his political ideas and opinions reflect his present ambiguous position within the business community. Unlike the big businessman who has achieved both status and prestige as part of his reward for having become financially successful, the small businessman has become neither an important source of influence or leadership in our present-day society nor the unequivocal economic success which was supposed to be his ultimate prize for hard work, initiative, and ingenuity. Individual competition between small merchants and proprietors, through which they and everyone else are presumed to prosper, has been upset by the mushrooming of large department stores and chain enterprises in practically every part of the country, with the result that the importance of small business has declined significantly while big

[1] See C. Wright Mills: op. cit., p. 51.

business has developed political power equal to its economic position. Under these circumstances it is easy to understand why the small businessman's political choices are not entirely irrespective of his economic grievances and why, to take a specific example which will be discussed in more detail, he responds to an assortment of political appeals demanding the curbing of the economic power of big business. But having said this, the fact remains that, in spite of major changes in the nation's economy during the last half century or more, the small businessman has kept much of his attachment to the values of pre-industrialism, something which cannot be explained by economic developments alone. To argue otherwise is to say that his political attitudes on a wide variety of current issues are motivated and shaped solely by his position in the economy. And while his economic fortunes (or misfortunes) certainly play a decisive role in his outlook on life, his strong belief in, say, the desirability of loyalty oaths cannot be fully explained either by his social origin or his economic situation.

It is frequently tempting to portray the small businessman as either very liberal or extremely reactionary in his politics—and leave it at that. There are those who will rush to defend one or the other of these descriptions, citing whatever evidence they can find to support their arguments, and thus make their case with seeming conviction if not persuasion. In point of fact there has been no thoroughgoing study of the politics of small business in the United States. This provides a kind of open season for anyone who wishes to present his own ideas or perhaps grind his own ax.

Certainly the present study makes no claim to offer anything like a final political judgment. One of its principal objectives, however, has been to examine the small businessman not merely in terms of his economic lot in society—which is generally the major if not the only concern of those who plead a case for small business—but also against the backdrop of the values of pre-industrialism, or what has been called here the agrarian spirit. In somewhat the same way that Bendix insists that the study of ideologies of management can provide an approach to an understanding of the social structure,[2] so a fuller understanding of the present-day small businessman can be achieved by considering the ideas and values to which he has been genuinely sympathetic. It is not suggested that the agrarian spirit represents an ideology peculiar *only* to small businessmen. It is more than likely that it fits other social or occupational strata equally well, but a project seeking data along these lines is beyond the scope of this study. However, inasmuch as there is a dearth of public-opinion material dealing with the political assumptions of small businessmen, an ideological approach may be suggestive and even useful as a guide for any further studies which may seek to correlate similarities and differences between small businessmen and other groups in society.

In any event it is considerably difficult to form a comprehensive picture of the politics of the small businessman or of his multiple opinions on the wide range of current political matters. For one thing, not only are small businessmen among the most volatile groups in the political community, but there is often some doubt as to whether, on a given occasion, any clear agreement can be reached as to who actually *is* a small businessman. For another, small businessmen do not share an important political advantage of big business: they have no comparable national organization of commensurate size or influence to represent their interests, to publicize their dissatisfactions, or to give voice to their feelings on the various domestic and international issues in which they are interested. Therefore, an early qualification must be placed on the generalized observations that follow, namely, that for our purposes the small businessman de-

[2] See Reinhard Bendix: *Work and Authority in Industry* (New York: John Wiley & Sons; 1956).

scribed here is representative rather than universal. There have been a number of small business organizations in the country whose activities and publications afford some valuable insight into the political principles and goals of small businessmen, two of them being the Conference of American Small Business Organizations (CASBO) and the National Federation of Independent Business, Inc. (NFIB). While in no sense the spokesmen for all small businessmen—no organization is—the former's vigorous activity in national politics for over ten years and the latter's continuing efforts to present to the members of Congress the views of small businessmen throughout the country make it possible to learn something of the political philosophy of small business, which both organizations have clearly articulated. Heavy use will also be made of several private surveys of small business attitudes on a number of issues which are closely bound up with the daily concerns of small businessmen. Finally, information gathered from other sources and studies, including some data from the Survey Research Center at Ann Arbor, Michigan, will be drawn on in attempting to determine not just the politics of small business but the political values to which the small businessman is largely committed.

2

For a number of years the Opinion Research Corporation in Princeton, New Jersey, has conducted studies of attitudes of small businessmen regarding what they have called "a familiar and long-standing problem: How to get small business support in the struggle to maintain business freedom." [3] The

[3] I wish to thank Mr. LeBaron R. Foster, vice president of the Opinion Research Corporation, Princeton, New Jersey, for special permission to make use of three of their confidential reports: *Small Business Thinking and the Free Market,* published in July 1950; *Socialistic Thinking in America—1953,* published in June 1953; and *Dealers in Hot Competition,* published in June 1957.

findings of one study were based on surveys of two separate small business groups, one constituting 237 interviews with small manufacturers employing from ten to 250 employees, and the other based on 1,000 interviews with a national cross section of owners and managers of all types of retail and wholesale businesses, plus additional interviews to permit separate reporting for auto dealers, filling station operators, appliance dealers, and grocers. The survey was conducted by means of personal interviews with owners of the business or active managers, all of whom were contacted in small, medium, and large cities across the nation according to their actual distribution as reported in U.S. Census figures. In another more extensive survey of dealers throughout the country the findings were based on 617 personal interviews with owners, managers, proprietors, or partners of business concerns in a representative sample of eighty-three cities wherein interviews with each type of dealer were allocated in proportion to the actual number of such dealers. These studies are of interest not only because they are among the few of their kind ever made, but because they also reveal many of the small businessman's feelings about certain economic matters which are of concern to him. With some 3,800,000 small business enterprises along the Main Streets of America, those who own and operate these firms are in a position to exert great influence through their participation in community affairs, by meeting and talking with millions of customers every day, as voters in State and national elections, and even as pressure groups attempting to shape legislation. In terms of sheer numbers, one of the reports makes clear, little businesses must be reckoned—at least potentially—among the strongest spokesmen for a "free economy." Yet small businessmen, like many big businessmen, have a fundamental conflict in their economic and political thinking. This conflict takes the form of "a tug of war of ideas, centering on short-term advantage *vs.* long-term values and principles. Much more than lip service is involved; the struggle has deep roots." Consequently there is serious concern in many quarters about one of the basic questions that prompted these particular surveys: how firm *are* the small businessman's "free market" convictions today? To gain even a partial answer to this question is to begin to get a perspective on his political thinking.

It is not surprising to learn that the small businessman says he believes in competition. In fact, he is quick to point out that business failure is "one of the risks of playing the game" and has to be accepted.[4]

"Suppose competition in one industry gets too tough and a lot of small companies start going out of business. Should that be accepted as part of the risk of doing business, or should the government do something to help them?"

	Small Manufacturers	Retailers, Wholesalers
THAT'S PART OF THE RISK	69%	62%
Government should help	20	29
No opinion	11	9

One small manufacturer put it this way: "Better to let a few go by the wayside than to let all of them starve with the government messing in them. Less taxes on all business would let more survive." Competition is good, the small businessman feels, because "it keeps you on your toes, holds prices down, and improves the product."

Many vigorous defenders of small business have frequently claimed that the role of the government in national affairs should be more positive in rendering increased aid and protec-

[4] All of the questions and responses used in this section, unless otherwise indicated, are from *Small Business Thinking and the Free Market* and *Dealers in Hot Competition.* For the convenience of the reader, specific page references to each of the poll questions in the reports have been omitted, inasmuch as the surveys themselves are not available for general use.

tion to different groups in society. "New Dealers" and "Fair Dealers" have often assumed that they have the support of the small businessman as well as the trade unions in their repeated efforts to obtain government help in counteracting the control and power of the large corporations. Yet the small business-man, except for specific self-serving purposes, "hates to have government in his hair" and is likely to be strenuously opposed to government regulation and control of almost any kind.

AGAINST . . .	Small Manufacturers	Retailers, Wholesalers
Close government regulation of business[5]	79%	78%
Top limit on salaries	92	83
Limit on profits	84	77
Price control	84	81
Government ownership (for basic industries)	88	85

When small businessmen are asked for their own ideas on the best thing the government can do for them, they are likely to think first of reducing taxes:

"The best thing the federal government could do for me . . ."

	All Dealers
Reduce taxes	41%
Enforce fair trade laws	13
Regulate big business	8
(top mentions)	

The strong demand for lower tax rates is common to most small businessmen and is the most immediate help they want from

[5] Small businessmen, like many other groups in society, are often pragmatic in their likes and dislikes. Thus it is not surprising to learn that dealers in 1957, while still strongly opposed to close regulation, softened somewhat in their opposition—from 78% in 1950 to 60% seven years la-ter. On this point they think much like business proprietors and managers nation-wide, 66% of whom are opposed to government regulation of business.

the government. More often than not they look to the government to stabilize prices, lower interest rates on loans, or reduce
government spending, all of which adds up to the idea of "less
government in business." As far as the small businessman is
concerned government regulation is not just something that
happens to the other fellow, but something he dislikes himself.
To him the lengthening arm of the government can very easily
reach back into his own shop.

The National Federation of Independent Business, whose
membership is almost exclusively small, independent enterprisers, has consistently argued that they are flatly opposed to
any further expansion of government controls. For example, in
its *Mandate* No. 215 (September 1955) the Federation polled
its members on a bill (S. 662) to extend federal minimum-
wage and maximum-hour control to larger retail, wholesale,
and service firms which operate four or more outlets. In another
Mandate they were asked for their opinion on a bill (H.R. 585)
to extend federal wage and hour controls to all retailers and
service establishments. On still another occasion the members
were polled on a bill (H.R. 83) that would require all businesses subject to federal regulations to pay their employees at
least $1.25 an hour instead of the $1 an hour minimum required then. The following is how they voted on each of these
proposals:

	For	Against	No Vote
S. 662. Extend wage-hour law to larger retail firms	42%	54%	4%
H.R. 585. Extend wage-hour law to retail-service concerns	28	67	5
H.R. 83. $1.25 minimum wage	30	66	4

The findings of these polls, as the vice president of the
NFIB explained to the Senate Committee on Labor and Public
Welfare, indicate that by and large the membership is opposed

to (1) wholesale inclusion of all businesses under federal wage-hour control; (2) expansion of this control to a limited number of larger independent firms; and (3) any further increase in the federal minimum wage, at least to the $1.25-an-hour level. These results are especially interesting, as Vice President Burger pointed out, when considered against the background of federation membership. There are all sizes and types of independent business and professional operations among the membership. Some of them, for one reason or another, are already subject to federal wage and hour control. Others are in the category of the larger independents thus far exempt from these controls. Many operate under contracts with labor unions. But the greatest proportion are the smaller-sized independents generally proposed for continued exemption from federal wage-hour controls. This might explain the two-thirds vote "against" the proposal for wholesale inclusion of all businesses under federal wage-hour controls. But, as Mr. Burger emphasized, it does not explain the majorities against the proposals for limited extension of the law and for the new $1.25 minimum hourly wage, except in the light of these important considerations: that among these smaller independents are many who fear that if their larger brethren go under control now, they may be next; that they fear this is part of a trend that will in time deprive them of necessary freedom of judgment in running their own businesses; and that it amounts to another step in the direction of complete government controls.

Mr. Burger made it clear that, from the point of view of the small businessman, these fears are thoroughly understandable. The history of recent years has been one of constantly expanding federal controls, controls which have become more extensive, to the point where the small businessman has no assurance they will stop spreading. Furthermore, Mr. Burger contended, most of those who opposed these bills are already paying at least the federal minimum-wage rate. As practical men they realize it costs money to live, to marry, and to raise families. They realize that employees burdened by financial difficulties are not at their efficient best. They also know that due to their size they have to live in intimate daily contact with their employees, whom they know "as human beings, not as mere statistics on a weekly payroll." If there are some who are paying so-called substandard wages, then they are doing so for reasons beyond their control. Mr. Burger insisted that when sales and profits were good in his own business, wages and bonuses were good. "But once the great automobile manufacturers stepped in and snapped up a goodly share of my customers, and once the depression struck, I had to cut, and cut all along the line. Given the opportunity I would have done better, and I think that given an opportunity they would be doing better." Putting it very succinctly, Mr. Burger expressed a feeling that is of paramount importance to the proprietor: denied the right to private judgment, he himself might have been driven to the wall; denied this right, today's small businessmen could be driven to the wall. What of the small minority of "chiselers" interested in getting the most for the very least? In stressing once more his opposition to further government controls, Mr. Burger expressed again the individualist ethic of the small businessman: "You know, our system of justice holds that it is better, in terms of legal safeguards, for 99 wrongdoers to escape punishment than it is for 1 innocent man to be convicted unjustly." [6]

In spite of his general opposition to "government in business" the small businessman is not averse to accepting government favors. "Fair trade" price fixing, for example, is not looked upon as government interference, but rather as a trade

---

[6] The comments of George J. Burger as well as the NFIB's polling results were inserted into the *Congressional Record*, July 1, 1959, by Senator William Langer.

practice which the manufacturer can choose to adopt if he wishes. In fact, many grocers, gas station operators, and other retail dealers believe that manufacturers should adopt minimum retail prices and enforce them.

"When products are fair traded, it's a big help to dealers," say . . .

Grocers, druggists	78%
Gas station operators	68
Appliance dealers	61
Building material dealers	48
Tire dealers	39
Auto dealers	37

This does not mean that dealers are unaware of the threatened collapse of fair trade, for more than one-third of them feel that fair trade is on the way out. But there is a strong tendency for the small businessman to rationalize the softening of competition in terms of "fair rules of the game," so as to permit both large and small units to compete on an equal basis. He looks upon the "fair trade" laws as a way of helping the "little man" and giving everybody the same opportunity as well as protection against the unscrupulous person working to sell a lot at a small margin.[7]

One of the most popular of government aids, of course, is loans to small business. Such proposals received the support of 54 per cent of the manufacturers and 59 per cent of the wholesaler-retailer group. Backing this demand is the feeling that small firms cannot obtain loans from banks or at least not at reasonable prices. Small businessmen are convinced that banks are reluctant to "take the risk" but that the government is in a

[7] 64% of those who have five employees or less feel that "fair trade" is a big help, as over against 39% of those who employ eleven persons or more.

position to do so and should back them up. "They lend it to big business, they should lend it to small ones," is the idea often expressed. Many small businessmen, however—and especially manufacturers—add the proviso that the loans should be on a "business basis" and "only so the owner can help himself and only if past performance justifies expansion." In other words, capital loans should be given to "those who can prove their fitness." Even though it becomes increasingly more difficult for the small businessman to prove his fitness in an age of large-scale industrial organization and competition, he continues to champion the cause of individual self-reliance and proclaim for himself the eternal verities of the Protestant ethic.

At the same time a large number of small businessmen feel that there is a real danger in accepting government assistance. Given a choice, dealers often show far greater preference for action undertaken by supplier companies, and they see the best chance of finding solutions to their problems by working directly with these companies. Among all dealers 43 per cent favored more active programs by large companies to assist their dealers, whereas only 17 per cent supported more direct federal financial aid for small business.[8] If dealers were to turn directly to political remedies for their grievances they might very well do so out of a sense of default on the part of the leadership they would prefer to follow. Despite any immediate economic benefits they might derive, many small businessmen are so strongly committed to the principles of free enterprise and competition in the marketplace that they are opposed to those who "want to get something for nothing" and to "the shortsighted, who don't see where all this leads." As a general proposition most small

[8] Another 68% favored either action by joint manufacturing and dealer councils or concerted action by dealer associations over any form of federal or State regulation of industry practices.

businessmen simply do not like government regulation and control and the interference with their business that it implies.[9]

The small businessman's commitment to the ideal of free competition, however, does not blind him to the fierce price competition that comprises his real world today and makes him seek some way out of his predicament. Unhappy dealers stress essentially three main points: (1) heavy price cutting, especially by the discount houses which have really hurt; (2) the small return on their initial investment; and (3) the increasing strength of monopolies. Only one dealer in five calls his line "one of the better ones" for a man going into business, and almost twice as many give it a low rating—"not so good."

"One of the better ones"		"Not so good"	Other answers
10%	Service stations	46%	44%
11	Appliance dealers	52	37
20	Tire dealers	39	41
25	Auto dealers	43	32
27	Grocers, druggists	28	45
35	Building material dealers	22	43
21	Six group total	38	41

Thus while dealers dislike being regulated, a growing number of them have been grudgingly persuaded that their salvation lies in various kinds of government action. Already a 53-per-cent majority of the surveyed dealers believe they would benefit if the giants of industry were broken up.[1] But it must be emphasized that attitudes of small businessmen toward the economic

[9] This finding has been revealed in both of the reports of the Opinion Research Corporation. For a different approach see Mills: op. cit., pp. 35–6. Mills contends that small businessmen really "do not believe in competition, and they have been doing their best to get away from it."

[1] In 1950 the figure was 33%. "Obviously," the report of 1957 points out, "it cannot be assumed that because dealers work hand in hand with industry, that they form a common ideological front in defense of the largest companies' rights to exist."

power of big business are largely dependent upon the line of work in which the individual is involved. The general public seems to feel that big business is squeezing out small business, and yet small businessmen do not speak with one mind on the matter. Small manufacturers tend to stress that small enterprisers have enjoyed an amazing growth since the end of the war, whereas many retail groups point to the number of small companies being pushed to the wall. The answers to the following question indicate in part the nature of the division in the ranks of small business on this point:

"Looking to the future, do you believe the smaller dealers in your kind of business will be squeezed out more and more by the larger outlets or will they be able to hold their own?"

	Will Be Squeezed	Hold Their Own	No Opinion
Appliance dealers	69%	28%	3%
Auto dealers	39	54	7
Gas station operators	66	30	4
Tire dealers	62	35	3
Grocers, druggists	65	33	2
Building material dealers	50	47	3
Total—Six dealer groups	59	37	4
Own the business	59	37	4
Manage, do not own	58	39	3
Years in business:			
5 years or less	53	41	6
6 to 15 years	58	40	2
Over 15 years	62	34	4
5 employees or less	63	34	3
6 to 10 employees	58	39	3
11 employees or more	48	47	5

The smaller firms unquestionably feel the competition from the large companies, as is clear from the responses below:

"Does your main competition come from large companies, or from other small firms?"

	Large	Small	Both	No Opinion
Appliance dealers	41%	29%	26%	4%
Auto dealers	35	38	21	6
Gas station operators	50	30	19	1
Tire dealers	61	19	20	0
Grocers, druggists	59	27	10	4
Building material dealers	48	32	17	3
Total—Six dealer groups	49	29	19	3
5 employees or less	52	29	16	3
6 to 10 employees	47	29	22	2
11 employees or more	45	31	21	3

Food and drug retailers understandably fear big company competition above everything else, and they mean the chains. Independent filling station operators feel the competition from large oil companies but also from other operators their own size. Other dealer groups, however, often blame the manufacturer who supplies them for instituting merchandising policies that foment their troubles. While all dealers generally fear the competition from the big outlets and see it increasingly driving small dealerships out of business, there is still a noticeable spirit of "live and let live" which, while it should not be exaggerated, reflects a hopeful belief that there is enough business to go around. Only among gasoline and appliance outlets is the feeling strong that their fields are overcrowded.

"There's enough business to go around in my line . . ."
Say
43% of appliance dealers
66 of auto dealers
32 of gas station operators
68 of tire dealers
62 of grocers, druggists
74 of building material dealers

Although dealers are not too happy with their present lot and generally feel they have worked very hard for very little gain, a surprising number of them voice optimism for the years ahead:

"What is the outlook for the year ahead—do you think your business will get better or not be as good?"

	Get Better	Stay the Same	Not Be as Good	No Opinion
Appliance dealers	51%	22%	27%	0
Auto dealers	47	30	20	3%
Gas station operators	50	23	22	5
Tire dealers	58	26	8	8
Grocers, druggists	46	25	24	5
Building material dealers	50	28	17	5
Total—Six dealer groups	51	25	19	5

In spite of the tendency in the last few generations toward economic and governmental centralization—resented more by the small businessman than perhaps by any other economic element in the country—the opportunity to go into business for oneself still stands as a symbol for the hired man. Many of those concerned with the future of small business would like to see the best minds of the present and future enter into self-employment and business ownership and thus "give full play to the capacities of people with courage, versatility and imagination."

In the infant stages of America's growth the small merchants typified the spirit of opportunity and enterprise in the new settlers. Today, notwithstanding the rapid changes in the economy that have diminished their importance, small businessmen still cling to this "spirit of young America" to protect their interests and to perpetuate the ideals of individualism. It is not particularly surprising that a new country would depend upon the entrepreneurs and small merchants for its major economic development. What is much more startling is that almost 200 years later the feeling is still widely shared that this form of economic enterprise is so necessary and beneficial that it must be preserved as a central ingredient of a nation's character. Some would have us believe that this "spirit of young America" must be preserved simply for the protection of economic endeavor; others claim that more than anything else it fosters the good life and if lost would jeopardize the country. In either case the small businessman is consistently looked upon as a standard bearer of the real American way of life.[2]

In this connection a revealing disclosure of small business feeling is contained in another report of the Opinion Research Corporation. The principal question investigated in this study was how far the government should go "in organizing our lives," with a view to pointing out which groups in society tend to be more "socialistic" in their attitudes and which groups are positioned toward the "free market" end of the attitude spectrum. Those who fall into the first category indicated a desire for the government to take a more active role in the American economy and voiced some criticisms about our business system generally, whereas those who hold "free market" ideas are generally opposed to government action or interference and speak highly of the advantages of our present economic system. A total of 3,095 general public interviews was taken, composing the national sample and distributed representatively by section of the country, occupation, size of the town, and rural and urban population.[3] The report found, not

[2] For a fuller discussion of this theme see Louis M. Hacker: *American Capitalism: Its Promise and Accomplishment* (Princeton, N.J.: Van Nostrand; 1957).

[3] The report referred to here is *Socialistic Thinking in America—1953*. Twenty-six questions made up the "Free Market" test. In scoring an individual's responses, one point was credited for each answer on the "free market" side, one point deducted for each "socialistic" answer, and zero given for each "no opinion." Thus possible scores ranged from 26 plus to 26 minus, a total of 53 possible scores. These scores were then converted to a 100 base, with 26 plus equal to 100% and 26 minus to 0%.

surprisingly, that the broad trend in the country is "anti-socialistic" and that public opinion has moved very definitely toward favoring the "free market" position.[4] The public today thinks much more highly of the American business system as a whole than it did twenty-five years ago, a finding that has also been confirmed by a study of the Survey Research Center.[5] At the same time, over the past twenty or thirty years the people have grown accustomed to "turning to government," and this

		Strongly Socialistic *	Strongly Free Market *
Should the government:			
Provide low-rent housing?	Yes, say	91%	39%
Control big business more strongly?	Yes, say	68	18
Place stiffer taxes on big incomes?	Yes, say	66	13
Provide government health insurance?	Yes, say	61	5

* Respondents were classified according to their answers to twenty-six separate questions covering various phases of "socialistic" vs. "free market" thought.

habit, the report showed, has become deeply ingrained to the point where a large majority of the people approve of government services like federal aid to State and local education, added tax advantages for small business, increases in Social Security coverage and benefits, and such things as more gov-

---

[4] For example, five indicators of this trend were (1) 62% *against* close government regulation of business in 1953, as compared with 54% in 1948; (2) 74% *against* government ownership of industry (63% in 1948); (3) 78% *against* top limit on salaries (67% in 1948); (4) 65% *against* limit on profits (53% in 1948); and (5) 53% favor less rather than more government lending (43% in 1948).

[5] See *Big Business from the Viewpoint of the Public* (Ann Arbor, Mich.; Public Affairs Group Survey Research Center, Institute for Social Research, University of Michigan; 1951).

ernment housing. The study points out that "socialistic" thinking on broad issues is translated into grass-roots support for welfare-state action by Congress, and that those who are "strongly socialistic" in their general thinking vote heavily for more government action on many of the leading issues of the day.

It is not necessary here to present a complete breakdown of the findings. What is of interest is the location of the small businessman on this particular scale. The chart below indicates the ideological cleavage that exists between small businessmen and other groups in the country.

SCALE OF SOCIALISTIC *vs.* FREE MARKET BELIEF *

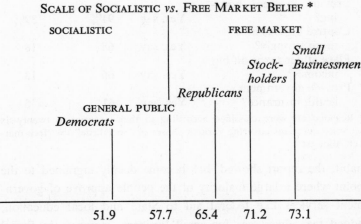

SOCIALISTIC   FREE MARKET

Small Businessmen

Stock-holders

Republicans

GENERAL PUBLIC

Democrats

51.9   57.7   65.4   71.2   73.1

* This chart, reproduced here in abbreviated form, shows how different groups in the population scored on a 26-question test. A person who gave "free-market" answers on all 26 questions scored 100%, while a person who gave all "socialistic" answers scored 0%. The vertical line represents the General Public—57.7. Among those well to the right, in addition to small businessmen, were business executives, upper-income people, clergymen, high-school teachers, and college graduates. Those farthest to the left included Negroes, foreign-born, the less educated, and low-income people.

The following are a sample of the specific questions asked in the survey, along with some comparative figures on the responses of small businessmen:

"One of the faults of the business system in this country is that the owners get too much of the money companies make compared to what employees get. Do you agree or disagree?"

	Agree	Disagree	No opinion
General public	46%	45%	9%
Small businessmen	22	68	10

"In the future, the government should pay more attention to encouraging opportunity rather than aiming at maximum security. Agree or disagree?"

	Agree	Disagree	No opinion
General public	65%	21%	14%
Small businessmen	72	18	10

"How about medical care—do you think that the federal government should provide government health insurance for everyone, or shouldn't they?"

	Agree	Disagree	No opinion
General public	30%	64%	6%
Small businessmen	20	78	2

"The federal government now owns a number of electric power plants, synthetic rubber plants, and barge and shipping lines. It's been said that the government should try to sell these to private companies. Should they do that, or shouldn't they?"

	Yes, Should	No, Shouldn't	No opinion
General public	53%	29%	18%
Small businessmen	67	23	10

"Do you think it is the responsibility of the federal government to see that everyone who is willing and able to work has a job?"

	Yes	No	Don't Know
General public	44%	50%	6%
Small businessmen	32	61	7

"How about making electricity with atomic power—should that be kept for the federal government to do or should private electric companies be allowed to do more and more of that?"

	Kept for Federal Government	Private Companies Allowed	No opinion
General public	45%	39%	16%
Small businessmen	33	51	16

If anything can be safely established about the small businessman it is that he belongs to one of the most heterogeneous groups in the country. When it is recalled that the Department of Commerce has classified approximately 92 per cent of all business establishments in the United States as "small" it can be readily understood why the term "small business" is often more of a rallying cry and slogan than anything else. For purposes of political analysis, the small businessman is difficult to evaluate and in some respects virtually impossible to pigeonhole. Perhaps the dominant characteristic of his political outlook is the same as that which pervades so much of the rest of his life—a pugnacious but proud individualism. Much more so than the big businessman, he tends to look out on a world which for him does not stretch very far, encompassing as it does essentially his own immediate personal interests and rarely touching the larger political and social considerations of the public as a whole. It is true that it has not been uncommon in our history for all businessmen, regardless of size, to put their private interests ahead of the public welfare. Today, however, there is evidence that a number of the larger firms are aware not only of their impact on the whole economic system, but of their own particular responsibility in helping to formulate some of its goals. The small businessman seldom demonstrates any such concern or vision, and when he does it is because he feels a given policy or program of the government is likely to have some direct effect on his own private enterprise. In an important sense he is like the great number of Americans who never go to college: both groups tend to take the short view of life and gear their expectations to the present, to what will happen to them today and tomorrow, since they feel anything beyond that is largely out of their hands and cannot be counted upon. But many big business leaders today, like the graduating senior from college, are more optimistic and willingly look to the future because they have some reason to feel confident of their own part in its unfolding as well as in its ultimate outcome. For this reason alone, the small businessman is more opportunistic in his needs and wants and responds quickly, either favorably or unfavorably, to what his representative is doing for him in Washington or, more likely, to what he feels the government itself is proposing to do *to* him.

The evidence is plain that the economic interests of small businessmen, far from being uniform, are generally in conflict. Some of them want the government to take a far more active role; others are firmly convinced the government is already too involved in their affairs. Those who clamor for financial assistance are opposed by those who feel overburdened by the weight of excessive taxes. The tie that so often binds them is the opposition they share to the large-scale operation, to the large company that so neatly and effectively has maneuvered them out of competitive equality into threatened bankruptcy. If the government is in a position to help them regain a healthy share of the market and thereby increase their profits, then plainly it should do just that.

In its election studies of 1952 and 1956 the Survey Research Center at Ann Arbor, Michigan, collected a small mountain of data from which it is possible not only to supplement some of the material already presented here but to make additional comparisons among occupational groupings within certain income ranges.[6] The most striking and obvious finding about small businessmen is that the lower their income, the more they favor a positive role for the federal government in the general area of social welfare. Small businessmen who earn less than $5,000 a year register strong support of the government's doing such things as seeing to it that everybody who wants to work can find a job or assisting people in getting medical and hospital care at low cost. More than one-half of those in this same income group feel that Negroes who are not getting fair treatment in jobs and housing should be given some kind of help by the government, whereas only 27 per cent of small businessmen making $7,500–$10,000 take this same position, in contrast to 37 per cent of big businessmen making over $10,000 a year. The importance of income in the determination of the small businessman's attitudes on a variety of domestic issues is perfectly apparent: the less he earns and the lower his socio-economic status, the more likely he is to support proposals leading to increased government activity in social welfare areas. The fact that many small businessmen earn less than $5,000 annually, have been raised in working-class families (or have parents who themselves were skilled or unskilled workers), and belong to minority ethnic or religious groups explains to a large degree not only why they might have some feeling for the lot of the Negro in America, but why they

[6] I am indebted to Warren Miller for his help in providing some of the pertinent interview data used here. Although again the information on small business attitudes is far from definitive—for example, some of the resulting occupation-income cells are too small to allow completely reliable estimates—it nonetheless adds that much more to our incomplete knowledge of the small businessman's thinking.

favor the extension of many government services and thus vote the Democratic ticket.

Yet the small businessman whose income is around $4,000 a year does not automatically welcome a heightened degree of government leadership in all areas.[7] For example, the attitudes of low-income small businessmen toward the government's cutting taxes is set apart and different from their generally affirmative feelings about governmental social welfare activity. While they strongly favor federal programs of aid to education, increased medical care, and employment guarantees, many of them approve of the government's cutting taxes, even if it means putting off some important things that need to be done. The higher their income, however, the more strongly they feel the government should *not* postpone taking whatever positive measures are needed. Thus 57 per cent of the small businessmen interviewed who fell in the $7,500–$10,000 income group disagreed strongly with the idea that the government should cut taxes in preference to taking care of some of the things which deserve federal attention, whereas only 37 per cent of the small businessmen in the $2,000–$5,000 group shared this view.

The data from the Survey Research Center show that, even among persons of equal education or with similar occupations, it is the high-income people who are relatively *more* willing to pay taxes than have the government fail to do what needs to be done. While this may seem to conflict with our more traditional assumption that those with the highest income have the

[7] This finding applies not only to small businessmen, but to other low-income occupation groups, e.g., skilled and unskilled workers, white-collar workers, etc. For a comprehensive analysis of attitude structures on a number of major issues relating to public policy, see Angus Campbell, Philip E. Converse, Warren Miller, and Donald E. Stokes: *The American Voter* (New York: John Wiley & Sons; 1960), pp. 168–87.

strongest interest in tax reductions, it is not hard to imagine that "willingness to pay taxes is dependent upon ability to pay, and that the present tax structure does not result in a perfectly progressive incidence of tax burden." [8] Therefore it is not difficult to understand why low-income small businessmen—or factory workers, for that matter—would favor cutting taxes, in contrast to those making $7,000, who have an additional amount of money to spend each year on some of the things they either need or want. The contradiction of the low-income small businessman's supporting the extension of government services while favoring postponement of important government activity so as to reduce taxes is actually more apparent than real, since the two responses may spring from the same motivation—"a simple desire for improvement of one's economic lot." [9] It is further confirmation that the small businessman tends to be parochial in his outlook because his immediate considerations are not apt to go much beyond his individual personal situation. For the lower-status small businessman, self-interest is the lowest common denominator and will virtually dictate a great many of his political feelings and responses. If he is out of work or afraid of losing his business he will turn to the government without hesitation, in the full expectation that it will take the necessary steps to guarantee his continued employment.

Where the small businessman's own self-interest is not directly affected, however, he is more likely to react in a way that reflects some of the political values he holds as an entrepreneur who believes in free enterprise and still has dreams of moving up the economic and social ladder, even though his

[8] Ibid., p. 196.

[9] Ibid. "As long as the structure of political attitudes is loose and specific evaluations have little cognitive contact, potential contradictions will not be confronted."

present status in the system is low. On questions which involve something more than his own short-run wishes he will often appear to be out of step in supporting a particular position or point of view that seemingly runs counter to his own interests. Only half of the small businessmen interviewed whose annual income is under $5,000 feel strongly that the government should see to it that big business corporations do not have much say about how the government is run. Similarly, the same number feel the government should leave things like electric power and housing for private businessmen to handle. It might be expected that all small businessmen in this low-income group would feel deeply—but in the opposite way—about these issues, since the position of big business in our economy clearly is a dominant one. Yet unlike the question of unemployment, where he can quickly see the personal threat it holds, the small businessman does not always perceive the role of big business as something that is immediately or directly related to his own self-interest. If he does not view the power of big business in our society as a particularly serious problem, it is because he has no real understanding of the complex relationship of economic power to politics which, at bottom, provides many of the advantages for big business. The low-income small businessman has had relatively little education, in many cases having only gone through grade school, and is therefore more confused than informed about many of the intricate and "distant" matters of governmental policy. In a word, his level of sophistication is low. He tends to view a political issue in simplistic terms and fails to differentiate significantly in the use of relevant political concepts. Thus he is often unable to see the breadth or appropriateness of meaning attributed to these concepts by others. When he votes for a political party—which, in the low-income groups, more often than not is the Democrats—he is essentially voting a single-group interest—his own—which is to say that he likes the Democrats because, as he sees them, they represent the "little man" or the "poor people" to whom they are willing to give help. Beyond that, there is no real conceptualization of the issues which distinguish between liberals and conservatives, and not even any explicit indication that he feels the Republican Party is opposed to him.

The small businessman who earns $5,000–$10,000 a year is not only better educated but more capable of perceiving such things as the relationship between means and ends in the political process. His support of a political party is not prompted just by the feeling that it favors the "common man," since he has some perception of the other party, its position, and its candidates. Significantly, the Survey Research Center found a higher proportion of small businessmen in this income range calling themselves strong Republicans rather than Democrats. Some 40 per cent of the small businessmen in the $7,500–$10,000 income bracket disagreed with the proposition that the government should guarantee employment, so that everybody who wants to work can find a job. In contrast, only 19 per cent of the big businessmen earning over $10,000 a year expressed the same view. In the same income group 40 per cent of the white-collar workers and 46 per cent of the skilled workers agreed strongly that the federal government should take measures insuring fair treatment in jobs and housing for Negroes; among small businessmen, however, only 27 per cent believed the government should definitely assume some responsibility in this area, whereas 37 per cent of the big businessmen felt it should. On the question of government aid to education, where only 7 per cent of the big businessmen disagreed that the federal government should provide money to help cities and towns around the country build more schools, 23 per cent of the small businessmen opposed any government assistance. Inasmuch as more than two-thirds of the small businessmen interviewed earned over $5,000 annually, these data lend some support to our earlier contention that many of the purported political attitudes of small businessmen are based to a large degree on a persisting and reassuring image, one that has long been cherished but is nonetheless grossly incomplete.

3

One of the strongest convictions held by the American small businessman is that free enterprise is a system that gives anyone at the bottom of the ladder a chance to rise to the top. He grew up under the impression that free enterprise meant "a man could buy a small supply of shoe laces, sell them house-to-house at a profit; buy more shoe laces, and in time become the owner of a shoe factory and live in a big white house on the hill." [1] Today his biggest worry is that this system of individual enterprise, of which he considers himself the hub, is well on its way toward being destroyed. He sees large numbers of people becoming less dependent upon themselves and more dependent upon huge corporations, big trade unions, and, above everything else, a powerful federal government. America, in his estimation, has sacrificed its birthright of freedom and has become a nation of dependents. The most urgent necessity, therefore, is to return to a system of widespread, independent ownership of business enterprise in order to restore freedom of opportunity to the country. The only alternative, in his opinion, is a continuous drift toward socialism and communism. A large number of his political views can be reduced for the most part to the central belief that the freest economy and the most democratic society is one which promotes a maximum of in-

[1] Edward Wimmer: "Freedom Depends on Business Independence," a talk delivered before the National Conference of Independent Shoe Retailers, in Chicago, on October 24, 1953. Mr. Wimmer is vice president of the National Federation of Independent Business, Inc.

dividual enterprise and a minimum of centralized power. It is because the small businessman holds strongly to these principles of free enterprise that his attitudes toward labor unions are essentially hostile and bitter.

The small businessman evaluates labor unions in much the same way that he judges his own economic problems, namely, in terms of whether or not the trade union is enhancing the workingman's own position in society as a free and enterprising individual.[2] The measure of small business support given to organized labor is largely dependent upon the amount of personal freedom the worker retains for himself. In his determination to uphold the unrestricted liberty of an individual to act in his own interest, even if it should entail sacrifice of the potential strength that lies in numerical unity, he has found it all but impossible to lend his support to the day-to-day struggles of organized labor. Nor do "milk and honey" testimonials to the "time-honored tradition" of American labor in any way mirror the feelings of the small businessman toward what has been happening in the past twenty-five years. As far as he is concerned, the very meaning of a strong, organized labor force is such as to

[2] In 1947 the Conference of American Small Business Organizations spelled out in some detail its position on labor. It began by freely admitting that "organized labor" is a "time-honored, traditional American institution," as much a part of "free, independent, competitive enterprise as enterprise itself. This combination of free labor and free enterprise, cooperating toward a common goal, has made this the most productive, progressive and prosperous nation, and has provided the highest standard of living enjoyed by any people on this earth. This combination must not be destroyed." *Report of Proceedings, Conference of American Small Business Organizations,* Eighth National Session (Washington, D.C.: February 18, 19, 20, 1947), p. 9. This approval and praise of "organized labor" calls to mind the many other kinds of present-day support given not only to organizations which have since become an accepted part of the national scene, but to social legislation which has largely been incorporated into the law of the land. It leaves unanswered the question of whether the small businessman, during the time labor was trying to *become* organized, actively supported its efforts, or, as is more likely, stood opposed to them.

threaten directly his own position as an independent businessman. CASBO continuously circulated to all of its members dramatic accounts describing the labor difficulties besetting the operators of one-man shops. These detailed reports of "labor coercion" are not lost on the small businessman, and the moral is always pointed up in bold black letters: *This can happen to you too!*

To the small businessman the issue is simple and clear-cut: why should "labor bosses" compel the proprietors themselves to become union members? To dragoon these owners into union membership is to make them subject to the mandates of union bosses and racketeers, thus imperiling free enterprise and endangering "the very existence of the great productive middle-class on which the preservation of our political and social institutions depends." Among the 3,000,000 or more small business concerns in the country, there are an estimated 1,800,000 owner-operators, some of whom have few employees and some of whom have none. The Conference repeatedly pointed out to its members that many of the largest concerns in the country began in just this way and were able to prosper and expand under the protection of "impartial laws." In the opinion of the *Los Angeles Examiner:* "The Conference of American Small Business Organizations is unquestionably right in blaming the Wagner Act for the oppression of little business and in demanding that Congress legislate a 'fair and equitable code of labor relations.' " [3]

CASBO's program for American labor was stated in much the same way in practically all of its annual convention reports. The touchstone of its position was that labor unions today have a "monopolistic stranglehold on the economy of the country" and, not content with "coercing employees to join their unions," are making a determined effort "to force the owner-

[3] Editorial in the *Los Angeles Examiner,* November 12, 1946.

operators of retail, personal service and other small establishments throughout the country to become members by intimidation, extortion, blacklisting and violence." The Conference also felt it is "general knowledge" that many labor unions have become "infiltrated by subversive agents" and that these agents have become the motivating power behind many strikes as well as the destruction of property. Consequently it believed that "labor unionism would be well served by being reconverted into independent autonomous units," supporting its argument with the following reasons:

(1) This would automatically give the local unions back to the workers' control.

(2) Workers would be enabled to elect their own local officers who would be responsive to local conditions.

(3) Workers would be enabled to purge their unions of racketeers, Communists, and other subversive elements, if any.

(4) Workers would still have the right to strike or bargain collectively on the local level.

(5) Workers would not become involved in jurisdictional strikes, sympathy strikes, or secondary boycotts.

(6) Workers' dues would not be used by unscrupulous mis-leaders against their political convictions.[4]

Any operation "short of removal of the infection which breeds labor monopoly and labor despots" would be merely a temporary palliative. The Conference firmly believed that in the best interests of labor, no less than in the welfare of the nation as a whole, new labor legislation is necessary to provide for local, independent union control for negotiating and voting at the plant level only, and without any interference or coercion from national or international affiliations.

The rest of CASBO's labor program followed consistently from its basic assumption that the combination of free labor

---

[4] *Report of Proceedings,* CASBO, Eighth National Session, p. 13.

and free enterprise has been destroyed by developments in the labor movement since 1932.

(1) Labor unions must be made subject to anti-trust laws.

(2) Unions must incorporate and become subject to state and/or federal regulations governing non-profit corporations.

(3) Foremen and supervisors must be prohibited from joining labor unions, or having joined, at the discretion of the employer be subject to reduction in rank to the status of an ordinary employee.

(4) Mass picketing must be outlawed.

(5) No employer should be required to employ workers who he does not consider necessary to his business.

(6) The matter of health, welfare, retirement, casualty and similar funds shall not be required subject-matter for collective bargaining.

(7) Industry-wide, nation-wide, and other strikes detrimental to public health, safety and welfare must be outlawed by statute.

(8) Jurisdictional and sympathy strikes and secondary boycotts should be outlawed by statutory act.

(9) Union membership should not be made a condition of employment, and the closed shop, union shop, check-off and maintenance of union membership should be outlawed by statute.

(10) Both union and company officials should be required to swear they are not members of, nor subscribe to, nor support directly or indirectly, any party or organization which plans or subscribes to any plan envisioning the overthrow of the Government of the United States.[5]

This "fair and equitable code of labor relations" makes a lot of sense to the small businessman. The issue, as he sees it, is not whether coal miners shall have higher wages or better working conditions or whether the railroad brotherhoods shall

[5] *Report of Proceedings,* CASBO, Fourteenth National Session (Washington, D.C.: March 23, 24, 25, 1953), pp. 18–19. See also *Report of Proceedings,* Eighth National Session, pp. 9–13.

have new work rules. The real issue "is whether they shall be condemned forever to live in fear of their Lewises, Whitneys, Petrillos and Reuthers." The small businessman believes that "if present laws and politics are not changed now, these men will be with us always—doling out to the American people what is already rightfully theirs, and getting abject gratitude in return. These are the methods of a Hitler and a Mussolini." [6]

In a "Declaration of Opposition" against "labor union coercion"—one of several full-page advertisements that appeared in many metropolitan newspapers under the headline "WAKE UP AMERICA!"—the Conference used strong words to make its position clear:

> Big Labor is Running Wild. It is drunk with power. It makes its own laws and compels obedience by force, frequently bordering on anarchy. It holds itself to be above the laws of the land and is aided and abetted by cheap, subservient politics. It assumes to hold in its hands the question of life or death over any small business which refuses to pay tribute in order to operate as a free American institution. THINK OF IT! Supposedly free American citizens, peacefully conducting their business, at the mercy of racketeers who presume to dictate who may or may not do business! . . . DO YOU KNOW WHAT THIS MEANS? Unless Big Labor is stopped NOW by force of public opinion and revulsion, and by united action of its intended victims, free independent business enterprise is DOOMED TO EXTINCTION! How? Big Labor is threatening America with labor dictatorship . . . the result will be the autocratic State— or COMMUNISM. The *Wagner Labor Relations Act* is the

[6] Editorial in the *Chicago Journal of Commerce,* May 16, 1946, which CASBO circulated to all of its members. One year later CASBO distributed a "Special Bulletin" to its membership "To Prevent the Recurrence of Another Public-Be-Damned Industry-Wide Strike." It asked three questions: "Who *Is* Running This Country Any Way? Is it the elected representatives of 160 millions of American citizens? Or is it the handful of power-drunk, self-perpetuating hierarchy of labor, constituting a Ruthless *Public-Be-Damned* Monopolistic Trust? Let's have a showdown on this question."

legislation under which coercion and rackets are whitewashed as legal. . . . IF YOU BELIEVE . . . That public rights come before the claimed rights of any labor union . . . in the inalienable right of every citizen to work where and for whom he wishes to work, without compulsion to pay tribute —If you believe in these fundamentals, then give your help AT ONCE. Free Enterprise is at the Crossroads! [7]

It is no accident that the Conference used such intemperate language. It knew very well that the strength of its appeal to small businessmen rested not on restrained analyses of labor relations but on a hard-hitting, "no pussy-footing" attack on "fundamentals."

Only once before in all our history—in 1776—have the American people been called upon to fight for their freedoms against Un-American radicals. We must revive the Fundamental Americanism of George Washington, Thomas Jefferson, Benjamin Franklin, Henry Clay, Patrick Henry, Abraham Lincoln and a host of other patriots of their day, who gave us "One Nation, Indivisible" and were not ashamed to fight for it. Are we? [8]

The time has come, CASBO pointed out, when every citizen and particularly every small businessman must take his stand. "He must decide whether he will play into the hands of the Communist-Radical-Labor-New Deal alliance to socialize America, or whether he wants to keep America American. The issue is now clear cut." It is no longer tenable for any American to claim nonpartisanship in politics. "States Rights Democrats, Republicans and loyal non-partisans generally will take one side. The new dealers, the radical labor element, fellow travelers and Communists will take the other side." To the small businessman the question is put simply: "Which side will you take?"

[7] Undated circular, "Wake Up Americans! Labor is Playing Right into the Hands of Communism," distributed by the Conference of American Small Business Organizations.
[8] Ibid.

It would be a mistake to assume that the labor program outlined here reflects only the opinion of CASBO. The National Federation of Independent Business, with a membership of over 100,000, has proposed virtually the same program with regard to labor as a result of the votes of its members cast in a number of secret ballots. For example, 93 per cent supported a bill to control union picketing, so that they would not

> open the door some morning and find a union picket line around your business . . . no warning, no effort to discuss things with your employees . . . no desire for union representation on their part. That's the thing that this bill aims to stop, and there are countless small businessmen today who would have been helped by such a law, and countless of thousands of others who will be helped by it.

On another ballot 85 per cent were in favor of a law prohibiting both the closed and union shop, supporting the argument that

> it's positively un-American and dangerous to our liberties to give labor and management the right to sign away a worker's freedom to get and hold a job without paying tribute to some union. This puts his livelihood right in the hands of someone other than himself. Let him step on the toes of some union "goon boy" and his choice is nothing but to go on relief.

They agreed with the contention that "these union and closed shop agreements promote the sort of racketeering and evil-doing that Congressional Committees have been uncovering, the stench of which has sickened the stomachs of our hardiest citizens." In addition to opposing the union and closed shop the Federation is against jurisdictional strikes, secondary boycotts, labor union "monopoly practices," and industry-wide "follow the leader techniques in wage negotiations." It favors subjecting labor unions to antitrust laws, and approves of injunctions to curb national emergency strikes, legislation working for the elimination of "Communist influence" in the labor movement, and curbing the power of the Secretary of Labor to raise minimum wages through the Walsh-Healy Act.[9]

In striking contrast to the approach of the small business-man is the more moderate tone of big business. It might be argued that big business is equally hostile to labor unions; certainly specific planks in the labor program of the National Association of Manufacturers are not significantly different from CASBO's. Yet such an interpretation overlooks a number of important considerations. The transformation of our economic system during the past several generations has laid to rest both the hopes of Adam Smith and the predictions of Karl Marx. Free enterprise is no longer as free or as enterprising for the little fellow as it once was, and the severe socio-economic divisions which were supposed to emerge to uproot our economic order have simply not emerged. Instead, big business and big labor today are in many crucial respects partners in an industrial system whose successful management is of common concern and a joint enterprise. This alliance is by no means permanent and in many areas is very shaky, but nonetheless, as Bernard Nossiter has said, the tacit collaboration between management and union officers has been thriving all through the period of postwar prosperity, is still spreading, and seems to be closely correlated with rising prices, persistent unemployment, and slow economic growth. "Stability" is what characterizes the new pattern.

> To the big corporation's managers, stability means ever-rising prices and profits, freedom from new competitive threats, and profitable stock options in an ever-rising stock market. To the big union's officers, stability means an ever-rising level of wages and fringe benefits for the members— with suitable rewards for the leader whose wisdom has

[9] See the "Outline of Testimony Presented before the Resolutions Committees of the Republican and Democratic Conventions," *National Federation of Independent Business, Inc.* (July 1952).

brought this about. Neither union members nor corporate stockholders complain much.[1]

To be seated on the opposite side of the bargaining table, insisting that the demands of labor are unjustified and unwarranted, is a far cry from opposing labor unions by constantly indicting their "Americanism" and the moral integrity of their leaders. When the opposition of big business to labor is voiced today it is largely motivated by economic self-interest; the small businessman, on the other hand, combines a fear of being liquidated by the intrusion of "big labor"—he has much the same fear of big business and big government—with an impassioned plea for a return to George Washington, Adam Smith, and God. His concern is more than economic; it is the concern of a man who is afraid that his entire way of life as an independent entrepreneur is being undermined. His condemnation of labor unions is an ideological reflection of his deep-rooted commitments to the values of pre-industrialism as well as to the immediate fear that his own shop or store may go union.

The different approaches of big business and small business to the problem of labor can be seen in an examination of their respective reactions to the widely discussed General Motors five-year agreement with the United Auto Workers. From the point of view of the small businessman the agreement was too generous to the unions and was regarded as another step in gradually forcing him to meet the same labor demands. In defending the fundamental principle of proprietorship, he looks upon such an agreement in the same way that he views industry-wide agreements in general: they constitute a pattern of relations that paves the way to big business paternalism and sacrifices in turn the rights of proprietors to be their own bosses

[1] Bernard D. Nossiter: "The Hidden Affair between Big Business and Big Labor," *Harper's Magazine* (July 1959).

on their own terms. Thus, the NFIB found that when it polled its membership on the question of the guaranteed annual wage 94 per cent were opposed to it. Not only did they feel it could lead to a drive by both big business and big unions for higher unemployment taxes, which small enterprises might also be forced to finance, but they feared it would be another step toward encouraging big business and labor leaders to consolidate their interests and move together at the expense of the little man.

Charles E. Wilson, at the time of the agreement president of General Motors and largely responsible for the new contract, expressed an entirely different attitude. From his point of view any good business transaction should work to the advantage and profit of the company, the employees, and the public. According to Henry T. Ewald, president of the Campbell-Ewald advertising agency:

> Back of the whole agreement is Wilson's desire for the good will of General Motors employees. He wants them to be contented, to be secure, to like to work for General Motors. He thinks that they, too, should share in the technological developments that go to make for better and more efficient production.[2]

Wilson acknowledged that he had been asked about the effect the contract would have upon small businesses. His answer, though perhaps not entirely satisfactory to small businessmen, revealed a philosophy suited to the needs of big business today.

> We are sure they have just as great an opportunity to improve their operations and take advantage of modern knowledge and techniques as we have. . . . We had good reasons for doing what we did. We thought we had a real opportunity to make progress in working out an American solution for labor-industry relations and to establish some

[2] Henry T. Ewald: "GM Finds Fairness," *San Francisco Chronicle,* August 27, 1950.

principles in collective bargaining which minimized pressure bargaining and rejected the false philosophy of class conflict.

We found the union leaders receptive to this thinking, and we have high hopes that between the unions and ourselves we have made real progress in this direction and that the agreement will be sound and constructive for all parties concerned.

I am sure that the men and women of the General Motors plants understand and that they are pleased with the results.[3]

Although big business and small business are in virtual agreement on such issues as the closed shop, secondary boycotts, the ill effects of the Wagner Act, and the desirability of a law such as Taft-Hartley, their respective objectives as businessmen are by no means identical. The similarity of their verbal hostility to certain labor practices is in no real sense indicative of their ultimate goals. The stake of big business in labor-management relations is significantly different from that of the small businessman, and to compare them only on the basis of formal policy declarations is to overlook this point. The small businessman's ideological allegiance to free enterprise and the entire pattern of living to which it is most easily accommodated impels him to regard not only labor unions themselves but the whole network of industry-labor arrangements today as a threat to his own private world. The violence of his denunciations merely reaffirms the depth of his fears. He is convinced that the "Communist-Big Labor alliance" represents one of the most critical and far-reaching tests for survival in the nation's history. That test is whether this nation "will continue as a Constitutional Republic, or whether we will substitute for it a Communist-Labor Government." It is high time, he feels, that "some one dared to call upon the American people to make war on this anti-American alliance." Steadily

[3] Ibid.

and consistently, the small businessman points out, the "Labor Hierarchy" is also propagandizing and promoting passage of "Communist-inspired bills" to bring about "economic regimentation" whereby the individual's liberty to run his own life is sacrificed for a pampering security. CASBO continuously opposed all legislative proposals which it felt would greatly diminish the area of individual discretion and choice. Among other things it applauded the termination of price and rent controls, called for an end to all Federal Housing activities, opposed "extension of Social Security laws to cover persons and occupations not now covered," as well as "any increase in present rates of taxation under this law." [4] In the opinion of the Conference, all of the "sugar-coated, sweet-sounding social legislation" fits into a "perfect pattern of a Communist system of 'Social Welfare' and a planned economy under which free, competitive enterprise cannot, and is not intended to, survive."

The opposition of big business to the welfare state is well known, but this opposition does not imply a flat disregard by a benevolent capitalism for the "welfare" of the American people. Moreover, the enlightened big business leader, while favoring a "sound" labor policy to further "good industrial relations," is well aware that "even *good* labor legislation does not automatically bring good employee relations." He believes that the problems of industrial relations cannot be solved in Washington, but is nonetheless convinced that big business has an obligation to take into full account the welfare of all of its employees.

> Industry has been making great progress in recent years in creating a working relationship and plant atmosphere which recognizes the dignity and importance of the individual employee, which builds a sense of teamwork in the

[4] *Report of Proceedings,* CASBO, Fourteenth National Session, p. 13.

plant. Advancement with employees, in research and understanding of human relations problems, have all been given concentrated attention, with the result that relations between employees and employers have been greatly enhanced.[5]

A report delivered to the 57th Congress of American Industry reviewed some of the recent achievements in industrial health and safety work. The emphasis throughout the report was on the individual, not in a manner to satisfy the small businessman —who would prefer to have the individual worry about his own needs in his own way—but by affirming that American industry's responsibility to take cognizance of the needs of each individual "must be considered an integral part of community relations, constituting a vital part of industrial citizenship." [6]

The growing concern of big businessmen for the welfare of their employees contrasts sharply with the small businessman's antagonism to the very conditions of modern industrialism, which breed, in his estimation, a degrading dependency. When the small businessman is told that the workingman today is caught in the labyrinth of modern industrialism and can attain freedom and dignity only through trade-union solidarity,

[5] George W. Armstrong, Jr.: "Present Status of Labor-Management Relations Act," *NAM—Employee Relations Division,* circular dated November 25, 1953. Mr. Armstrong is president of the Texas Steel Company and chairman of the Industrial Relations Committee of the National Association of Manufacturers.

[6] *Human Relations on the Industrial Health Front,* Highlights of Presentation before the 57th Congress of American Industry [NAM], November 20, 1953. "American industry is on the threshold of a period which calls for vision, leadership and positive action. The duration of this period will be influenced in large degree by the performance of business leaders and the degree in which they measure up to the hopes and confidence vested in them by the people. We face a challenge. . . . So long as a finger can be pointed at industry because it is not moving adequately to safeguard its employees, so long will industry be vulnerable to attack and, indeed inviting the very threat of unsound legislation it decries." Ibid.

he answers that the worker has lost both his freedom and his dignity and is a tool in the hands of irresponsible labor leaders. He is convinced that the American worker himself is confused and frustrated by the situation in which he finds himself, and is looking for a way out of the political and economic enslavement in which he is bound by one-sided labor laws. He firmly believes the American worker wants to *work* and to buy the products of other workers.

> How many so-called labor unions dare poll their membership on whether they oppose the closed shop and the check-off? And what a short life there would be for some of these so-called labor unions (which are really political organizations of a foreign ideology), if the American worker realized he was being used as a political pawn in an attempt eventually to control government itself.[7]

The anger of the small businessman is directed with particular force at the industrial unions throughout the country. His complaints about local and independent craft unions are relatively minor compared to his blanket condemnation of the mass-base unions in industry. In his concern for the individual's freedom of choice and action he continually points to what he regards as the flagrant undermining of this fundamental principle. If a plant has 2,000 employees and 1,500 vote to join a certain union, then that union has the sole right to make an agreement representing not only its own membership, he points out, but the other 500 employees who voted against the union. And if the 500 do not like the agreement, they then have the choice of joining the union or quitting their jobs. In the eyes of the small businessman they are helpless. The only course of action remaining "to keep America American" is to curb the ir-

[7] Undated circular, "A Real Look at the Books, or . . . America's Eleven Years under the 'Wagner Labor Relations Act,'" distributed by the Conference of American Small Business Organizations.

responsible labor leaders who are depriving millions of workers of their rights and liberties.[8]

It is not surprising to find that small businessmen are often more worried over the imminent danger of "Moscow's trained Communist cells" disrupting America's industrial plant than are the leaders of big business. The latter are certainly aware of the problem of communism, but their concern is overshadowed in many instances by the pleas of small businessmen for instant and drastic action. Mr. Fred A. Virkus, chairman of the Conference, spoke before a meeting of the Union League Club in Chicago in 1953 and made it clear that nobody—including big business leaders—has had the guts to face the facts of communist infiltration and sabotage in American industry to the point of doing something about it. The Conference, ac-

---

[8] In connection with the question of industrial unionism, an analysis of the relative merits of the philosophy of both the AFL and the CIO appeared a few years ago in a monthly publication of the Chamber of Commerce. The pronouncements of these two labor organizations—in this case on the issue of productivity and wages—"are as opposite as those emanating frequently from the White House in Washington and the Politburo in Moscow." The AFL was commended for wanting to make certain that wage increases, resulting from more efficient production, would not force price increases. But the Chamber was not so flattering in its opinion of the CIO's philosophy: "In sharp contrast to the AFL is the policy of the CIO. Recently Philip Murray, President of the CIO, called together a cadre of top leaders and filled them . . . with feelings of exploitation, hatred and class conflict. He got them excited and angry. . . . In a recent CIO publication a calculation was made for the meat-packing industry which showed how much wages could increase if the owners gave up all returns—a Marxist idea! This idea of confiscation, by one productive factor, of the earnings of the other productive factors is a foreign ideology. . . . In spite of a partial house cleaning, the CIO has never rid itself of its Marxist economics. Virtually every important speech and publication . . . instead of being designed to improve the position of the workers, is replete with class consciousness, hatred for employers and is designed to further and intensify the class struggle—things foreign to most Americans. All of this is in sharp contrast to the statesmanlike pronouncement of the AFL." *Economic Intelligence,* monthly bulletin of the Chamber of Commerce of the United States (December 1951).

cordingly, proposed a bill specifically designed to "hamstring the traitorous Communist Cells." [9]

> Regardless of whether or not your business is directly threatened by Communist infiltration in your plant, I am calling on you as anti-Communist Americans to help [CASBO] to do the only thing that can be done legally to put the Communist traitors on trial in a Federal Court, and, if convicted, behind the bars.
>
> This Small Business Conference is prepared, it has what it takes, it has the legislative know-how and the ability to organize the Congressional support necessary to do this job. But it must have the cooperation of the businesses of this country . . . to break the stranglehold of Communists, pinks, punks, psychopaths and traitors in manufacturing plants.[1]

Mr. Virkus pointed out that the NAM and the Chamber of Commerce had both warned of the dangers of communist infiltration in industrial plants, but that "no business organization has taken the initiative . . . to do these things which this Conference has done on each of these vital matters." CASBO alone has acted vigorously in this patriotic matter because small businessmen, if no one else, are fully aware of this "damnable anti-Americanism." [2]

The small businessman's bitter feelings about the American labor movement today reflect a basic hostility to the social and economic developments of the last three decades. Americans have had a ringside seat, the Conference has stated, at the battle being waged in the country between

> the New Deal and its allies, Radical Labor Leaders and their allies the Communists, Fellow Travelers and other

[9] Congressman Lane (D., Mass.), in the First Session of the 83rd Congress, introduced H.J.R. 247 for the establishment of a commission on sabotage in war-production plants.

[1] An address delivered by Fred A. Virkus, chairman of the Conference of American Small Business Organizations, to the Union League Club, Chicago, February 10, 1953.

[2] Ibid.

Left Wingers on the one side, to promote what these call the "Welfare State," and the Republicans and States Rights Democrats on the other side, to prevent out-and-out State Socialism.

The number one creed in Moscow's textbook of subversion is to take over the control of labor unions one by one; and certain "misleaders" in the ranks of labor "lend themselves to dissension between management and employees, to class consciousness and race consciousness, to strikes, riots and revolution—the first communist principle of divide and conquer." Big business may be in a position to "co-operate" with these trade unions and to provide them with "security" and welfare services, but to the small businessman there is really but one issue—"the preservation of overall free enterprise and our Constitutional Republic." [3]

4

In the nature of things today it is difficult to categorize either people or ideas into rigid, airtight classifications. This is especially the case with issues that bear directly on international affairs in general and the foreign policy of the United States in particular. Perhaps no other question so confuses the average

[3] CASBO COMMENTS, Special Bulletin (undated), entitled: "Toward Soviet America." The head of the Communist Party in America, William Z. Foster, the Conference points out, "wrote a book in 1932, entitled 'Toward Soviet America,' in which he outlined the program and the strategy of the Communist Party to Sovietize the United States. 345 pages of detailed instructions to Communists and their Fellow Travelers on how to infiltrate into government offices, labor unions, colleges and schools ('to catch them young'), Church groups, women's groups and wherever else possible, 'to soften up' the American people for the Red Revolution to exterminate the 'Middle Class.' Small, independent business is particularly referred to as 'Middle Class.' . . . The parallel between the Communist's program as outlined in the Foster textbook . . . and the New Deal's program . . . stripped of all camouflage, is so specific that even some former ardent New Dealers gag when they mention it." Ibid.

American as does the problem of this country's relations with the rest of the world. Certainly there is little doubt that the present international situation has aroused strong feelings throughout the country, but it is equally true that these feelings are mixed with a real sense of frustration and have often been without a satisfactory emotional outlet.

The small businessman is often more easily angered by what happens in international affairs than by any other political considerations. The reason is not hard to find: the sense of complete futility in such matters is strongly felt, and his feeling of helplessness is abetted by the conviction that America is being pushed around by "foreigners" at the same time that it is playing Santa Claus to the rest of the world with his money. Big businessmen themselves are by no means sanguine in their attitude toward foreign entanglements, but their annoyance is likely to be tempered by a realization that in the long run they have more to gain by patience and persuasion than by an abrupt withdrawal from all international dealings. It is illuminating in this regard to compare the views of big business and small business on the problem of foreign relations in order to demonstrate once again that their general outlook is dissimilar in many respects and reflects a different set of political values.

The division in the Republican Party between the supporters of President Eisenhower's foreign policy and those of the so-called "isolationist" wing serves as a yardstick against which it is possible to determine the nature and extent of the cleavage. In the Presidential campaign of 1952 Eisenhower's initial financial support came from the big moneyed interests centered on the Eastern seaboard, with big business as the dominating force behind the President, constituting the core of the more "liberal" international wing of the Republican Party. By and large it coincided with the urbanized elements within the party, as evidenced by the fact that it had the support of such men as Senator Ives of New York, Senator Duff of Pennsylvania, and Henry Cabot Lodge of Massachusetts. As Samuel Lubell has pointed out, this alignment represents an exact geographical reversal of the division in the 1920's, when the progressive Republicans came from the Midwest and the Old Guard strongholds were in the industrialized East. The "revolt of the city" in the industrial areas of the nation "shifted the balance of political power from employers to labor, from the descendants of the 'old' Americans to the offspring of the former minority groups." To survive politically, "the Eastern Republicans have had to adjust to the issues and conflicts of that change." [4]

The big business wing of the Republican Party has been determined to do all it can, without endangering its own interests, to prop up Europe's economy and at the same time to support the colonial powers. The men supporting Eisenhower have generally believed that the best way to deal with explosive nationalist movements is through the nations that now control the so-called "backward areas." They are not blind to the importance of colonial reform, and they fully understand the need for developing a fairly prosperous and trained middle-class element among native populations. Where reforms are needed, however, they believe that the controlling powers should make them.

> In their view, France, Holland, Belgium, and Great Britain must be supported, not only in order to tighten the bonds that hold the Western alliance together and to save Europe for the capitalist world, but as a means of controlling areas for which the United States should have no direct responsibility.[5]

[4] Samuel Lubell: op. cit., pp. 230–1.

[5] Barrow Lyons: "The Men behind the Money," *The Nation* (July 5, 1952). Mr. Lyons served as an economist for the Securities and Exchange Commission under President Roosevelt and for several years was chief information officer of the Bureau of Reclamation.

In contrast to the "liberal" elements in the Republican Party are the groups which gravitate in the opposite direction. Not only are these the "rugged individualists," the isolationists, and the super-patriots, but they are the ones who are most antagonistic to all kinds of international commitments and who prefer tough talk to diplomatic finesse. They are far more concerned with the domestic market than they are with international finance, and they are not overly interested in the "survival value" of European capitalism. The small businessman, for one, can find deep satisfaction in this corner because these men are not afraid to have America stand up for her rights in the face of world opposition.

The "isolationist view" is part of a political philosophy which traces its lineage back to the earliest days of the republic. Irving Pflaum has shown that

> at its core lies an idealistic vision of America as the New Jerusalem, a fresh and gleaming experiment in civilization cherished by generations of immigrants who peopled the center of the continent. They left the Old Country (which might be any place from Minsk to Dublin) in bitterness; and they believed profoundly that the American Dream could survive only if it avoided all contamination from the corruption, quarrels, and oppression which they had fled.

To the small businessman and other groups which share his feelings, "the real reactionaries are those people who seek to entangle us in the hopeless affairs of Europe—thus sidetracking (probably for selfish or sinister reasons) the march of America —from Greenland to Cape Horn—toward liberty, equality, and progress." [6]

---

[6] "Although this philosophy often has been kidnapped by a variety of reactionaries, it was originally a liberal doctrine. Its disciples have ranged from Thomas Jefferson to Charles Beard, William Jennings Bryan to the LaFollettes (father and sons), ex-Senators Borah, Wheeler, Lamke, and Nye, and even that grand old saint of the Liberals, George Norris." Irving Pflaum: "The Baffling Career of Robert E. Wood," *Harper's Maga-*

The National Association of Manufacturers and the Chamber of Commerce have taken positions on a number of issues relating to foreign affairs which suggest a difference in attitude and approach from that of many small businessmen. Both organizations are on record as supporting the United Nations, albeit with a number of reservations from time to time, and they have actively participated in such United Nations agencies as the International Labor Organization and the International Monetary Fund. The NAM, desirous of spreading knowledge everywhere of the "beneficent results for everyone of the workings and techniques of private capitalism," has expressed a real interest "in economic developments in Western Europe following an early conviction that its rehabilitation was essential to the prosperity and security of the United States—indeed of the entire Western World." [7] Far from espousing a narrow isolationist attitude, the NAM has recognized that "Western Europe has never been and cannot become a self-contained economic unit," and that America's interest and world interest "lie in the success of moderate governments in power in Western Europe and we should cooperate with them in solving their problems within the framework of expanding world trade." [8] The NAM affirmed and reaffirmed its support of the European Recovery Program, and acknowledged that ECA

---

zine (April 1954), p. 72. In a study of American isolationism, Professor Smuckler has shown that the districts dominated by urban populations are found in relatively larger numbers in the anti-isolationist group. On the other hand, the isolationist group is dominated by a preponderance of semi-urban and rural districts. "The obviously frequent coexistence of isolationist strength and rural population dominance in a district point to the same conclusion as stated previously. Non-urban and rural areas are more frequently isolationist in Congress than urban and metropolitan communities." Ralph H. Smuckler: "The Region of Isolationism," *American Political Science Review* (June 1953), p. 399.

[7] *Industry Believes,* policy statement of the National Association of Manufacturers, approved December 1952, p. 68.

[8] Loc. cit.

achieved marked success in improving Europe's production and standard of living. In May 1949 the NAM published a report entitled: *The Bold New Plan, a Program for Underdeveloped Areas,* in which it outlined its own program for fostering private-enterprise development abroad through the encouragement and protection of American private investments.

The United States Chamber of Commerce, in April 1953, approved a new and more "liberal" policy on trade and tariffs favoring increased American imports. It also advocated an end to foreign economic aid and approved limited trade by the free nations with the Soviet bloc. The new trade policy was more liberal than the Chamber's former position in that it called for outright repeal of the "Buy American" Act and advocated increased imports as an alternative to tax-supported foreign aid. The Chamber stated that protection to domestic producers from import competition should be "judged in the light of the national interest." [9] Even more forthright in its international leanings has been the United States Junior Chamber of Commerce. It has pledged full support to the United Nations, has given strong endorsement to both the Point Four Program and the Voice of America, and has urged Congress "to continue to support the principles of the International Trade Organizations as a means of insuring the prosperity of all the nations of the world." [1]

It need not be maintained that big business has a record of distinguished internationalism to show that its general outlook on America's relations with the rest of the world is con-

[9] Both the NAM and the Chamber of Commerce have been extremely cautious in their pronouncements on the question of tariff reductions, in most cases preferring to leave the final decision on this matter to the individual industries and business firms themselves.

[1] Resolutions adopted by the Board of Directors of the United States Junior Chamber of Commerce, in Tulsa, Oklahoma, on August 4, 5, 6, 1950.

siderably different from the viewpoint of a large number of small businessmen. Nor is the suggestion being made that big businessmen should be the architects of American foreign policy because of their deep insight into world affairs. One could too easily advance arguments to demonstrate that big business has not been in the forefront of the groups in this country which have continually stressed the importance of closer co-operation with our foreign allies. Yet it did not pass without notice that in the fall of 1959 when Soviet Premier Khrushchev visited the United States he received a warm and enthusiastic welcome from a great many of America's big businessmen. The New York *Herald Tribune,* in a survey of forty-eight top business executives from companies doing an annual business of more than $25,000,000, found that seven out of eight supported the thirteen-day visit of the communist leader as a step that might ease cold-war tensions and lead to greater East-West trade.[2]

The point to be made is that in comparison with the international perspective of big businessmen as it has developed and manifested itself in the postwar years—limited, imperfect, and self-interested as it may be—the attitude of small businessmen stands out all the more sharply. In general their point of view is at odds with the cautious "internationalism" of big business, not to mention the firm internationalist convictions of the United Nations and its most ardent defenders.

The Conference of American Small Business Organizations, in its usual candid manner, made clear not only its views on many specific international controversies, but also the basic assumptions on which its entire position rested. The general objective of the foreign policy of the United States, it maintained, should be a world of "free sovereign nations." To achieve this goal, the Conference felt, it is necessary to reaf-

[2] New York *Herald Tribune,* September 14, 1959, Section 3, p. 6.

firm a belief in the traditional policy laid down in the Farewell Address of George Washington:

> It is our true policy to steer clear of permanent alliance with any portion of the foreign world; so far, I mean, as we are now at liberty to do it; for let me not be understood as capable of patronizing infidelity to existing engagements. I hold the maxim no less applicable to public than private affairs, that honesty is always the best policy. I repeat it, therefore, let those engagements be observed in their genuine sense. But in my opinion it is unnecessary, and would be unwise, to extend them.
>
> Taking care always to keep ourselves by suitable establishments, on a respectable defensive posture, we may safely trust to temporary alliances for extraordinary emergencies.[3]

CASBO also believed in the soundness of the Monroe Doctrine enunciated in 1823 and therefore opposed "further extension of territorial holdings of any European power or further extension of any European system in the Western Hemisphere." In addition, it supported the Open Door policy for the Far East, signed in 1922, "to wit: 'To respect the sovereignty, the independence and the territorial and administrative integrity of China.' "

In the light of these pronouncements CASBO took an outspoken stand on a number of international issues and advocated the following program as America's foreign policy:

(1) The United States should include only "temporary alliances" for extraordinary emergencies and only with nations taking the measures set down here to eradicate the Communist conspiracy in their midst;

(2) The United States should cancel all diplomatic and trade relations with the Soviet bloc and insist that our temporary allies do the same and permit no economic, military or charitable aid to any nations except such allies;

[3] Quoted in *Report of Proceedings,* CASBO, Thirteenth National Session (Washington, D.C.: April 21, 22, 23, 1952), pp. 21–2.

(3) Legal measures should be taken to eradicate completely the Communist conspiracy in the United States;

(4) The United States should propose at the earliest possible moment the ousting of the Soviet Union and its satellites from the United Nations;

(5) As the United Nations represents a permanent alliance rather than a temporary alliance for emergency purposes to which we subscribe, subsequent withdrawal of the United States from the United Nations should take place as early as circumstances and conditions permit, and the headquarters of the United Nations should be removed from the boundaries of the United States;

(6) There should be an amendment of the Constitution of the United States providing that neither the charter of the United Nations nor any treaty to which the United States is a party shall supersede the Constitution of the United States;

(7) Within the limits of our ability, the United States should aid every nation and every force actively fighting the Kremlin, both outside and inside the Iron Curtain, using counter-subversion to meet Communist subversion.[4]

The Conference's distrust of international dealings on the part of the United States caused it to seek a change in the Constitution to "protect the Domestic Law of the United States and the Constitutions of the Several States Thereof from Invalidation by Reason of Treaties Concluded with approval of the United States Senate or by Force of Executive Agreements, etc." It has now become evident, stated CASBO, that "sinister forces" are designing "to destroy our form of government and put in its place some form of Socialistic or Communist dictatorship by misuse of the provisions of Article Six of the Constitution of the United States relating to the making of treaties." Furthermore, the decisions of the United States Supreme Court and of certain State courts have shown the "imminent danger" of these "sinister forces" realizing their objective "without the

[4] Ibid.

consent of the people and without Congress being aware of the import of certain provisions of the Charter of the United Nations, the Genocide, Human Rights, Right to Organize, International Trade Organization Conventions and other covenants and conventions upon our form of government." Accordingly, CASBO urged "recapture, by the Congress, of its sole power to declare war" and endorsed the passage of the Bricker Amendment to the federal Constitution.[5]

In 1953 the Conference went on record as being increasingly concerned over "the disparity between the grave issues debated during the 1952 political campaign and the legislative measures so far proposed by the newly elected administration," and urged the incumbent administration "to come to grips with the problems facing the nation . . . stamp Communist influences and corruption out of government agencies, and actually reduce spending to absolute necessities to avoid outright confiscation of the people's income." At the same time the

---

[5] *Report of Proceedings*, CASBO, Twelfth National Session (Washington, D.C.: April 2, 3, 4, 1951), pp. 24–5. CASBO offered its own amendment in three parts:

(1) The basic principles of this Constitution, namely, the establishment of a representative form of a Federal Government, consisting of the Legislative, Executive, and the Judicial, and of the sovereignty of the governments of the several states of the character guaranteed by the Constitution; the express limitations of the Constitution on the powers of Congress; the guarantees of individual liberties contained in this Constitution and in the Bill of Rights, set forth in the first Ten Amendments, and the independence of the Federal Judiciary, shall not be abolished nor altered by any treaty or executive agreement.

(2) The power of the Senate to ratify treaties shall be exercised only by two-thirds of the entire membership of the Senate and not by two-thirds only of the members present.

(3) The Supreme Court shall have and promptly exercise original jurisdiction to pass upon the validity of all treaties and executive agreements upon application by the President or of the Governor of any state made within six months of the date of the proclamation of any treaty or executive agreement. Ibid.

See also *Report of Proceedings*, CASBO, Fourteenth National Session, p. 19.

Conference (1) strongly endorsed the McCarran-Walter Immigration Act; (2) urged that "all bills which carry appropriations for foreign aid carry in their title the clause in the federal Constitution by which such aid is justified"; (3) urged that the treaty by which the United States endorsed the United Nations Charter be declared null and void; and (4) urged that "the Trade Agreements Act of 1943, as amended, and which expires on June 30th, 1953, be permitted to expire." [6]

Of particular importance to small businessmen is the whole question of foreign trade. CASBO long felt that the "selective free trade policy" adopted by the State Department and based upon the International Trade Agreements Act was impairing wages and investments and causing unemployment and loss of taxable property in this country. The Conference declared that

> the proposed International Trade Organization, consisting of 58 nations, each with one vote, to which it is suggested that this nation assign all of its right to adjust tariffs and import fees involving the protection of the working men and investments in the United States of America, would complete the job of wrecking our economy.

CASBO also opposed the policy of "making up the trade balance deficits of the European nations (16 ECA nations) in cash each year without definite conditions for its utilization," in the belief that it simply re-establishes "the century-old feuds and rivalries among such nations." Consequently the Conference passed the following resolution:

> BE IT RESOLVED, that the Conference of American Small Business Organizations records its opposition to the continuation of the Reciprocal Trade Program and the holding of membership by the United States in the International Organization, and recommends to the Congress that the *flexible import fee* principle, based upon "fair and reason-

[6] Ibid.

able" competition, be substituted for the 1934 Trade Agreements Act as extended, and be administered by a reorganized experienced tariff commission, to be known as the Foreign Trade Authority (operating in the same manner as the long established Interstate Commerce Commission which adjusts freight rates for the carriers on a basis of a "reasonable return" on the investment).[7]

The National Federation of Independent Business has taken a strong stand on a variety of proposals relating to international affairs in response to direct, signed ballots from its members. A bill requesting that the President tell the people through Congress "just what our foreign policy is" was approved by 80 per cent of the members voting, reflecting the deep distrust of Presidential leadership in foreign affairs that is felt by a great many small businessmen. This view is frequently expressed in the argument that ours is a government of the people and the people have a right to know what our foreign policy is—"if we have one." Any secret, zigzag course followed by the administration, the NFIB has warned, will leave our country weak and alone. The only way to get this information is for Congress to be kept fully and currently informed. Then if the people find our foreign policy a failure, they can turn it over to Congress and thereby strengthen our nation and restore public confidence. In keeping with this position is the vote of 72 per cent of the small businessmen in the NFIB to support the "Bricker Amendment," which would require House and Senate approval of treaties and executive agreements. On the over-all question of whether or not they favored maintaining foreign aid itself as a permanent feature of our nation's foreign policy, 80 per cent replied in the negative. In the secret ballot they agreed with the expressed idea that those who espouse aid forget that you cannot finance or

[7] *Report of Proceedings,* CASBO, Eleventh National Session (Washington, D.C.: March 27, 28, 29, 1951), p. 41.

buy friendship. In Korea, it was said, "the United States bore almost 90% of the burden but where were our European allies?" Now they see the switch is to Asia, where a number of countries are flirting with Communist China. To the small businessman the question here seems simple enough: who is kidding whom?

Other votes which small businessmen in the Federation have cast over the years, indicating their general feelings on matters relating to foreign affairs, include the following:

	For	*Against*	*No vote*
No U.S. aid to a European nation until it can demonstrate "maximum self-help"	95%	4%	1%
That Congress require foreign nations receiving American aid let their people know that the aid-goods are from the U.S.	96	2	2
Limit foreign aid to military assistance only	61	31	8
Grant foreign aid to only those nations lined up with us in the "cold war" against Communists	73	17	10
Extend the Reciprocal Trade Act for 3 years	28	66	6
Admit another 300,000 displaced persons into the United States	28	66	6

When the position of CASBO and the NFIB on foreign affairs is placed alongside that of such conservative organizations as the NAM and the Chamber of Commerce, one fact emerges with exceptional clarity: small business's bitter opposition to many policies is prompted to a large extent by ideological considerations, while the NAM and the Chamber seem to be more rationally motivated in their over-all outlook. If the NAM or the Chamber of Commerce favor a given policy or program, their reason is apt to be that it is good for business and therefore deserves to be supported. CASBO, on the other hand, not necessarily looking at a particular international proposal or trade agreement from the point of view of economic self-interest alone, appraised any situation with harsh and extreme ideological language and tended to look for Marxist plots. It was "unalterably opposed" to the Point Four Program, for example, because this "fantastic program . . . is a Marxian planned Utopia to 'equalize' the standards of living of the countries of the world, and once begun would have no foreseeable ending." [8] And what particularly angers the small businessman about all of America's commitments around the world is that he can see no profitable ending for any of them. The leaders of big business at least have a vision of what tomorrow may bring, and they also see a good chance of being able to influence the course of events. The small businessman, however, reacts with impatience to what happens in the rest of the world. The more economic trouble he sees in foreign countries, the more he is convinced that America should devote her energies to strengthening her own free-enterprise economy at home and preserving the economic rights and liberties of Americans. His heaviest attack on America's foreign policy is that it is more foreign than American. If he has viewed domestic developments of the past twenty years as conclusive proof that America has forsaken her long-standing tradition of individual liberty in exchange for the dubious industrial blessings of big government, big labor, and big business, he is even more antagonistic to what he considers to be the un-American "ideologies" emanating from foreign shores. That he has advocated a tougher and more belligerent course of action for the United States in Asia and a weaker and more "isolationist" stand in Europe may indicate some contradiction and confusion in his thinking, but the motivation underlying both posi-

[8] *Report of Proceedings,* CASBO, Twelfth National Session, p. 26.

tions—indeed, his whole attitude toward America's role as a world power—is that his country has been kicked around long enough and should demonstrate to the rest of the world that it believes in America first, last, and always.

5

In defending the principle of proprietorship as the common denominator of his entire way of life, the small businessman has taken an active interest in a wide variety of problems. However, with the advances of industrialism, the areas in which he can effectively exercise his own discretion as an individual proprietor have been steadily reduced, resulting in his conviction that this drift away from proprietorship has amounted to a betrayal of the fundamentals of "Americanism." Feeling that what is really at stake for small business is more than the "ebb and flow of dollar totals," he has even entered the field of education.

The small businessman's interest in education reflects his concern for what has been happening to traditional American principles of government in the last twenty or thirty years. He sees in this country an educational movement which is identified with the national "social planners," as he might call them, and from his point of view it is totally "subversive" because of its success in "undermining allegiance and faith." The issue is more than communism in the schools; it is what he often calls "leftism" in education, and to the small businessman and many other like-minded Americans at the grass roots, this is the real poison.

Over a century ago Horace Mann expressed the belief that education was an instrument of indoctrination and propaganda, his views then being of particular interest to the business community. Education, he pointed out, had a "market value" of its own: it could instill common values, uphold the institution of property, and prevent the uprising of dangerous ideologies. Today the small businessman is convinced that there is a trend in American education whose purpose is to remake society by converting the public schools and colleges into an agency to promote socialism, a planned collectivist economy, government regimentation, or the welfare state. The new educational philosophy, he feels, not only brands the capitalist the implacable foe of human rights, but insists that the only solution to the contemporary problem of self-government and social well-being lies in increasingly bigger government. Furthermore, he is particularly incensed by what he feels is the open promotion of world government or some supranational sovereignty as a subtle way of eradicating—"beginning in the kindergarten" —American nationalism and the deep loyalties it involves. He agrees with Representative Paul W. Shafer that an educational movement and philosophy which "attributes supreme virtue to the new, to the attitude of critical skepticism, to cynical distrust of human motives and impulses, and which, at the same time, belittles the old, decries inherited loyalties, and minimizes truths and values established by past experience, is subversive." [9]

The Conference of American Small Business Organizations repeatedly challenged "the very cloak of immunity from criticism under which the educational world is sheltering the deteriorating tendencies in American education." The initial issue between the educational world and its critics, CASBO believed, is "whether or not teaching is the sole possession of teachers." In this regard the Conference claimed that certain so-called "leaders" are asserting this proprietorship by means which "gravely and unfairly reflect on the character and ability

[9] Paul W. Shafer: "Is There a 'Subversive' Movement in the Public Schools?" Speech delivered in the House of Representatives, March 21, 1952, pp. 4–5.

of thousands of loyal, competent and self-sacrificing teachers."
In 1953 the Conference reaffirmed and detailed its attitude
toward the whole subject of education. "The profoundest
danger to the American educational world today," it stated,
"lies in confusion of thinking." This is partly a "planned confusion" on the part of a small minority, "but mostly it results
rather from the mixture and compounding of three diverse
tendencies in the teaching world," each of which CASBO opposed and deplored.

(1) The so-called "progressive" or "soft" method of teaching basic skills and disciplines;
(2) The conviction that free enterprise has come to an end
and that pupils must be prepared for the "bright, new
(collectivist or socialist) world of tomorrow";
(3) The claim—in fact the exclusive claim—to such characteristics as "intellectual," "liberal" and "progressive," by left-wing professional educators and their
friends outside the profession.[1]

The Conference claimed that in order to defend this state
of confusion from inquiry and probing, "some so-called educational leaders—aided and abetted by organizations and
publications claiming the 'intellectual' label—have resorted
to smear tactics, guilt by association, innuendo, distortion,
'the big lie'—anything and everything to avoid meeting the
real issue." CASBO stated "the real issue" in unequivocal terms
and put it in capitals: "DO YOU OR DO YOU NOT TEACH, SUPPORT
AND BELIEVE IN ANY OR ALL OF THE THREE OBJECTIONABLE
TENDENCIES LISTED ABOVE?"[2] To evade this issue, "left-wing
leaders—whether or not they are communists—have used
Communist tactics," the Conference said, but quickly added
that "by their fruits ye shall know them."

[1] *Report of Proceedings*, CASBO, Fourteenth National Session, pp.
23–4.
[2] Ibid.

The attitude of the Conference on the question of education was further amplified by its insistence that every American family has a proper interest in education and its processes, pointing out again that the latter are not the sole property of educators.

> Education takes place in the home, in the Church and even "on the job" for many youngsters, as well as in the schools. Educators are the partners of, not the sovereigns of, the father, the mother, the minister and the taxpayer in the raising of America's children. The cloak of immunity and the arrogant front of certain professional "educators" do not cover a true educator. They are rather a confession of intellectual and probably moral bankruptcy on the part of the individual in question. By no means all, or even most, educators are like this. But they have gotten into a situation where many who claim to be their leaders do so. Such persons, and those outside the educational world who aid them, stamp themselves accordingly.[3]

Many members of the Conference—"businessmen and fathers, and patriotic citizens"—became so alarmed at the "prevalent favorable attitude toward collectivist doctrines" in the schools that they took vigorous action in countless communities across the country to protect the American school system "from the inevitable deterioration which will otherwise occur." [4]

It is of no small interest to note at this point that the National Association of Manufacturers does not share the feeling that the educational system in this country is in the process of deteriorating. For that matter the position of this big business organization with regard to American education and its role in our present-day society contrasts strikingly with the viewpoint of small business. Charles R. Sligh, Jr., president of the NAM in 1953, told an education-industry conference that his organiza-

[3] Ibid.
[4] *Report of Proceedings,* CASBO, Twelfth National Session, p. 38.

tion was opposed to any "wholesale indictment" of American colleges and universities by anti-communists. The fact that some college faculties probably include professors with "communist leanings" or who expound "socialist ideas" in the classroom, he said, "should not cause a general condemnation of our educational system." Increased support of higher education, he contended, is the "positive approach to the left-wing problem." [5]

The NAM has long recognized that American industry must extend financial support to higher education. Far from having any deep fears about American education subverting our way of life, the NAM has generally expressed strong confidence in our schools, in the practical belief that prosperity will continue as long as the nation has greater production, better education, and better leadership. "The ascending spiral of greatness in America," another past president of the NAM has remarked, "has risen because industry has produced wealth, which in turn has supported educational institutions, which in their turn have supplied leadership to industry in order that with each succeeding generation it might produce more wealth." [6]

The "market value" of education is more than apparent to many big business leaders. "If you harbor the thought that business is interested exclusively in profits," Sidney P. Allen, financial editor of the *San Francisco Chronicle,* remarked, "or that the National Association of Manufacturers is 'reactionary' in its approach to the problems of the day, you might pause for a moment and heed Karl Bunting." [7] Mr. Bunting, another former president of the NAM, sees education as the NAM's principal program. Big business has a self-interest in its edu-

[5] *San Francisco Chronicle,* April 15, 1953.

[6] "Industry Is Urged To Back Colleges," *The New York Times,* November 29, 1949.

[7] Sidney P. Allen: "NAM Pushing Profits for College Training," *San Francisco Chronicle,* March 10, 1954.

cational efforts and donations, and many business leaders would like to see the program of support from corporations on a current basis. "A good, smart liberal arts graduate will deal in terms of human problems," Mr. Bunting said. "And we need a better understanding and relationship between employer and employee. We need more understanding of human motivation." [8]

In February 1954 the NAM issued a pamphlet entitled *This We Believe about Education*.[9] In many ways it is a remarkable document, and if the source were not known it might conceivably be difficult to believe that many of the statements within its pages actually came from the NAM. To many small businessmen the pamphlet would confirm what they have long suspected—that many big businessmen have taken a "leftward slant" on American education. There is little doubt that, in comparison with the bitter and emotional pronouncements of CASBO, the statements of the NAM are models of restraint and reason.

> It is the responsibility of Education to support, and frequently to lead, the necessary and continuing fight to preserve freedom of expression and freedom of inquiry. Even tolerance of intolerance must be safeguarded. . . . All educators should oppose any attempt by either government or public opinion to repress expression of honest views or to curtail scientific studies and researches. An educator must stand ready to fight for his right to pursue knowledge in the true scientific spirit. Because education has a centuries-old familiarity with the struggle to achieve and maintain freedom for the human mind, the American people rightfully look to educators for leadership in that continuous battle.[1]

[8] Ibid.
[9] *This We Believe about Education*, A Statement Concerning Education in America, by the Educational Advisory Committee and the Educational Advisory Council of the National Association of Manufacturers, New York, February 1954.
[1] Ibid., p. 16.

Every teacher in America, the NAM declares, should have the "unquestioned right to impart knowledge objectively concerning all matters related to the subject he teaches." Completely objective teaching, however, especially for the social sciences, "while a desirable goal, can scarcely be expected or achieved in actual practice by teachers who are also thinking human beings; reasonable deviation from this absolute standard should not expose any teacher to attack, intimidation, or insecurity of his position." Short of advocacy of the overthrow of the government, "no attack on any teacher or on his teaching because of his individual ideological convictions, should be supported or condoned." Furthermore, the NAM believes that "businessmen, the public, and educators should view with proper and customary caution sweeping charges made by any group which studies the educational system and publishes adverse findings as to its methods, purposes, or practices, or as to the ideological loyalties of some of its leaders." [2]

The NAM, contrary to CASBO, feels that with few exceptions all of the major goals and objectives of American education have been endorsed by a sufficient percentage of the American people to assure those goals a "justified place in the over-all design." It would seem wiser, the NAM advises, if all persons concerned with education would recognize the advantages of a "heterogeneity of ideas as to the purposes of education." Another group of prominent big businessmen, aware of the serious financial problems facing the American educational system, announced the "reluctant conclusion" that federal aid is "necessary" to provide adequate schools in low-income States. This conclusion, a departure from the opposition to federal aid for education usually taken by much of the big business community, was the major point of a ninety-page report released by the research and policy committee of the Com-

[2] Ibid., pp. 29–30.

mittee for Economic Development.[3] The research committee, which included corporation executives and industrial leaders, proposed that the federal government distribute about $600,-000,000 in string-free grants to strengthen public schools in "states where incomes are lowest." It said that there is a clear and urgent "national interest" in insuring adequate schools in all parts of the country, and it is therefore appropriate for the federal government to step in. But CASBO, speaking for those who have what it calls a "deep allegiance to the governmental and economic principles on which the United States were founded, which stem from an abiding faith in individual liberty," regarded the current "trend in education" as something to which all patriotic citizens must be inevitably and forcefully alerted. To this end the Conference established a Committee on Education, one of whose principal projects was to examine the contents of textbooks through its own quarterly publication, *The Educational Reviewer.*

The Educational Reviewer was launched by the Conference with the central purpose in mind of exposing the "collectivist doctrines" being taught in the schools. It stated in its first issue that it was ferreting out the "concealed theories of collectivism" as a service to teachers throughout the country. It stated frankly that the *Reviewer* "is to be biased in favor of both personal liberty and economic liberty," the twin touchstones of the American system. "On that issue, the *Reviewer* will not be partisan or even bipartisan." It would rest its case on the premise that the encroachment of centralized political power upon the initiative of the individual and groups of individuals is the greatest threat both to liberty and to material well-being.

[3] *We Can Have Better Schools,* A Summary of the Statement on National Policy issued by the Research and Policy Committee of the Committee for Economic Development (New York: 1960).

It will measure school and college materials by the criteria of liberty and responsibility, rather than by the currently voiced standards of "rights and duties" to be parcelled out at the hands of bureaucrats. No one need be amazed, therefore, that these columns will reflect the views of believers in the American constitutional system.[4]

Communism was not singled out as the main issue. "Our most dangerous subversives in this country," CASBO had already announced, "are not the out-and-out Communists but the men and women who, knowingly or unknowingly, through indifference or apathy, vote for, or in other ways sponsor the trend toward socialism."[5] Speaking for "businessmen and fathers" who have become alarmed at the propaganda being taught to their sons and daughters, the *Reviewer* was concerned primarily with attacking "all shades and degrees" of "collectivism," the real destroyer of individual liberty and freedom. These businessmen and parents

> know that they and their country prospered under the economic aspect of liberty, the private enterprise system, and they wish their children to enjoy the same advantages. But the questions at the family dinner table, the quotations from certain teachers, began to sound strange. An examination of some of the textbooks which were the source of those ideas led to further study and to the present effort to evaluate current textbooks and supplementary materials.[6]

Mrs. Lucille Cardin Crain, secretary and editor of the *Reviewer,* explained why the need for such a publication became urgent. In a radio interview in 1950 she cited the case of a Middle Western small businessman, a member of CASBO, who was "shocked when his daughter came home from college full of un-American doctrines. . . . He looked into the textbooks that his daughter had been made to study. The history books

---

[4] *The Educational Reviewer,* Vol. I, No. 1 (July 15, 1949).
[5] *Report of Proceedings,* CASBO, Eleventh National Session, p. 39.
[6] Ibid.

were slanted toward the revolutionary 'new order.' The textbooks on government pleaded for 'change' and for giving more power to government." He "hit the ceiling," Mrs. Crain said, when he discovered that his daughter had been taught "a lot of economic nonsense" in textbooks in which he found "general condemnation of the system of which he is a part."

BILL SLATER: Then what did he do?

MRS. CRAIN: First, he read the economic textbooks used in the high school of his home town. Then he asked his school officials why they used them. They said there was nothing better— that there hadn't been a sound, new textbook on economics for high school pupils in the last ten years.

BILL SLATER: That's about the story all over the country, so far as I've heard it. But this man found a way to do something, did he?

MRS. CRAIN: Yes. Mutual friends brought us together and we planned the work of *The Educational Reviewer*.

. . .

BILL SLATER: What about the argument that's heard these days about presenting "all sides of every question"?

MRS. CRAIN: I'm awfully glad you brought that up. One of my favorite teacher-reviewers gave me her interpretation of that trick—it is a trick— and I shall be eternally grateful to her for her answer.

BILL SLATER: How did she explain the trick?

MRS. CRAIN: She pointed out that giving the same emphasis to all points of view, good and bad, and letting immature minds make decisions without guidance, is just what the propagandists want. And I remember her adding something like this: "Truth and falsehood are *not* equal; there is no equality between right and wrong." [7]

[7] Excerpts of a radio broadcast entitled: "What Is Taught Your Children," reprinted in *The Educational Reviewer,* Vol. II, No. 2 (Octo-

In keeping a militant watch on American education the Conference proclaimed its belief that the public school system is an important bulwark of American democracy. One of its primary functions is to teach "American ideals, U.S. History, U.S. Constitution and the principles underlying the basic liberties we enjoy." In furtherance of this traditional policy, the Conference declared, specific courses in American history, geography, civics, and allied subjects have been an integral part of school curriculums for more than a hundred years. It has only been in recent years that " 'left-wing' educators, known as 'Frontier Thinkers,' have sought to reconstruct our educational system with the avowed purpose of bringing about a new social order based upon principles of collectivism or Marxism." These educators, announced CASBO, frankly admit that "the first step in their scheme is to demolish faith and belief in many of our existing social, economic and political principles and traditions in order to pave the way for the 'new society.' " The Conference maintained that this plan has already been adopted in many public schools by the elimination of specific courses in American history and civics, and that in their place have been substituted "certain courses known as Social Science, which do not impart a faith in present American institutions, but in effect undermine the belief of our children in their country and its time-honored institutions, including our system of free enterprise." It is this "alarming condition," CASBO concluded, that is "largely responsible for the spread of Marx-

---

ber 15, 1950). For an attack on *The Educational Reviewer* and other organizations operating in this field, see Arthur D. Morse: "Who's Trying To Ruin Our Schools?" *McCall's* (September 1951). See also Robert A. Skaife: "They Sow Distrust," *The Nation's Schools* (January 1951). For the story of the "Phony Three-R Fight" see Ernest O. Melby: *American Education under Fire,* a Freedom Pamphlet printed by the Anti-Defamation League of B'nai B'rith in 1951.

ism and subversive doctrines now evident in schools, colleges and youth organizations, and also deficiencies in the fundamentals of education." [8] Therefore the Conference urged every precaution possible to prevent anyone who subscribes to "any of the ideologies of Communism or any other governmental philosophy at variance with our form of government" from being appointed to a position of trust or influence. "Only Americans should be employed to handle Government affairs and to teach our youth; only those persons who are glad to turn their faces toward the rising sun every day and swear allegiance to our country, are suitable for such employment." [9]

The "subversion" of American principles taking place in the classroom is seen by the small businessman in much the same way that he has viewed the destruction of individualism and personal liberty throughout society in the last twenty or thirty years. The schools are poisoning the minds of young people today because they are not teaching the benefits of our private enterprise system, with the result that the future managers and employees of American industry will not believe in the economic system in which these enterprises were created and in which they have prospered. As far as the small businessman is concerned, the practical every-day world outside the classroom is not much better at instructing the independent proprietor. Society, he has concluded, has lost faith in its traditional values and ideals, for the individual today can always turn to the government for help in what he cannot do by himself. From the point of view of the small businessman, no more damaging indictment of present-day America can be made.

[8] *Report of Proceedings,* CASBO, Tenth National Session (Washington, D.C.: February 21, 22, 23, 24, 1949), pp. 41–2.
[9] *Report of Proceedings,* CASBO, Eleventh National Session, p. 40.

6

In a recent book Daniel Bell argues persuasively that few serious intellectuals in the Western World any longer believe ideology to be *truth* and consequently few of them have any ideological allegiances.[1] Conscious ideology has passed from the present scene and what has taken its place, if anything, is the "middle way" between left and right that is predominant in Western Europe as well as in America. It is a happy development, as Bell points out, because those who tend to think in airtight ideological terms have a passion for certitude, which Justice Holmes long ago pointed out is never the test of certainty, and thus are led to divide political, social, or intellectual situations into heroes or villains. In the enthusiasm to proclaim their "true beliefs" they not only succeed in reducing ideas to a distorted simplicity, but they sacrifice the ability to perceive the complexity that is at both the core and periphery of our modern industrial life. In short, the end result of ideology is extremism, left or right. Therefore, in Bell's own words, we must confront individual issues on their individual merits rather than from general formulas. It is the substitution of the experimental and the pragmatic for the programmatic and the apocalyptic.

The small businessman, in fighting for nothing less than his own survival, is a contemporary example of the commitment to a particular kind of American ideological thinking. No one could claim that the ideology of the small businessman or the consequences of his commitments bear any resemblance to the peculiar fanaticism of many of the leaders of socialism or the cruel results of the abstract ideology of Marx and Lenin. The small businessman, rather, looks at his own problems and the special conditions of his emancipation as the *general* condi-

[1] Daniel Bell: *The End of Ideology* (Glencoe, Ill.: Free Press; 1960).

tions—to borrow a phrase from Marx—through which alone the modern society of the United States can be saved. To this extent he has an ideology: he claims national if not universal validity for his particular interest. His dilemma and his frustration lie in his not being able to see his "particular interest" in its true proportions. Where Marx promised that the future, "the day after the revolution," would usher in the Utopia without conflict, the small businessman clings more to visions of the past, when life was more simple, more rewarding, and, in fact, more American. The "angry young men" of Great Britain are angry today because they are desperately in search of a "cause" that will satisfy their youthful ire against a world that to them seems middle-aged. The small businessman is angry too, but his, ironically, is the anger of middle age against the innovations of a still young corporate society.

When the Lynds studied "Middletown" in the 1930's they found that most citizens shared the belief that the small businessman was the pillar of the American economic system. Today the small businessman is no longer that sure of himself, and he is bitter. He is bitter because he sees himself constantly surrounded by big business, big labor, and big government, each of which he feels has taken the road of paternalism or something even worse. The different kinds of "appeasement" practiced at intervals by organizations like the NAM and the Chamber of Commerce are simply paving the way to cartelization. "If the hired big boys want that, OK, let them want it," a former official of a small business organization explained, "but we will fight them tooth and nail. If you want a Mussolinic America, then go along with the 'go along' boys. If you want proprietorship, stand with us." [2] The desire of the NAM's "hired management" to keep its job, the small businessman will argue, even explains the NAM's (as he would say) "soft"

[2] Letter to author, dated June 16, 1953.

thinking on education. His argument is that because "left-wing educators" proved themselves capable of creating a big fuss about anybody who cared to inquire into their professional work, the more timid slunk away, including the hired management of the NAM. One of the reasons they were hired in the first place, he points out, is that they had skillfully avoided becoming public targets by avoiding bad public relations. But when the "leftists" in education proved conclusively that "bad public relations" was exactly what they could and would create for any critics, the public relations experts ran for cover. This phenomenon, he feels, could be multiplied indefinitely; it is part and parcel of the drift of things today. Independents are always in the minority; leaders are always in the minority (by definition); orthodoxy (of the moment) is always in the majority (by definition). This at least is part of the answer the small businessman gives to explain the paradox of "soft" leadership on the part of big business.

> Why did the horse out-survive the mastodon? Why do feeble new species eventually duplicate "tough" old ones? Why is communism a threat only many years after Lenin and Trotsky were allowed sealed passage to Russia by the Allies? Why can a microscopic organism destroy big throbbing "healthy" bodies? The phenomenon is ideological as well as tangible.[3]

The small businessman, on the other hand, regards himself as a "hard" thinker and very often will admit that in the common parlance of politics he is to the right of center. Big business is less right-wing than small business, he says, because its managers do not need to be right-wing in order to keep their jobs. But the proprietor must be right-wing or he will cease to be. He has a motive; the big corporation president does not. And while there are exceptions on both sides, this is the preponderant tendency. He is opposed to FEPC; he is a States'-

[3] Ibid.

rights Constitutionalist, and he supports the Bricker Amendment. If such positions as these are right-wing, he argues, then he could not be anything but right-wing and still be *for* the "proprietary principle." The "left-winger" is the proprietor's enemy because he holds to more government whenever there is a choice. The small businessman, however, always holds to less government, preferring rugged individualism whenever a choice can be made, but in any event seeking the survival of the proprietor as such. By necessity he feels he must be against collectivism, mild or severe, since the proprietor's survival *as such* depends on profits. Thus he is strongly in support of the profit system. However, since the survival of the profit system depends in its turn on the survival of the very society of which it is a part, all small businessmen must necessarily be (in their view) "enlightened." Their ideological conviction in this regard is strong: "We must pass the test of *being for a basic principle even when the particular application is against us;* or must qualify the principle so much as to make it again of general application if we find that it cannot be strictly applied." [4]

It makes little difference in what direction the small businessman turns or in what particular political or economic controversy he may become involved; he can find ample proof all about him that the virtues and inducements of an earlier, more American way of life have been traduced by alien ideologies and severely damaged by the regimentation and bureaucratization of an industrial social order. His politics reflect a deep hostility to anyone or anything that shows a contempt for the principles of individual independence and achievement, as well as pride of family and of country. Those who stand apart from him he feels are willing to trade the "ideal of liberty for the false bait of a security which no political power can ever give." [5]

[4] Ibid.
[5] *The Educational Reviewer,* Vol. II, No. 2 (October 15, 1950).

Retrospect
and Prospect

<u>1</u>   Almost forty years ago Thorstein Veblen pointed out that the "country-town situation of the nineteenth century" was being left behind and that the salvation of twentieth-century democracy would depend upon the satisfactory resolution of technological problems and crises generated in a society increasingly dominated by large vested interests. He was at the same time fully aware that the country town, with its community life and self-sufficiency, had been for many generations the center of American life, indeed a great American institution, and that it would continue to play an important role in shaping public sentiment and giving character to the nation's culture. The road to success, he wrote, ran into and through the country town, or its equivalent in the cities. "Habits of thought engendered by the preoccupations of the retail trade" molded popular sentiment and morals and clearly dominated public policy regarding what was to be done and what was to be left undone, locally and at large, in political, civil, social, ecclesiastical, and educational concerns. This,

Veblen said, was what was meant by democracy in American parlance, and it was for this small-town pattern of democracy that "the Defender of the American Faith once aspired to make the world safe."[1]

To the small businessman, as we have seen, this same pattern remains the bedrock of many of his deepest convictions. He has roots in what Veblen called the "masterless country town," and it has been a real and continuing revolution for him to live and prosper in a society that has changed its basic economic ways and evolved into a complex social order. He has reacted almost instinctively to the demands of modern industrialism with suspicion and outright resentment. His lament for the simpler days of the small town at the turn of the century, with its pleasant social life of hay rides, chicken-pie suppers, and church socials, as well as the masculine gatherings on Saturday night at the store or barbershop to discuss politics—where people could listen to each other because there was no manufactured noise to keep them from hearing—this lament of the small businessman and others like him is sung today in many different refrains.[2] "I'm just a little country dealer in Mill Valley with low overhead and I do my own selling," ran a recent radio commercial in the San Francisco Bay area. "Like I said before, that beautiful Pontiac looks just as nice in my little showroom as it does in any of the big city dealerships around."

The social prestige and personal satisfaction of owning a small independent enterprise have been diminished by the advances of corporate technology. The small entrepreneur has

---

[1] Thorstein Veblen: *Absentee Ownership and Business Enterprise in Recent Times: The Case for America* (New York: B. W. Huebsch; 1923), p. 151.

[2] For a good-natured and perceptive discussion of small-town nostalgia, see R. L. Duffus: "Lament for the Old Style Small Town," *The New York Times Magazine,* December 13, 1959.

come to feel that both his own private world and the long tradition of American individualism have been overthrown in the growth of organization and the resulting quest for security. He is among those who have been most severely affected by the industrial revolution, in that as an individual he has been uprooted, almost literally, from the social soil in which he has grown. Many of his cherished values have been devalued, but even more discouraging to him has been the painful realization that much of his customary independent behavior has been paralyzed. The small businessman, in a word, has generally found it difficult to see or understand that an advanced industrial system is incompatible with the structure, status, and class system of pre-industrial society.[3] The individual today, unlike the heralded individual of the past, is likely to be, in Drucker's words, an employee in an impersonal system of mass production, receiving a pay check that his union has gotten for him from an employer he himself may never see. The small businessman's reaction to this and other similar developments of our time is to fight any tendencies toward the "welfare society," which he sees as threatening the total loss of individual liberty. Thus what is at issue for him is the enduring question of how the individualist creed of nineteenth-century democracy, with which he has long been identified, can be reconciled with both the collectivism of economic organization and the practices of a mass industrial democracy.

In the transformation of American capitalism from what Berle calls private business to public enterprise the whole basis of individualism itself has been changed until today it is the organization and not the individual alone that is central to our industrial system. As Drucker has pointed out, the industrial principle—the mass-production principle—is much more than a mechanical principle. It is a social principle, a prin-

[3] For a fuller treatment of this point, see Peter Drucker: op. cit.

ciple of *human* organization. It was not the organization of mechanical forces that was so revolutionary in Ford's plant, Drucker observes. It was the organization of human beings working together and performing a common task. This more than anything else explains the shattering impact of the new principle "on the relationship between man and society, and on the family." [4] The impact on the small businessman has been no less severe. Striving to maintain his position as an independent proprietor, he has been faced with the fact that the overwhelming trend of modern industrialism is to divorce the individual worker from his product to the point where to-day he can no longer produce by himself. He needs the tools and equipment of the modern plant, and the product that is finally turned out is not *his* work; it is a collective product that has been mass-produced. In the process the traditional society of pre-industrialism has been dissolved, and the individual entrepreneur has been dislodged from the more peaceful world of free and private enterprise.

To the small businessman, whose mode of living and entire outlook on life have always been synonymous with the freedom to do or become whatever he wants, organization by its very definition is considered a threat to everything he believes in. He scans the horizon of modern society and sees everywhere a proliferation of organizations, and to him their presence is not a blessing but a form of coercion that prohibits him from exercising his individual choice in all those matters in which he feels he has a direct concern. His strong attachment to an unfettered individualism has prevented him from seeing many of the positive effects that have accrued to the individual today as a consequence of the growth of corporations, trade unions, and other large-scale organizations. Part of the price one pays in joining any organization is the sacrifice of decision-making

[4] Ibid., p. 4.

at the individual, personal level, and the small businessman is usually unhappy about paying the price. He sees large aggregates of impersonal power dwarfing the individual, which is about all he sees. He calls it bureaucracy, stoutly opposes all forms of it, and attacks it with solemn regularity. It is an attitude that is reflected in his estimate of labor unions and the damage they purportedly cause the individual union member. Whatever benefits trade unions may have brought the workingman, most of them are offset in his mind by the feeling that, above everything else, the individual union member suffers a cruel loss of individuality and freedom in submitting to union discipline. It is often the big businessman who is able to perceive what the small businessman does not: that in an industrial age where organization and power predominate, where economic mobility as a road to success is declining, and where new independent enterprises are difficult to launch, bureaucratization generates sources of freedom for the individual which are denied those who remain outside any organized structure. Lipset and others have pointed out that bureaucracy, by establishing norms of fair and equal treatment, often reduces the arbitrary power which is characteristic of many non-bureaucratic organizations. Trade unions, in their imposing on the work situation a rational scheme of rules that protects the union member from the indiscriminate use of power by the employer, have significantly enlarged rather than diminished the meaning of freedom for the individual worker. "In many ways, the employee of a large corporation who is the subject of controversy between two giant organizations, the company and the union, has a much higher degree of freedom than has the man who does not work for such a large organization." [5]

[5] Seymour M. Lipset: *Stability in the Midst of Change,* reprint No. 142 of the Institute of Industrial Relations (Berkeley, Calif.: University of California; 1960), p. 37.

The small businessman has not really accepted the fact that the individual lives a more specialized life in the industrial society of the twentieth century or that he is more and more incapable of understanding—and controlling—*by himself* all the disturbances and complexities which are a part of his daily life. He has not understood that a person gains in rational insight when he joins a group or organization and actually acquires more control. For the small businessman it has been difficult to accept the idea that the individual can no longer live off his own resources as was perhaps his good fortune a hundred years ago, and that the advances of industrialism and mechanization have made the individual person, as a lone force in society, increasingly ineffective. In fact, an added touch of irony for the small businessman today is the realization that the individual union member probably carries more weight in our political affairs than the small shopkeeper or independent proprietor.[6]

Anything that appears to whittle away at the small businessman's prized independence is deeply resented, and very often his lament is both plaintive and shrill. The vice president of the National Federation of Independent Business sounded a typical and recurring note of bitterness in an address to a convention of independent bankers in which he pointed to the American farmer today—it could just as easily have been the

---

[6] I am indebted to Lloyd Fisher for many of these observations. Herbert Simon has dealt at length with this question—that is, the problem of man without an organization, or, more properly, the encounter between irrationality (man) and rationality (organization)—in his *Administrative Behavior* (New York: Macmillan; 1957); *Models of Man, Social and Rational* (New York: John Wiley & Sons; 1957); and, with James G. March, *Organizations* (New York: John Wiley & Sons; 1958). Since individuals by themselves are not capable of exercising a high degree of rationality in the modern world of buzzing confusion, rational choice, Simon argues, "can hardly exist without a theory of organization." *Models of Man,* p. 196.

small proprietor—as little less than a slave to one of the small businessman's major ogres, the perfidious chain store.

> He gets up in the morning, puts on his chain store pants and shirt, socks, shoes and cap. He picks up his chain store milk bucket and goes out to milk a subsidized cow. He pours the milk into a can that came from Sears Roebuck or Montgomery Ward, loads it into a truck tired by Sears Roebuck and run on Standard Oil gasoline. He sells the milk to National Dairy or Borden, and takes his money to Kroeger, or some other chain, and buys his food. His wife cooks it for him on a chain store stove and serves it with chain store utensils. After supper, instead of reading the Bible, he looks at the pictures of the pretty girls in the catalogue.
>
> Later, he crawls into his chain store bed, turns off his chain store radio, sets his chain store alarm clock, and rests his head on a chain store pillow. And do you know what Sears and Montgomery Ward have done to show their appreciation? They are printing their catalogues on slick paper.[7]

[7] Ed Wimmer: *Now or Never, Mr. Independent Banker,* an address delivered at the National Convention of the Independent Bankers Association of America at Detroit, Michigan, reprinted and distributed by the National Federation of Independent Business. On another occasion Mr. Wimmer made his point in this way: "In Redlands, California, there is a clothing merchant named Milton Gair, who has gained an international reputation as a fighter for independent business and ethics in business. Let me read you one of his ads: 'This institution was founded on the conviction that the economic health of every community in America would be bettered if thousands of men each owned his own business—keeping his profits where given—creating his own business policy—rather than having a few giant corporations thousands of miles away, owning thousands of stores, dictating management policy by remote control, continuously syphoning retail profits from where given, and under absentee ownership making colonies of every community they penetrate. We proudly claim that we do not undersell any one. Our merchandise is not made that way. We don't buy our suits by the carload. We hand pick them. A necktie is something more than to keep your neck warm. It should be an expression of your personality. Our kind of merchandise will never, never give you that cut-price look. We are proud of our kind of customers and our kind of goods.' A short time ago, Mr. Gair republished

Does the American farmer know what has happened to him? Does he know what he has done to his town, "his sons who might have started a little business in the neighborhood town and raised their families where he could enjoy his grandchildren, and watch them all become responsible, accountable citizens?" Of course not. He has no idea what he has done to himself "because the bankers, the grocers, the hardware men, and the rest of the independent business people of America have been sitting on their hands and remaining silent on the most momentous question ever to face a free people." In the opinion of this small business leader the trouble is that no one today knows the true meaning of the word "capitalist."

> I think we need to tell them that the little colored boy walking down the street in Alabama, looking up at a man on the street and saying, "Shine, sir?", is a capitalist in business for himself, on his own initiative. That he is just as much a capitalist as John D. Rockefeller ever was, in the true meaning of the word, and that men who own lawn mowers, or anything else they can say is their own, that they, too, are capitalists, and this is one of the stories we must tell while there is still time.[8]

---

an ad which was run by Sears Roebuck, in a statement by General R. A. Wood, of that big chain. Here is what General Wood said: 'Our one and only purpose is to bring quality merchandise at real savings. That is why we carry our own brands. In order to insure quality for Sears products we select the best makers of merchandise nationally advertised. . . . Then we give these manufacturers our orders during their slack season. It would not be good common sense for the maker of well known merchandise to allow us to sell his goods under his own nationally advertised name at our low prices. So, to protect his business, and, at the same time, give our customers real savings, we sell these products under our brands.' Now, which of these two advertisements would you select as being representative of the things that go into the building of a better community, a better nation? You've got to make up your mind on this question, and again I say, IT'S NOW OR NEVER." Wimmer: "Freedom Depends on Business Independence," pp. 12–13.

[8] Wimmer: *Now or Never, Mr. Independent Banker,* p. 19.

But it is now or never, he warns.

> Again I repeat, it isn't important what happens to me. Personally, I am willing to scratch with the chickens, wash dishes in a restaurant, or do anything else in case of a depression, but I want my kids to have an education. I want to help them to become accountable, responsible citizens in this community and nation. And when my boy walks down the street holding the hand of a girl, I want him to be able to look at a vacant store and say: "Here we will build our future." [9]

Yet the small businessman is not very confident of the future because whatever hopes for himself he may have are dimmed by his nostalgia for the vanished simplicity of an earlier time and his distrust of the forbidding structures of large corporate enterprises that virtually run modern society. The entrepreneurial capitalism of liberal economics, which measured a man's worth almost solely by the goods he produced and the profits he made, has been replaced by a new principle of industrial capitalism that is becoming an integral part of the creed of many contemporary big businessmen: that men and not just money, services and not just goods, must be the concern of enlightened corporate managers who are responsible not only for the nation's economic soundness but for governing a new "social system" which will foster human values that ultimately will enrich the lives of workers and owners alike, as well as everyone else. *Fortune* magazine, already alert to the collective implications of modern industrialism, has stated the dilemma of the small businessman acutely:

> In the age of the professional manager, what does it take to be an entrepreneur? Habitually, Americans praise the man who starts and runs his own business, the man who "works for himself." He is admired for his daring, his initiative, his rugged individualism. Yet many who praise him wonder if

[9] Ibid., p. 21.

his virtues have not become just a little anachronistic: fine once, but somewhat out of joint with the temper of the times. Question: To survive, doesn't he have to become more like the professional manager? Or does he flourish by remaining different? [1]

As contrasted with the former society of free and equal individuals competing in harmony against one another in the name of the common good, or of individuals pursuing with few restraints their own selfish ends—whichever description is preferred (and very often the two were the same)—today's society has seen the qualities of acquisitiveness and rational self-interest challenged not simply by Marxist dreamers or other self-styled dreamers but by many practical, hardheaded big business leaders whose more farseeing vision has compelled them to acknowledge that individual egoism and desire, whatever their virtues in the past, cannot be elevated above the social needs of the present. They have also recognized that our industrialized capitalist economy is made up in large part of enormous power groups constantly struggling with each other, a struggle which necessitates the careful scrutiny and increasing intervention of the government to mitigate the conflicts. They may not be happy with this situation, but a great many of them are prepared to live with it if for no other reason than that they accept the facts of life. In contrast, the small businessman feels virtually helpless before the agglomeration of huge corporations, with their mass advertising and high-powered salesmanship trained on him by a wide assortment of efficient groups. Just as nature was unintelligible to primitive man and his feelings of anxiety arose from the incalculability of the forces of nature, so it can be said without too much exaggeration that for the small businessman today "the incalculability of the forces at work in the social system under which he

[1] "The Entrepreneurial Ego," *Fortune* (August 1956), p. 100.

lives, with its economic crises, inflation and so on, has become a source of equally pervading fears." [2]

In spite of the steady advance of bigness and organization it is still the fashion, certainly the political fashion, to point to the small businessman and the small enterprise as the life blood of our economic system. Senator John Sparkman, chairman of the Select Committee on Small Business, voices the sentiment of every officeholder and office seeker in proclaiming that small business concerns "are and always have been the foundation of our capitalist system." [3] Whatever the merits of this argument may have been in the past—and there were many—the legendary virtues of small businessmen, no matter how poignantly they are extolled, are likely to be irrelevent to a realistic appraisal of our present social order. It is big businessmen far more than small businessmen who occupy the central positions of power and influence in the country, demonstrating clearly, no matter how one may feel about it, that we live in a highly developed capitalist system which no longer bears much resemblance to the individualist democracy of an-

[2] Karl Mannheim: *Man and Society in an Age of Reconstruction* (New York: Harcourt, Brace; 1951), p. 59. "The petty entrepreneurs, who direct their own tiny individual economic units, the small shopkeeper and the artisan, whose enemies are technical invention and large-scale production, have a quite different attitude towards further industrialization and rationalization. To maintain their independence they must destroy the big concerns, the great factories, and the department stores. If they were to have things their own way, technical rationalization would be brought to a standstill. Anyone who is at all capable of thinking in sociological terms knows that rationality cannot be suppressed in one sphere without causing a corresponding regression in the whole of man's cultural and spiritual life." Anyone who wants to return to the social and economic life of a bygone era, Mannheim observes, must also remold our whole outlook along such lines. "In order to save himself he must artificially arrest the whole process of social development which, impelled by technical rationality, is moving more and more rapidly towards further industrialization and large-scale organization." Ibid., p. 105.

[3] Statements of this sort can be found practically any place. This one appeared in a letter from the Senator in *Harper's Magazine* (July 1960).

other era, much less the economic philosophy of another century. Small business is on the periphery of modern society not only in this country, but in many of the industrialized nations of Europe as well. The small businessman lacks any deep roots because the security he wants for himself cannot be easily found in the declining world of individual proprietorship. Nor can the corporate structure of big business offer him any measure of security, since it is this very segment of the economy that has upset his traditional way of life and made his position so precarious. It is not too outrageous to say that the small businessman lives in the industrial world but does not belong to it. He is a man without a class, caught as he is in the squeeze between big business, big labor, and big government. It is a position of despair rather than hope because there are no clear avenues open to him that hold out the promise of improving his lot. Where industrial workers and many others can turn to organizations to help attain their ends, small businessmen are reluctant to join forces, since their temper as well as the nature of their individual enterprises and the long hours they put into them make it difficult for them to join together to use collective means. Furthermore, many small businessmen and a great many of those who speak for them are unhappy about the growing dependence on the government on the part of those they distastefully refer to as "special interest" groups. Small businessmen are frequently told that they can perhaps seek tax equity when the issue is one of survival, but they should not join the mob that goes to Washington demanding special treatment.

Historically this has been a nation of entrepreneurs—fiercely independent businessmen, proud of their self-reliance, their ability to accomplish miracles against overwhelming odds, their competitive spirit, and their single-mindedness of purpose. Now, however, aided and abetted by politicians who have placed the aura of motherhood around small business, many of the qualities which made for successful enterprise seem to be diminishing.[4]

The small businessman, in conflict with so much of the modern world, does not really know where to turn. He may blame the government in Washington, but a greater danger is that, in his frustration, he may turn to extremist anti-democratic movements in response to a yearning for vigorous action that will set things right once and for all.

It is no longer a revelation that the right-wing Poujadists in France, the neo-Fascists in Italy, the Nazi movement in Germany, and McCarthyism in this country all received heavy support from small businessmen.[5] Almost thirty years ago Harold Lasswell described how the small proprietors of the lower middle class, along with many others who found themselves pushed and pulled by the industrial workers on one side and the powerful industrialists on the other, turned to Hitler when he promised to protect them from the harshnesses of industrialism.[6] It was a stirring appeal and the small businessman responded, but it was also an empty promise. Hitler had no intention, once in power, of curbing Germany's industrial growth. The small merchants in France, deeply resentful of the power of big business and the large industrial unions for reaping all of the rewards of modern industrialization, looked to Poujade to put a stop to it and make it possible once again for the entrepreneur to run his business and live his life free

[4] Paul Donham: "Whither Small Business?" *Harvard Business Review* (March–April 1957), p. 81.

[5] Statistical data in support of this observation can be found in Seymour M. Lipset: *Political Man* (New York: Doubleday; 1960), Chapter v; and in William Kornhauser: *The Politics of Mass Society* (Glencoe, Ill.: Free Press; 1959), Chapter xi. I have drawn on both of these works here.

[6] Harold D. Lasswell: "The Psychology of Hitlerism," *Political Quarterly*, IV (1933), pp. 373–84.

from the coercions of governmental bureaucracy. Of the fifty-two Poujadists elected in 1956, twenty-six were merchants and twenty-four more were either artisans or heads of small or medium-sized enterprises.[7] Thus it has been the marginal elements of the middle class in France who, besides their resistance to concentration and specialization and to the rationalization of business enterprise that has accompanied the advance of modern capitalism, have also been most impatient with many of the political features of contemporary society, which they view as long on parliamentary discussion but short on decisive action that will bring immediate results. Kornhauser makes the important point that the anti-democratic responses of small businessmen in Nazi Germany were a reaction not so much to the *crisis* of industrial capitalism, which was the case with white-collar employees who were not marginal to large-scale enterprise, but to the *order* of industrial capitalism itself. The observation applies to small businessmen and their support of "radical" movements in other countries equally well, including the United States.

The sources of support given the late Senator McCarthy in this country have commanded the attention of a number of social scientists who have been interested in determining the nature of American right-wing movements and their potential for permanence on the political scene.[8] A study conducted in Bennington, Vermont, in 1954 showed that those who strongly approved of McCarthy were the ones who were most hostile to the political, economic, and social direction of our present society, with small businessmen first in both respects.[9] While there was considerable support for McCarthy among white-

[7] Quoted in Kornhauser: op. cit., p. 205.

[8] See especially Daniel Bell (ed.): *The New American Right* (New York: Criterion Books; 1955).

[9] Martin Trow: "Small Business, Political Tolerance, and McCarthy," *American Journal of Sociology* (November 1958), pp. 270–81.

collar people in every educational category, there was a good deal more among small businessmen in particular, no matter what level of formal education they had completed. Small businessmen who had not gone to college were much more pro-McCarthy than manual workers of a similar educational background. Among the groups who had gone to college, the support of McCarthy by small businessmen was stronger than among salaried employees. The figures below tell the story: [1]

SUPPORT FOR MCCARTHY BY OCCUPATION AND EDUCATION

	Less than 4 years of High School			High School Graduates			Some College and More		
	Man.*	Sal.*	S.B.*	Man.	Sal.	S.B.	Man.	Sal.	S.B.
Favor McCarthy's Methods	53%	38%	65%	49%	36%	58%	32%	22%	32%

* "Man.": manual workers; "Sal.": salaried employees; "S.B.": small businessmen, including merchants and other small proprietors.

It is significant that in interpreting these findings Professor Trow rejected a number of hypotheses often advanced to explain the actions of small businessmen, one of them being the notion that they identify with and take on the values of big businessmen, which are also the values of the radical right. He concluded that their heavy support of McCarthy arose from the fact that "small businessmen in our society disproportionately tend to develop a generalized hostility toward a complex of symbols and processes bound up with industrial capitalism." Specifically, he refers to a number of tendencies characterizing our contemporary social order which we have previously indicated are resented by small businessmen—"the steady growth and concentration of government, labor organizations, and business enterprises; the correlative trend toward greater rationalization of production and distribution; and the

[1] Ibid., p. 274.

men, institutions, and ideas that symbolize these secular trends of modern society." [2] It is further confirmation that small businessmen, isolated from the cultural sophistication, or "cosmopolitanism," of our time, project their grievances and insecurities into the political arena and thereby reaffirm the provincialism of their outlook and the intemperateness of their mood.

The bitterness of the small businessman makes him receptive to a variety of political appeals that provide more emotional release than intellectual substance. The independent proprietor, who for many years enjoyed a measure of influence and prominence in his local community, today has neither. Just as the small enterprises in the smaller cities are now owned and controlled by the big corporations in the large cities, so the small businessman himself feels controlled by the big industrialists who wield their influence from plush offices in New York or Chicago or San Francisco. In his anger at a modern world that has brought him little but declining prestige and power, the small businessman is likely to be swift in his response to ideological attacks on big business and, of course, big unions. The Bennington study showed that small businessmen, more than either salaried employees or manual workers, are hostile to both, reflecting again a generalized fear of the dominant currents of present-day society. Unlike those who are reconciled to the continued existence of big companies and trade unions—and are represented in both the Republican and Democratic Parties—small businessmen are considerably more susceptible to a political orientation which, as Trow has said, has no institutionalized place on the political scene and little representation or leadership in the major parties. Therefore they sought that voice and place through McCarthy

[2] Loc. cit.

who "expressed for them their fear and mistrust of bigness and of the slick and subversive ideas that come out of the cities and the big institutions to erode old ways and faiths." [3]

The mistrust of bigness by the small businessman not only reflects his general hostility to the principal direction of modern industrialism, but is also an expression of his long-standing conviction that our antitrust laws are the guardians of the American way of life. Republicans and Democrats alike are fully aware that in appealing to the small businessman they must advocate a program of trust busting as the way to protect him from the evils of big business. They know that suspicion of bigness has been a strong feature in our political history and are more than willing to attack—the language may vary but the message is loud and clear—the powerful influences inside and outside the government that are exerting great pressure to scuttle the Sherman Act, the Clayton Act, the Robinson-Patman Act, and any other laws which are seen as the remaining bulwark of our free-enterprise system. To the small businessman the one escape from the danger of great masses of people becoming more and more dependent upon large corporations and, in turn, on the big trade unions is to return to a system of widespread independent ownership of farm, home, and business enterprise. "Our recommendations," the vice president of the National Federation of Independent Business has declared, "are that we unwind the whole show; that we put every bank and every corporation in this country back on its own feet again where Jefferson, Lincoln and Andrew Jackson would ask that they be put, if they were alive today." [4]

The feelings of small businessmen on this matter deserve

[3] Ibid., p. 276.

[4] Ed Wimmer: *Now or Never, Mr. Independent Banker*, p. 9. I have relied on many of Mr. Wimmer's comments because they are a clear statement of the small businessman's attitude on this question.

some attention because they represent a point of view that has become one of the cardinal tenets of their political faith. To restore freedom of opportunity and representative government in this country is, in their opinion, the only remaining course that has a chance of becoming a universal pattern for free men throughout the world. To produce an economy founded on the principle that no nation is free unless its economy promotes a maximum of small enterprises and a minimum of power in the hands of the few requires a decentralization program that will not compromise with the principles involved, and to the small businessman this means the participation of the greatest number of people, as independent individuals, in the production and distribution of goods and services. As far as he is concerned, big business must either voluntarily unwind itself into a system of independent companies or be forced to unwind under government supervision. Who are the ones who must lead the fight against big business? They are the small hardware men, the small grocers, the furniture men, "all the men of Main Street" who are still running their businesses, who believe that "the only answer to Communism is in a better idea, the American idea that Washington and Jefferson believed it to be," and who are ready to tell the rest of the world about the Sermon on the Mount, the Declaration of Independence, the Constitution, and the Bill of Rights.

The small businessman's intense dislike of communism has led him to view its spread throughout the world in very narrow terms. The president of the National Federation of Independent Business has explained the Russian revolution with the argument that for generations the individual Russian had little opportunity to engage in free enterprise. Every nation that has gone communist, he says, did not have antitrust laws, which is to say that when the people of these nations rebelled against the concentration of economic power "they

went either to Communism or to its half-brother, Socialism."
With this in mind he insists that certain prestigious people in
America today are actively engaged in cultivating communism.

> They are not only the poor warriors that parade on May
> Day with clenched fists and carrying real cards. Those doing
> the most in preparing the seedbed for the harvest of Com-
> munism are found holding office in government, finance and
> industry.
> More potential Communism is spawned within the wal-
> nut panelled luxury of offices where monopoly procedure
> and protection are devised, than in a grubby cell head-
> quarters in the skid-row section of some city.
> Whether these people are activated by malicious greed,
> by fear or stupidity, it makes little difference. They are as
> much assassins of the American system as a Bolshevik.[5]

It is at this juncture, as we have suggested, that the views
of small businessmen and big businessmen need most to be
weighed in order to appraise their respective responses to the
particular demands of our advanced industrial order. In this
regard there is a question which perhaps comes as close as any
other to raising one of the crucial issues of our time: Is bigness
in itself a necessary evil? Or, stated another way, can bigness
be used for positive good and put to the service of a democratic
mass society? It seems unlikely that small businessmen are in
a position, either ideologically or economically, to provide the
necessary answers. David Lilienthal, who claims that the program of trust busting in behalf of the small businessman is fu-
tile, also feels that it is a social evil that might threaten national
security and deprive the nation of all the goods and services
from which it benefits daily. No amount of nostalgia for the
good old days, he warns, can change the fact that small busi-

[5] C. Wilson Harder: *Monopoly Breeds Communism,* pamphlet distributed by the National Federation of Independent Business.

ness today is not the norm and that big business is the driving force of our economic life.[6]

This is not the place to review the diversity of ideas which have been advanced to deal with the problem of corporate power in our economy or to evaluate the various remedies proposed by business executives, political scientists, economists, and lawmakers.[7] Our concern is with the attitude of small businessmen who look upon bigness, whether it be in business, labor, agriculture, or the government, as a serious threat to individual freedom across the board. In their unceasing demand for the vigorous enforcement of the antitrust laws to preserve local, independent, owner-operated small enterprises, they have found themselves in conflict with both the logic and direction of our industrial system. In keeping with the nineteenth-century liberal outlook they have demanded the suppression of concentrated economic power wherever and whenever they have found it.[8] Fifty or sixty years ago, when monopolies were relatively scarce and free competition in the marketplace was still the pervading norm, such demands may have served some useful purpose. But today concentrated economic power is not the exception but the rule of our economic system. The business corporation which Brandeis distrusted and condemned as socially unhealthy and economically wasteful has become the nucleus of our economic way of life. As Galbraith has said, the ancient liberal formula of trust busting has been dealt a serious blow, for while it is possible to prose-

[6] David Lilienthal: op. cit., p. 6.

[7] For an extended analysis along these lines see Theodore J. Kreps: "Types of Attitudes towards Corporate Giantism," in *Proceedings of the Thirty-Second Annual Conference of the Western Economic Association* (1959).

[8] For an analysis of varying approaches to this question, see John H. Bunzel: "Liberal Ideology and the Problem of Power," *Western Political Quarterly* (June 1960).

cute a few evil-doers, it is not so practical to indict a whole economy. "To suppose that there are grounds for anti-trust prosecution wherever three, four, or a half dozen firms dominate a market is to suppose that the very fabric of American capitalism is illegal. This is a notion which can seem sensible only to the briefless lawyer." [9] The small businessman, however, fearful of communism slipping through the back door, looks upon the antitrust laws as our only real fortress. He is convinced that, unless there is an immediate showdown with the "cannibalism of monopoly," the generation of Americans now developing may very easily be forced into the slavery of industry solely because there will be no opportunities left for the starting of any venture on Main Street or the continuation of existing small businesses. The antitrust laws "are the real weapons of Democracy and those who seek to destroy them deserve no more consideration from their fellow citizens than any other wartime saboteur." [1] Their feelings run deep on this subject because they believe nothing less than a thoroughgoing economic reorganization of the economy matched by "a spiritual mobilization the likes of which has never been witnessed anywhere else in the world" are necessary to make "this America of ours the land of the free and the home of the brave, and not the land of the chain and the home of the slave." [2]

This is heady stuff, but like the preaching of the antitrust laws themselves, it does little more than reassure the virtuous that evil is under attack. Thurman Arnold, who was a vigorous head of the Antitrust Division of the Justice Department in the 1930's, claimed that the actual result of these laws "was to

[9] J. K. Galbraith: *American Capitalism* (London: Hamish Hamilton; 1952), p. 58.
[1] C. Wilson Harder: op. cit.
[2] Ed Wimmer: *Now or Never, Mr. Independent Banker*, p. 14.

promote the growth of great industrial organizations by deflect-
ing the attack on them into purely moral and ceremonial chan-
nels." Whenever concentrated economic power has become the
whipping boy of politicians whose public mission is to defend the free-enterprise system, the cry has been for tougher
enforcement of the antitrust laws rather than a program leading toward more effective techniques of control. "The antitrust
laws, being a preaching device, naturally performed only the
functions of preaching"[3]—and meanwhile "bigness" in business, reflecting the practical need for large-scale organization
in an industrial society, has grown steadily bigger.

A serious danger for any society is confusion about the
nature and implications of existing institutions and practices.
On the question of antitrust policy itself, small businessmen
are not unequivocal in their support. While many of them unquestionably owe their existence to the benefits they have derived from this policy, others have wanted less competition
than the combination of economic forces and antitrust policy
imposed on them. Unable through their own resources to
achieve the kind of market restraint often gained by larger businesses, small businesses have turned to governmental assistance
in seeking to eliminate price competition. Yet any such program necessarily implied a substantial breach in antitrust
policy. "Small businessmen themselves seldom advocated an
end to competition in general," it has been pointed out. "It was
only the competition immediately confronting them that they
wished to attack; elsewhere it was to be supported."[4]

[3] Thurman Arnold: *The Folklore of Capitalism* (New Haven, Conn.:
Yale University Press; 1937), pp. 211–12.
[4] Merle Fainsod, Lincoln Gordon, and Joseph P. Palamountain, Jr.:
Government and the American Economy (New York: W. W. Norton;
1959), p. 568. For a detailed review of some of the more technical problems of small business in our economy, particularly what is called "the retreat from competition," see Chapter xvii. The authors close their discus-

The truth about our economy has too often been obscured by the romantic visions of those who clamor for a free competitive economy whereby decisions will be made through the mechanism of a free market. Their invective against the predominant features of our corporate society serves to perpetuate many irrational appeals to political values and economic conditions which characterized our early history but which no longer exist. All of the testimonials to the creative potential of small business do not alter the fact that our political and social institutions today have been shaped by the economic structure we have developed in the last sixty years. Moreover, there has been no sustained or effective opposition to this development on the part of the American people, and no important organized group has used its political power to work for a restoration of an older version of free enterprise.

Professor George Stocking has presented a minimum agenda of what would have to be done if we really wanted to dismantle our present institutional structure and begin anew with a truly competitive economy:

(1) Revise our patent laws so as to give venture capital easier access to modern technology.

(2) Prohibit mergers so as to make business firms as small and numerous as is consistent with the economies of mass production.

---

sion with the following comments: "Granted that there are compelling reasons, political, social, and economic, for the preservation of small business, it can be argued that the public interest will be better served by affirmative assistance than by legislation which restricts competition and perpetuates inefficiencies and waste. Small businesses typically do not possess the managerial skills, technical information, research facilities, access to highly qualified outside counsel, and financial resources generally available to larger corporations. This lack is now increasingly, but unevenly, met by trade associations, chambers of commerce, state and federal Departments of Commerce, and the Small Business Administration. Assistance of this type could be substantially broadened. Competitive policy, while inhibiting the predatory and the restrictive, might more properly strengthen the weak than hobble the able and strong."

(3) Require federal incorporation for firms the assets of which exceed a specified minimum and which do business in interstate commerce, and limit the use of the holding corporation.

(4) Supply more adequate funds for the enforcement of antitrust. Eternal vigilance is the price of liberty.

(5) Curb labor monopolies. Specifically, prohibit industry-wide bargaining. The ideal unit of bargaining would probably be the firm and the size of the firm would be limited in accordance with the principle set forth under (2) above.

(6) Lower tariffs.

(7) Through monetary and fiscal policies, stabilize the general price structure; but leave individual prices to seek competitive levels and perform their proper function of allocating resources and distributing income.

(8) Curb monopolies of prestige created by advertising where the main effect is to increase costs by diverting customers from one product to a substantially similar product. This might involve limiting or taxing advertising expenditures, government grading to prevent misleading advertising, or service by a Bureau of Standards like that of Consumers' Research.[5]

T. K. Quinn, lamenting the major changes which have moved us "from a nation of small capitalists into a nation of hired employees," would begin with a planned program of decentralization of our large corporations.[6] Whatever may be the attraction of one scheme or another for those who want a return to the "democracy of smaller units," there is no serious likelihood that we will turn our efforts to changing the whole economic foundation of American society. And even if it were feasible it is not entirely clear that it would be desirable.

In our economy, as Kaplan and others have consistently

[5] George W. Stocking: "The Effectiveness of the Federal Antitrust Laws: A Symposium," *American Economic Review* (June 1949), pp. 719–20.

[6] T. K. Quinn: *Giant Business—Threat to Democracy* (New York: Exposition Press; 1953).

stressed, it is big business which undertakes the major role of co-ordinating individual efforts and resources into collective achievement. Furthermore, under modern technology it is a function which *must* be undertaken, whether by private corporate power or by the state.[7] It may very well be that in the years to come the government will assume a larger role in the planning and regulation of our enormous economic resources not only to make the most efficient use of our productive capacity, but to make certain that political power does not become the handmaiden of economic power. In any event the collective enterprise, whether it be the corporation or the government or some viable combination of the two, will play not a smaller but a larger role in the years ahead. Berle has said that a system like ours "is just as good as the ideas and strength of the body politic behind it. The same system in the hands, for example, of a Latin American dictator could produce terrible oppression."[8] In other words, a fundamental task of highest priority is to devise both a doctrine and a practice that will make it possible to control the power we have created. It seems unlikely that the voice of small businessmen, based on what has been heard from them up to now, will carry a great amount of weight in the resolution of this problem.

The small businessman, who, paradoxically, talks as if he had a monopoly of his own on the prescription for preserving individual freedom, approaches many of today's problems in the light of what he would prefer the world to be like if he could push a button and start all over again. But the temper of big businessmen is again strikingly different, not because their motives are more noble or their interest in making money less acute, but because they are impelled for the most practical

[7] A. D. H. Kaplan: *Big Enterprise in a Competitive System* (Washington, D.C.: The Brookings Institution; 1954), p. 248.

[8] A. A. Berle, Jr.: *Economic Power and the Free Society.*

reasons to look at the present situation as it actually exists and to consider what can and cannot be done about it. For one thing, they look upon bigness as more creative and considerate of human needs than smallness. In terms of individual freedoms—and it is important to emphasize that small businessmen continually talk only about *freedom*—many big businessmen feel that never before has so much been done to provide the individual worker with the necessities and in many cases the luxuries of modern living. Only large organizations, they would claim, can make year-round agreements with their employees, guarantee annual wages and medical provisions, and maintain decent retirement funds. It may still be a debatable point whether big or small business is more economically efficient, but there seems little reason to doubt that large organizations are far more prepared to take an imaginative approach to the long-range future and have a realistic appreciation of the need, for example, to conserve the country's supply of raw materials. As we have previously noted, it is small business that is more intent on making a fast dollar and most likely to take a "buccaneering view" of the nation's treasures. The owner-operator, whose interests are bound up essentially with the welfare of the local community and with the profits he can make in the immediate present, has less understanding of the economic system as a whole than is found in the big businessman.

Still another distinctive feature of the small businessman's ideological perspective is his paradoxical combination of extreme faith in individualism in business and his customary role as an inveterate joiner in his own home town. He is the foundation of the service club, the fraternal orders, the Chamber of Commerce, and the veterans' posts, and through these he does good for the community on a vast scale, raising funds for the blind, the crippled children, and so on. He can thus fulfill his social obligations through civic and service clubs which function apart from his business. But any thought that business itself is a social instrument which might be used to discharge some social or non-business responsibility is foreign to his thinking, and anyone advocating such a radical idea would be looked upon with suspicion.

The small businessman has not been able to appreciate the compelling need to redefine contemporary American politics in terms of group rights as well as individual liberties. He has clung to a host of popular phrases—"the land of individualism," "free private enterprise," "the American Dream"—as if they applied with equal relevance to an industrial capitalist economy as they might have applied to the democracy of the nineteenth century. The truth is that they are of little use in helping to recognize those continuing structural changes which require a re-evaluation of democratic methods and goals. In contrast, a growing number of big businessmen have learned that democracy can no longer be measured exclusively in economic terms or defined simply as liberty of contract. They have realized many of the implications of an important development which small businessmen have not to this day fully understood: that the pure and perfect market society, if it ever existed at all, has been transformed into a politically managed economy in which, as Daniel Bell has observed, the distinction between the "sum total of individual decisions" and the "social decision" is more than a semantic one. Small businessmen have failed to grasp the degree to which an administered economy imposes a particular type of dependency upon everyone. Big businessmen, however, have realized that the political, economic, and social world in which they operate is in many important respects similar to a "collective" economy in the sense of being a whole, interdependent system. This does not mean that important spokesmen for the big business community no longer subscribe to the symbols of the age of individualism or that leading business journals or Chambers of Commerce have suddenly discarded their traditional belief that expanding governmental activity is a sinister force that can only lead to socialism. The regular torrent of words dedicated to the elevation of rugged individualism as the businessman's cult is still useful in a variety of ways. For one thing, as Charles Adrian has pointed out, it seeks to preserve and perpetuate the essentially unnatural alliance of friendship between big and small business. For another, the language of individualism, in addition to seeking to prevent the adoption of proposals that would lead to increased governmental intervention in private business, promotes public goodwill by using meaningless but immensely reassuring symbols to which all pay lip service whether they live by them or not.

> Yet, the big-business bureaucrat, in contrast to the small-business proprietor, has no strong motivation to fight the social service state. Organized labor is not his problem— unless he serves in the industrial relations department— and big business has by and large accepted the existence of big labor and feels able to live with it. . . . Because he must conform to the expectations of his bureaucracy, he will likely speak in traditional individualist terms, but he has far less incentive to take political action in support of these views than has the small businessman.[9]

This different orientation of small business and big business helps explain, at least in part, why the small businessman is so hostile to the present and despairing of the future, just as it helps explain why the big businessman is more self-confident and optimistic.

[9] Charles R. Adrian: *State and Local Governments* (New York: McGraw-Hill; 1960), pp. 69–70.

2

Like death and taxes, the small businessman will always be with us, if only to serve as a reminder that his own life expectancy as a free enterpriser is growing shorter. The burden of the argument presented in these pages, reduced to its barest essentials, is that the preservation of democracy, liberty, and freedom in America is no longer dependent upon the survival of small business. Whether there is agreement with this statement or not, it is important that there be no confusion about its meaning. No claim is made that small business is a detriment to our way of life or that small businessmen have no place in our future. The contention, rather, is that small business is not, today, the basis of our economic system and that the growth of large business units is neither the death blow to a free society nor the inevitable road to socialism. There remains, then, the question of what place small business will have in our industrial society in the years to come. While no complete or perhaps even satisfactory answer can be given here, a number of concluding observations can be advanced which may suggest at least the growing difficulties which will beset the small businessman and some of the questions of public policy which will have to be weighed.

Small businesses outnumber all other forms of enterprise, but they are also a declining influence in our society. No matter how it is scrambled, this remains a statement of fact. Politicians in and out of season may come to the rescue of small businessmen with promises of aids and subsidies as well as vigorous pronouncements in behalf of decimating the giants, but no amount of governmental action is going to enhance the small businessmen's position, transform them into a dominant force, or arrest what is indisputably a high mortality rate. It has been estimated that only one of every five small businesses will survive a full decade and that the great majority last but seven years. In a normal year over 300,000 go out of business and approximately 400,000 more are sold or transferred to someone else. In the shadow of these statistics is still another: 400,000 pin their hopes each year to the American Dream and take a flyer at being small and independent. Most of these self-styled businessmen have no business going into business, since they not only have insufficient capital but are lacking in training and experience. They do not know very much about the market into which they are entering, frequently cannot be bothered to keep records, and would not recognize a constructive management plan if one were handed them. Taxes are high and profits are low, which means the local banks, taking a dim view of the small businessman's chances for survival, are reluctant to stake him to his dubious venture. When the conventional sources of credit dry up, the Small Business Administration is called upon annually to disperse hundreds of thousands of dollars to stem the tide of small business failures, but these business and disaster loans have met with little permanent success. George S. Odiorne, who is a professor at the University of Michigan's School of Business, makes the point that the small businessman has today acquired a privileged position in Washington comparable to the farmer's—but with an important difference.

The farmer is subsidized for hardships resulting from superior ability to produce. In most instances the small businessman is shored up with tax money because of his incompetence in management. And the present pattern of government aid does nothing constructive about converting a losing small business into a stable and profitable one. The Small Business Investment Companies [created by Congress in 1959 and operating under the supervision of the Small Business Administration] in fact merely assuage symptoms without getting at the underlying malady which is partly a matter of hard economics, partly the fruit of the small businessman's peculiar philosophy and limitations.[1]

There is one similarity between the farmer and the small businessman that is by way of being both an economic fact and a political hot potato: there are too many of both. The small businessman, whose economic position in our economy is marginal at best, is nonetheless important politically not only as a favored constituency in the eyes of Congress but as a significant numerical force—small business has upwards of 3,500,000 votes. Consequently governmental policy decisions affecting small business, made inevitably against the backdrop of political considerations, rarely focus on the harsh conditions which have made free entry into business a disastrous venture for countless thousands and have forced those who somehow manage to get started to accept an increasingly smaller and unprofitable share of the market. One result has been that small businessmen have fallen back upon an outmoded frontier individualism, exemplified by both their passionate defense of an older way of life and their expression of distrust of foreign ideologies, internationalism, cosmopolitanism, urbanism, collectivism, and almost everything else that comprises the world in which they must live.

The average small business, if one can talk in relative terms, is neither very efficient nor profitable. Those which do well do extremely well and also demonstrate a particularly high standard of efficiency, but these are still a small proportion and generally are not in competition with the greater efficiency of the mass-production industries. It is precisely this point which needs to be kept in mind when considering what to do with small business today. It has been almost an annual ritual in Congress

---

[1] George S. Odiorne: "How Small Business Cuts Its Throat," *Harper's Magazine* (April 1960), p. 47.

on both sides of the political aisle to rush to the aid of the small businessman with impressive sums of money on the grounds that he is especially needed to help preserve the middle class in the struggle against communism and thereby save our American Way of Life. Put this way, who in the political arena is going to argue that the price tag is too high? "It is one thing to write a book pointing out the incredible waste involved in the way we deal with small business," a prominent legislator commented privately. "Most small businessmen don't read anyway. But they vote, and few of us here are going to commit political suicide by being unfriendly to them. It would be smarter to come out against the Fourth of July." If small business is to be aided and protected because it is viewed, almost reverently, as the mainstay of our economic system, there is no clear limit to the funds that one can demand in its behalf and no possible way of measuring logically the amount of assistance which can be afforded. If on the other hand it were recognized that our economy is one in which large-scale enterprise predominates and small enterprises will remain important primarily in those areas where it is not feasible for large firms to move in and take control, then it would be possible to look at the problem of small business in less emotional and flag-waving terms. For example, it has been pointed out that in many of the rural areas there is a place for small firms which may or may not be efficient but which supply a small-scale local need. There are many accessories which can be made by small firms and supplied to large ones, and small businesses often make satisfactory distributors. "But it is absurd," Professor Richard Osborn remarks, "to envision small firms as attaining a dominant position or to conclude that their practices will have a major determining influence on the large firms." [2] Viewed in this light, small busi-

[2] Richard C. Osborn: "The Plea for Small Business," *The Accounting Review* (October 1951), pp. 10, 18. Professor Osborn has presented an

ness should be maintained as a part of our economy if it meets one essential condition: that it performs a useful function. Basically, hope for the great majority of small businesses lies in a high level of employment and national income, which will increase the value of their sales to the point where a sufficient proportion of their capacity will be utilized to keep them in business. It remains one of the ironies of our day that most of the political measures which could most help to advance these necessary economic and social conditions are the very ones to which small businessmen generally are bitterly opposed.[3]

Clark Kerr has written that the world is currently witnessing the greatest ideological struggle of all history—the ideological struggle over how best to organize industrial society. At bottom the issue is twofold: how should responsible power—the authority to make decisions—be distributed in our modern pluralistic society, and how can the American industrial system best preserve and augment the freedom of its individual members in the face of large-scale organizations? Many big businessmen have already suggested an answer by claiming that the

---

extremely able and thoughtful review of specific forms of economic aid to small business today. It should be pointed out that after analyzing the dearth of equity capital for small business, the problems of raising loan money, the implications of recent tax adjustments, and the potential forms of legislative assistance, he is not hopeful about the prospects for shoring up this segment of our economy. "The impression may have been gained," he says at the conclusion of his essay, "that the writer feels there are very distinct limits within which small business can be assisted. This is a correct impression."

[3] Ibid., p. 18. Ernest G. Draper has observed that "an amazing amount of hokum, excited arguments and wild conclusions" have filled the air any time the problem of small business is discussed, "with little sustained effort to study in a realistic setting or arrive at conclusions that bear some relation to the background of proven facts." The truth is that "everyone seems ready to die for little business but few are willing to sit down and work out constructive proposals that are in line with reality. This is another way of saying that there has been a great deal of maudlin discussion about the present and future of smaller business and only a modest amount of anything else." Weissman: op. cit., Introduction, p. ix.

welfare corporation is prepared to assume the necessary leadership to advance the needs of the country. But there is nothing in our commitment to democracy that implies that big business should be vested with either the power or prestige to organize society on its own terms.[4] Small businessmen admittedly contribute little by their repeated denunciations of any form of "collectivizing" society, but this is no reason to permit or encourage a pyramiding of this complex collective process on big business. To do so might eventually lead the public to accept big business as an elite best qualified to foster the values and purposes of our democracy, when in fact the potential richness of our industrial society might be better achieved by depriving the economic sector of its present role in influencing and in many cases deciding major public policies in terms of what is favorable to its own interests. If our pluralistic society is to be preserved it will need a diversity of expertise and leadership.

It is clear that the American people have some important choices to make about the future direction of our society and the dispersal of power within it. It is also clear that the small businessman is many steps removed from the central problems arising out of a social order far more complicated than he is willing to admit or able to accept. His fears, misgivings, and doubts, expressed in moralism and skepticism, prevent his being able to provide a positive program which might in any sense answer our present needs. As a result he can do little more than oppose the main drift of current events. Small businessmen claim to be the cornerstone of American democracy, but it is doubtful if they can be counted upon to furnish imaginative and constructive leadership. There is little reason to assume, on the basis of their current performance, that they possess the qualities necessary to guide a great democracy in a time of crisis.

[4] See Theodore Levitt: "The Dangers of Social Responsibility," *Harvard Business Review* (September–October 1958).

APPENDIX
BIBLIOGRAPHY
INDEX

TABLE 1

Growth of United States Business, 1951–9

INDUSTRY	1951	1953	1955	1956	1957	1958	1959	% GROWTH 1951–9
All industries	4067.3	4187.7	4286.8	4381.2	4470.7	4534.4	4589.2	12.8
Mining and quarrying	37.0	37.6	37.8	40.9	42.2	42.3	42.0	13.5
Contract construction	377.3	405.3	429.8	451.7	465.4	467.6	475.9	26.1
Manufacturing	322.8	330.7	326.1	327.3	332.3	333.0	331.0	2.5
Transportation, communication, and public utilities	180.7	192.2	193.4	200.1	208.4	209.5	211.8	17.2
Wholesale	268.6	283.1	291.9	296.9	303.7	310.9	317.0	18.0
Retail	1820.9	1846.1	1874.5	1903.2	1925.6	1947.8	1956.3	7.4
Finance, insurance, and real estate	326.9	342.8	359.5	371.5	383.0	393.3	403.3	23.4
Service	733.0	749.9	772.6	789.6	810.0	830.1	851.9	16.2

Column header: NUMBER OF FIRMS IN OPERATION (THOUSANDS)

SOURCE: Betty C. Churchill: "Rise in the Business Population," *Survey of Current Business*, XXXIX (May 1959), p. 18.

TABLE 2

EMPLOYMENT CLASSIFICATION BY SIZE AND INDUSTRY, 1956

INDUSTRY	% OF FIRMS WITHIN INDUSTRY HAVING			
	0–3 employees	more than 20	more than 100	more than 500
All industries	75.3	5.0	.9	.2
Mining and quarrying	62.1	11.9	2.3	.4
Contract construction	72.6	4.8	.5	*
Manufacturing	43.0	23.7	6.1	1.1
Transportation, communication, and public utilities	78.7	5.6	1.4	.4
Wholesale	61.9	7.4	.7	*
Retail	79.2	2.4	.2	*
Finance, insurance, and real estate	81.1	3.1	.7	.2
Service	83.1	2.8	.3	*

SOURCE: Betty C. Churchill: "Size of Business Firms," *Survey of Current Business*, XXXIX (September 1959) p. 16.
* Less than 0.05%.

TABLE 3

INCORPORATED AND UNINCORPORATED BUSINESS BY INDUSTRY, 1952

	Incorporated Numbers (thousands)	%	Unincorporated Numbers	%
All industries	526	12.8	3595	87.2
Mining and quarrying	9	23.7	29	76.3
Contract construction	29	7.4	365	92.6
Manufacturing	111	33.9	216	66.1
Transportation, communication, and public utilities	28	15.5	153	84.5
Wholesale	75	27.2	201	72.8
Retail	126	6.9	1711	93.1
Finance, insurance, and real estate	94	28.3	238	71.7
Service	54	7.3	681	92.7

SOURCE: Betty C. Churchill: "Business Population by Legal Form of Organization," *Survey of Current Business*, XXXV (April 1955), p. 18.

TABLE 4

BUSINESSES BY EMPLOYMENT SIZE AND LEGAL FORM OF ORGANIZATION, 1947

SIZE CLASS	A. WITHIN SIZE CLASS (%)				
	All Forms	Corpora-tions	Proprietor-ships	Partner-ships	Other
All Classes	100	11.3	69.8	17.0	1.9
0–3 employees	100	3.7	79.6	15.3	1.3
4–7	100	19.4	55.8	22.3	2.4
8–19	100	35.9	38.0	22.2	3.8
20–49	100	50.5	22.7	21.4	5.5
50–99	100	65.7	13.0	16.3	5.0
100 or more	100	82.6	3.1	10.7	3.6

SIZE CLASS	B. WITHIN TYPE OF ORGANIZATION (%)				
	All Forms	Corpora-tions	Proprietor-ships	Partner-ships	Other
All Classes	100	100	100	100	100
0–3 employees	73.5	24.0	83.8	66.4	52.4
4–7	13.1	22.6	10.5	17.3	17.0
8–19	8.2	25.9	4.4	10.7	16.6
20–49	3.2	14.3	1.0	4.1	9.3
50–99	1.1	6.1	.2	1.0	2.8
100 or more	1.0	7.0	*	.6	1.8

SOURCE: Betty C. Churchill: "Business Population by Legal Form or Organization," *Survey of Current Business*, XXXV (April 1955), p. 19.
* Less than 0.05%.

TABLE 5

CORPORATION ASSETS BY INDUSTRY, 1957–8

INDUSTRY	% OF CORPORATIONS HAVING	
	less than $250,000	more than $1,000,000
All industries	80.5	5.1
Mining and quarrying	67.6	11.3
Contract construction	83.5	3.8
Manufacturing	70.0	10.4
Transportation, communication, and public utilities	80.3	6.9
Wholesale	76.2	5.1
Retail	87.3	1.9
Service	89.6	2.2

SOURCE: *Corporation Income Tax Returns, Statistics of Income* (1957–8), pp. 41–66.

TABLE 6

EMPLOYMENT BY INDUSTRY DIVISION, 1948–56

INDUSTRY	NUMBER OF EMPLOYEES (THOUSANDS)		
	1948	*1951*	*1956*
All industries	36,475	38,390	40,667
Mining and quarrying	896	844	767
Contract construction	2,074	2,407	2,582
Manufacturing	15,864	16,820	17,661
Transportation, communication,			
and public utilities	4,115	4,119	4,094
Wholesale	1,985	2,212	2,414
Retail	7,097	7,430	7,914
Finance, insurance, and real			
estate	1,742	1,910	2,326
Service	2,702	2,649	2,910

SOURCE: Betty C. Churchill: "The Size Characteristics of the Business Population," *Survey of Current Business*, XXXIV (May 1954), pp. 22–3; and Churchill: "Size of Business Firms," *Survey of Current Business*, XXXIX (September 1959), p. 19.

TABLE 7

EMPLOYMENT CLASSIFICATION BY SIZE AND INDUSTRY, 1956

INDUSTRY	% OF EMPLOYMENT IN FIRMS HAVING			
	0–3 employees	*more than 20*	*more than 100*	*more than 500*
All industries	6.5	76.4	58.9	43.7
Mining and quarrying	2.7	84.0	63.2	42.8
Contract construction	11.6	56.7	27.6	10.8
Manufacturing	.9	93.3	79.1	60.4
Transportation, communication, and public utilities	2.3	91.2	83.0	72.8
Wholesale	7.4	60.2	29.4	14.2
Retail	14.7	51.8	32.6	24.2
Finance, insurance, and real estate	12.5	68.0	52.8	37.6
Service	15.8	54.5	28.7	12.4

SOURCE: Betty C. Churchill: "Size of Business Firms," *Survey of Current Business*, XXXIX (September 1959), p. 16.

TABLE 8

THE UPPER 1% OF FIRMS, 1956

INDUSTRY DIVISION	Number of firms	Lower size limit (employment)	Average size (employment)	% of total employment
Mining and quarrying	410	220	1,000	53.2
Contract construction	4,500	69	190	33.7
Manufacturing	3,300	570	3,200	58.8
Transportation, communication, and public utilities	2,000	150	1,600	80.4
Wholesale	3,000	84	260	32.1
Retail	19,000	36	180	43.4
Finance, insurance, and real estate	3,700	57	360	57.8
Service	7,900	46	150	40.1

SOURCE: Betty C. Churchill: "Size of Business Firms," *Survey of Current Business*, XXXIX (September 1959), p. 17.

TABLE 9

RETAIL ESTABLISHMENTS BY SALES SIZE, 1954

SALES SIZE	Number of firms	Sales by firms in sales class (thousands of $)
All retail establishments	1,721,650	$169,967,748
Operating all year:	1,614,504	162,508,375
with sales of		
more than $5 million	1,068	12,698,766
$2 million to $5 million	4,927	14,206,911
$1 million to $2 million	12,974	17,782,832
$500,000 to $1 million	30,122	20,787,448
$300,000 to $500,000	42,046	16,068,870
$100,000 to $300,000	231,230	37,512,849
$50,000 to $100,000	317,230	22,206,519
$30,000 to $50,000	287,192	11,095,921
$20,000 to $30,000	220,137	5,284,695
$10,000 to $20,000	252,491	3,617,821
$5,000 to $10,000	144,815	1,007,807
Less than $5,000	70,272	237,936
Not operating all year	107,146	7,459,373

SOURCE: *Census of Business, 1954*, Vol. I, *Retail Trade—Summary Statistics* (Washington, D.C.: U.S. Department of Commerce, Bureau of the Census; 1957), p. 2–2.

TABLE 10

MERCHANT WHOLESALERS BY SALES SIZE, 1954

SALES SIZE	Number of firms	Sales by firms in sales class (thousands of $)
All merchant wholesalers	165,153	$101,100,941
Operating all year:	159,687	99,619,703
with sales of		
more than $10 million	815	18,584,598
$5 million to $10 million	1,638	11,223,011
$2 million to $5 million	6,609	19,940,896
$1 million to $2 million	11,969	16,741,594
$500,000 to $1 million	19,663	13,952,367
$300,000 to $500,000	19,583	7,656,795
$200,000 to $300,000	17,886	4,424,833
$100,000 to $200,000	31,174	4,532,948
$50,000 to $100,000	25,011	1,857,660
Less than $50,000	25,339	705,001
Not operating all year	5,466	1,481,238

SOURCE: *Census of Business, 1954*, Vol. III, *Wholesale Trade—Summary Statistics*, p. 12.

TABLE 11

SERVICE ESTABLISHMENTS BY SALES SIZE, 1954

SALES SIZE	Number of firms	Sales by firms in sales class (thousands of $)
All establishments	785,589	$23,487,419
Operating entire year:	748,266	22,658,319
with sales of		
more than $500,000	4,383	7,704,019
$300,000 to $500,000	4,047	1,539,806
$100,000 to $300,000	24,203	3,906,640
$50,000 to $100,000	38,590	2,653,703
$30,000 to $50,000	49,525	1,877,044
$20,000 to $30,000	56,316	1,345,554
$15,000 to $20,000	49,063	824,697
$10,000 to $15,000	82,023	963,849
$5,000 to $10,000	177,506	1,166,615
$3,000 to $5,000	135,293	467,199
$2,000 to $3,000	82,123	164,246
Less than $2,000	45,194	44,947
Not operating entire year	37,323	829,100

SOURCE: *Census of Business, 1954*, Volume V, *Selected Service Trades—Summary Statistics*, p. 2–2.

TABLE 12

SALES BY SIZE CLASSES, SELECTED INDUSTRIES, 1954

SIZE CLASS	% of firms in size class	% of sales
A. *Retail establishments*		
More than $1 million	1.1	26.3
More than $100,000	18.7	70.0
Less than $30,000	39.9	5.6
B. *Merchant wholesalers*		
More than $5 million	1.5	29.5
More than $1 million	12.7	65.8
Less than $100,000	30.5	2.5
C. *Selected services*		
More than $300,000	1.1	39.4
More than $50,000	9.1	67.3
Less than $10,000	56.0	6.2

This table was compiled from Tables 9, 10 and 11. Percentages are based on total number of establishments and sales.

TABLE 13

COMPARATIVE RATES OF EARNING BY SMALL MANUFACTURERS, 1947–59

YEAR	*Assets under $1 million*	*Assets over $1 million*
1947	16.3	15.5
1948	12.6	16.3
1949	7.0	10.6
1950	12.5	15.7
1951	9.0	12.5
1952	7.9	10.6
1953	7.1	10.8
1954	5.4	10.3
1955	7.5	13.0
1956	10.4	12.4
1957	——	——
1958	4.4	8.9
1959	8.3	10.5

SOURCE: "How Healthy Is Small Business?" *Congressional Quarterly Weekly Report*, XIV (May 25, 1956), p. 592; *Fourteenth Semiannual Report*, Small Business Administration (1960), p. 13. Data is taken from Federal Trade Commission and Securities and Exchange Commission figures covering about 3% of the total business population.

TABLE 14

SMALL BUSINESS SHARE OF DEFENSE CONTRACTS, 1951–9

YEAR	Total Contracts Awarded (billions of $)	Contracts Awarded to Small Business	
		(billions of $)	(% of contracts)
1951	$30.8	$6.4	20.9
1952	41.2	7.1	17.1
1953	28.4	4.6	16.2
1954	11.6	2.9	25.1
1955	14.8	3.2	21.8
1956	17.5	3.4	19.6
1957	19.1	3.7	19.8
1958	21.8	3.7	17.1
1959	22.7	3.7	16.6

SOURCE: "How Healthy Is Small Business?" *Congressional Quarterly Weekly Report*, XIV (May 25, 1956), p. 593; *Small Business Administration—1960*, Part I (March 22, 1960), p. 3.

TABLE 15

SEARCH FOR BUSINESS CREDIT, JULY 1953–JUNE 1954

Size of firm by employment	% of firms getting all funds desired	% of firms getting none of funds desired
1–3 employees	48.8	19.9
4–19	50.3	14.9
20–49	55.8	11.0
50–99	59.3	9.2
100 or more	68.4	5.3
Age of firm		
Established	55.2	15.4
Newer	47.6	16.4

SOURCE: Loughlin McHugh and Jack Ciaccio: "External Financing of Small and Medium-size Business," *Survey of Current Business*, XXXV (October 1955), p. 18.

Bibliography

A.   BOOKS AND ARTICLES

Adams, Brooks: *The Theory of Social Revolutions.* New York: Macmillan Co.; 1914.

Agar, Herbert, and Tate, Allen (eds.): *Who Owns America?* Boston: Houghton Mifflin Co.; 1936.

Allen, Sidney: "NAM Pushing Profits for College Training." *San Francisco Chronicle,* March 10, 1954.

Andrews, Robert Angell: "The Community Industrial Financing Plan as a Source of Funds for Small Business." Unpublished Ph.D. thesis. Stanford University; 1950.

Arnold, T. W.: *The Folklore of Capitalism.* New Haven: Yale University Press; 1937.

——, and others: *The Future of Democratic Capitalism.* Philadelphia: University of Pennsylvania Press; 1950.

Auerbach, Morton M.: *The Conservative Illusion.* New York: Columbia University Press; 1959.

"Auto Dealer Franchises in Peril." *Business Week* (March 23, 1957).

Bain, Joe Staten: *Barriers to New Competition, Their Character and Consequences in Manufacturing Industries.* Cambridge: Harvard University Press; 1956.

——: "Industrial Concentration and Government Antitrust Policy." In Harold F. Williamson (ed.): *The Growth of the American Economy.* New York: Prentice-Hall; 1947.

Barnes, W. B.: "Small Business in America: Its Place and Problems." *Advanced Management,* Vol. XXI (July 1956).

Barrett, E. T.: "Who Speaks for Small Business?" *Management Review,* Vol. XLVII (May 1958).

Basel, Amos: "The Unseen Revolution." *New Republic* (May 2, 1949).

Basil, Douglas Constantine: *Organization and Control of the Smaller Enterprise.* Minneapolis: University of Minnesota Press; 1959.

Begeman, Jean: "Big Business 'Fronts.'" *New Republic* (February 13, 1950).

Bell, Daniel: "America's Un-Marxist Revolution." *Commentary* (March 1949).

Bell, Daniel (ed.): *The New American Right*. New York: Criterion Books; 1955.

Bellamy, R.: "The Changing Pattern of Retail Distribution." *Bulletin of the Oxford University Institute of Statistics*, Vol. VIII (August 1946).

Bendix, Reinhard: *Work and Authority in Industry*. New York: John Wiley & Sons; 1956.

———, and Lipset, Seymour M.: "Social Status and Social Structure: A Re-examination of Data and Interpretations." *British Journal of Sociology* (June 1951).

Benton, William: "Young Man, Be Your Own Boss." *Reader's Digest* (September 1944).

Berle, A. A., Jr.: "Businessmen in Government: The New Administration." *The Reporter* (February 3, 1953).

———: *Economic Power and the Free Society*. New York: Fund for the Republic; 1957.

———, and Means, Gardiner C.: *The Modern Corporation and Private Property*. New York: Macmillan Co.; 1933.

Bernheim, Alfred L. (ed.): *Big Business: Its Growth and Its Place*. New York: The Twentieth Century Fund; 1937.

Billington, Ray Allen: "The Origins of Middle Western Isolationism." *Political Science Quarterly* (March 1945).

Black, Nelms: *How To Organize and Manage a Small Business*. Norman, Okla.: University of Oklahoma Press; 1946.

Blair, John M.: "Relation Between Size and Efficiency of Business." *Review of Economic Statistics*, Vol. XXIV (August 1942).

———: "Technology and Size." *American Economic Review*, Vol. XXXVIII (May 1948).

Block, Herbert: "Industrial Concentration Versus Small Business." *Social Research* (May 1943).

Blough, Roger M.: *Free Man and the Corporation*. New York: McGraw-Hill Book Co.; 1959.

Bone, Hugh A.: *American Politics and the Party System*. New York: McGraw-Hill Book Co.; 1949.

Boulding, Kenneth: *The Organizational Revolution*. New York: Harper & Brothers; 1953.

Bradley, Albert: *Let's Stop Taxing Progress*. Pamphlet issued by General Motors (*c.* 1947).

Brady, Robert A.: *Business as a System of Power*. New York: Columbia University Press; 1943.

Burgess, Ernest W.: "The Family in a Changing Society." *American Journal of Sociology* (September 1948).

Burns, Robert Arthur: *The Decline of Competition: A Study of the Evolution of American Industry*. New York: McGraw-Hill Book Co.; 1936.

"The Business Population." *Survey of Current Business,* Vol. XXXI (February 1951).

Butters, J. Keith, and Lintner, John: *Effect of Federal Taxes on Growing Enterprises.* Cambridge: Harvard University Press; 1945.

Capital for Small Business. Chicago: Investment Bankers Association; 1945.

Cassady, Ralph, Jr., and Jones, Wylie L.: *The Changing Competitive Structure in the Wholesale Grocery Trade.* Berkeley, Los Angeles: University of California Press; 1949.

Cates, John: "Politics of American Business." *New Statesman and Nation,* Vol. XLIV (March 7, 1953).

Centers, Richard: *The Psychology of Social Classes.* Princeton: Princeton University Press; 1949.

Chamberlain, John: *The Roots of Capitalism.* Princeton: D. Van Nostrand Co.; 1959.

Churchill, Betty C.: "Age and Life Expectancy of Business Firms." *Survey of Current Business,* Vol. XXXV (December 1955).

————: "Business Population by Legal Form of Organization." *Survey of Current Business,* Vol. XXXI (June 1951).

————: "Business Population by Legal Form of Organization." *Survey of Current Business,* Vol. XXXV (April 1955).

————: "Recent Business Population Movements." *Survey of Current Business,* Vol. XXXIV (January 1954).

————: "Rise in the Business Population." *Survey of Current Business,* Vol. XXXIX (May 1959).

————: "Size Characteristics of the Business Population." *Survey of Current Business,* Vol. XXXIV (May 1954).

————: "Size of Business Firms." *Survey of Current Business,* Vol. XXXIX (September 1959).

————: "State Estimates of the Business Population, 1944–1951." *Survey of Current Business,* Vol. XXXII (January 1952).

————: "Survival Patterns of the Postwar Business Population." *Survey of Current Business,* Vol. XXXII (December 1952).

————, and Foss, Murray F.: "The Size Distribution of the Postwar Business Population." *Survey of Current Business,* Vol. XXX (May 1950).

Cleveland, A. S.: "NAM: Spokesman for Industry?" *Harvard Business Review* (May 1948).

Cochran, T. C.: "Cultural Factors in Economic Growth." *Journal of Economic History,* Vol. XX (December 1960).

Cole, Arthur Harrison: *Business Enterprise in Its Social Setting.* Cambridge: Harvard University Press; 1959.

Commager, H. S.: *The American Mind.* New Haven: Yale University Press; 1950.

Converse, P. D.: *Should I Start My Own Business?* Urbana, Ill.: University of Illinois Press; 1945.

Corey, Lewis: *The Crisis of the Middle Class.* New York: Covici Friede; 1935.
———: "The Middle Class." *Antioch Review* (Spring 1945).
Cowing, Cedric: "The Idea of Competition in America, 1865–1917." Unpublished M. A. thesis. Stanford University; 1950
Crum, William L.: *The Effect of Size on Corporate Earnings and Condition.* Harvard Business Research Studies No. 8. Cambridge: Harvard University Press; 1934.
Davenport, Russell W.: "The Greatest Opportunity on Earth." *Fortune* (October 1949).
Davis, Jerome: *Capitalism and Its Culture.* New York: Farrar & Rinehart; 1935.
Dean, J.: "Competition, Inside and Out." *Harvard Business Review,* Vol. XXXII (November–December 1954).
Denison, Edward F.: "Service Industries—Trends and Prospects." *Survey of Current Business,* Vol. XXV (January 1945).
Dever, H. F.: "Automation and Small Business." *Instruments and Automation,* Vol. XXX (September 1957).
Dobb, Maurice: *Studies in the Development of Capitalism.* New York: International Publishers; 1947.
Donham, Paul: "Looking Around." *Harvard Business Review,* Vol. XXXIII (November–December 1955).
———: "Whither Small Business." *Harvard Business Review,* Vol. XXXV (March–April 1957).
Dorfman, Joseph: "The Economic Philosophy of Thomas Jefferson." *Political Science Quarterly* (March 1940).
Drucker, Peter: "Care and Feeding of Small Business." *Harper's Magazine,* Vol. CCI (August 1950).
———: *Concept of the Corporation.* New York: John Day Co.; 1946.
———: *The End of Economic Man.* New York: John Day Co.; 1939.
———: *The Future of Industrial Man.* New York: John Day Co.; 1942.
———: *The New Society.* New York: Harper & Brothers; 1949.
Edgerton, John: "Annual Address of John E. Edgerton, President of the N.A.M." *American Industries* (October 1930).
Editors of *Fortune:* "The Class of '49." *Fortune* (June 1949).
———: "U.S.A.: The Permanent Revolution." *Fortune* (June 1950).
Edwards, Corwin D.: *Big Business and the Policy of Competition.* Cleveland: Press of Western Reserve University; 1956.
———: *Maintaining Competition.* New York: McGraw-Hill Book Co.; 1949.
Eells, Richard: *The Meaning of Modern Business.* New York: Columbia University Press; 1960.
Elliston, H. B.: "Little Businessman, What Now?" *Saturday Evening Post,* Vol. CCX (April 16, 1938).
Engler, Robert: "The Farm Bloc." *Nation* (September 19, 1953).
———: *The Politics of Oil.* New York: Macmillan Co.; 1961.

Evans, G. H., Jr.: "Business Entrepreneurs, Their Major Functions and Related Tenets." *Journal of Economic History,* Vol. XIX (June 1959).

Evans, T. M.: "Corporate Socialism Threatens To Eliminate Small Firms; Small Business Financing." *Commercial and Financial Chronicle,* Vol. CXXCIV (November 8, 1956).

Fitzgerald, C. L., Jr.: "Problems in Review: Small Business Financing." *Harvard Business Review,* Vol. XXXVII (March 1959).

Fitzhugh, George: *Sociology for the South.* Richmond: A. Morris, Publisher; 1854.

Fitzwilliams, Jeanette: "Employment in Corporate and Non-Corporate Production." *Survey of Current Business,* Vol. XXXIX (November 1959).

Friedrich, Carl J.: "The Agricultural Base of Emotional Nationalism." *Public Opinion Quarterly* (April 1937).

Gable, Richard W.: "NAM: Influential Lobby or Kiss of Death?" *Journal of Politics* (May 1953).

Galbraith, J. K.: "Businessman as Philosopher." *Perspectives U.S.A.,* No. 13 (1955).

Gardner, B. B.: *Human Relations in Industry.* Chicago: Richard D. Irwin; 1945.

Gaus, John M., and Wolcott, Leon: *Public Administration and the United States Department of Agriculture.* Chicago: Public Administration Service; 1940.

Graham, Frank D.: *Social Goals and Economic Institutions.* Princeton: Princeton University Press; 1942.

Green, Arnold: "Why Americans Are Insecure." *Commentary* (July 1948).

Grimshaw, Austin: *Problems of the Independent Businessman.* New York: McGraw-Hill Book Co.; 1955.

Griswold, A. Whitney: "The Agrarian Democracy of Thomas Jefferson." *American Political Science Review* (August 1946).

———: *Farming and Democracy.* New York: Harcourt, Brace & Co.; 1948.

Hacker, Andrew: *Politics and the Corporation, an Occasional Paper on the Role of the Corporation in a Free Society.* New York: Fund for the Republic; 1958.

Hacker, Louis M.: *The Shaping of the American Tradition.* New York: Columbia University Press; 1947.

———: *The Triumph of American Capitalism.* New York: Simon & Schuster; 1940.

Hamilton, D.: "Entrepreneur as Cultural Hero." *Southwestern Social Science Quarterly,* Vol. XXXVIII (December 1957).

Harris, Herbert: "Small Business: America's Biggest Business." *Nation's Business,* Vol. XLII (April 1954).

Hart, H. H.: "New Legislation Brings Relief to Small Corporate Taxpayer and Owner." *Journal of Taxation*, Vol. IX (October 1958).

Hatt, Paul K., and Reis, Albert J.: *Reader in Urban Sociology*. Glencoe, Ill.: Free Press; 1951.

Heimann, Eduard: "Theorie des Mittelstandes, by Fritz Marbach." *American Economic Review*, Vol. XXXVI (December 1946).

Henry, K.: "What Small Business Really Wants." *Dun's Review and Modern Industry*, Vol. LXXIV (July 1959).

Hertzler, J. O.: "Some Tendencies Toward a Closed Class System in the United States." *Social Forces* (March 1952).

Hewitt, Charles M., Jr.: *Automobile Franchise Agreements*. Homewood, Ill.: Richard D. Irwin; 1956.

Hoad, William M.: *Small Business Case Book*. Third Edition. Ann Arbor: Bureau of Business Research, University of Michigan; 1955.

Hofstadter, Richard: *The Age of Reform*. New York: Alfred A. Knopf; 1956.

————: *The American Political Tradition*. New York: Alfred A. Knopf; 1948.

Hopkins, Ernest J.: "Long-term Needs of Small Business." *Private Capital Requirements*. Postwar Economic Studies No. 5. Washington, D.C.: Board of Governors of the Federal Reserve System; 1946.

Houser, Theodore V.: *Big Business and Human Values*. New York: McGraw-Hill Book Co.; 1957.

"How Healthy Is Small Business?" *Congressional Quarterly Weekly Report*, Vol. XIV (May 25, 1956).

Jenkin, Thomas Paul: *Reactions of Major Groups to Positive Government in the United States, 1930–1940*. Los Angeles: University of California Press; 1945.

Jones, Griffith: "Why Do Businesses Fail?" *Dun's Review* (September 1952).

Jones, Rudolph: *The Relative Position of Small Business in the American Economy since 1930*. Dissertation abstract, Studies in Economics, Series 5, No. 5. Washington, D.C.: Catholic University of America; 1952.

Judkins, C. J.: "Do Associations Represent the Small Business Firm?" *Domestic Commerce*, Vol. XXXIV (July 1946).

Kaplan, Abraham D.: *Big Enterprise in a Competitive Society*. Washington, D.C.: The Brookings Institution; 1954.

————: "The Role of Small Business and Free Enterprise." *Proceedings of the Academy of Political Science*, Vol. XXII (May 1947).

————: *Small Business: Its Place and Problems*. New York: McGraw-Hill Book Co.; 1948.

Kelley, Pearce Clement, and Lawyer, Kenneth: *How To Organize and Operate a Small Business*. Third Edition. Englewood Cliffs, N.J.: Prentice-Hall; 1961.

Ketchum, Marshall D.: "The Financial Problem of Small Business." *Journal of Business of the University of Chicago,* Vol. XVII (April–July 1944).

Klein, L. R., and Margolis, J.: "Statistical Studies of Unincorporated Business." *Review of Economics and Statistics,* Vol. XXXVI (February 1954).

Kornhauser, William: *The Politics of Mass Society.* Glencoe, Ill.: Free Press; 1959.

Krusen, H. Stanley: "Equity Financing for Smaller Businesses." *Dun's Review and Modern Industry,* Vol. LXXIII (May 1959).

Lane, Robert: "Government Regulation and the Business Mind." *American Sociological Review* (April 1951).

Laski, Harold J.: *The American Democracy.* New York: Viking Press; 1948.

Lauterbach, Albert T.: *Man, Motives and Money: Psychological Frontiers of Economics.* Second Edition. Ithaca, N.Y.: Cornell University Press; 1959.

Law and Contemporary Problems, Vol. XXIV (Winter 1959).

Lazarsfeld, Paul F., and Stanton, Frank M. (eds.): *Communications Research.* New York: Harper & Brothers; 1949.

Lebow, Victor: "The Nature of Postwar Retail Competition." *Journal of Marketing,* Vol. IX (July 1944).

Lederer, Emil, and Marschak, Jacob: "The Middle Class." Translated by S. M. Ellison (mimeographed). Columbia University; 1937.

Lemmon, S. M.: "The Ideology of the 'Dixiecrat' Movement." *Social Forces* (December 1951).

Lent, George (ed.): *A Tax Program for Small Business: How Should Small Corporations Be Taxed?* (Pamphlet.) Hanover, N.H.: Amos Tuck School of Business Administration, Dartmouth College; 1958.

Lerner, Max: *America as a Civilization.* New York: Simon & Schuster; 1957.

Levitt, Theodore: "The Dangers of Social Responsibility." *Harvard Business Review* (September–October 1958).

Lewis, G. F.: "Comparison of Some Aspects of the Backgrounds and Careers of Small Businessmen and American Business Leaders." *American Journal of Sociology,* Vol. LXV (January 1960).

Lilienthal, David E.: *Big Business: A New Era.* New York: Harper & Brothers; 1952.

Lubell, Samuel: *The Future of American Politics.* New York: Harper & Brothers; 1951.

Lumer, Wilfred: *Small Business at the Crossroads.* Washington, D.C.: Public Affairs Institute; 1956.

Lynd, Robert S.: "Can Liberalism Do It?" *New Century.* Publication of the Princeton Liberal Union (Spring 1948).

———: "Leadership in a Free Society." *Political Science Quarterly* (December 1937).

————: *Knowledge for What?* Princeton: Princeton University Press; 1946.

————, and Helen M.: *Middletown in Transition*. New York: Harcourt, Brace & Co.; 1937.

Lyons, Barrow: "The Men Behind the Money." *The Nation* (July 5, 1952).

McConnell, Grant: *The Decline of Agrarian Democracy*. Berkeley: University of California Press; 1953.

McConnell, Joseph L.: "Corporate Earnings by Size of Firm." *Survey of Current Business*, Vol. XXV (May 1945).

MacDonald, Dwight: "The Defense of Everybody." *The New Yorker*, Part I (July 11, 1953); Part II (July 18, 1953).

McHugh, Loughlin, and Ciaccio, Jack N.: "External Financing of Small and Medium-Size Business." *Survey of Current Business*, Vol. XXXV (October 1955).

McKean, Eugene C.: *The Persistence of Small Business: A Study of Unincorporated Enterprise*. Kalamazoo, Mich.: The W. E. Upjohn Institute for Community Research; 1958.

Mannheim, Karl: *Man and Society in an Age of Reconstruction*. New York: Harcourt, Brace & Co.; 1951.

Marcus, Sumner: *The Law of Small Business*. Missoula, Mont.: Bureau of Business and Economic Research, Montana State University; 1958.

Margolius, Sidney: "Super Business of Supermarkets." *The New York Times*, Sunday Magazine Section, March 29, 1959.

Mason, Alpheus T.: *Brandeis*. New York: Viking Press; 1946.

————: "Business Organized as Power: The Imperium in Imperio," *American Political Science Review* (June 1950).

Mason, Edward S. (ed.): *The Corporation in Modern Society*. Cambridge: Harvard University Press; 1959.

Masuoka, Jitsuichi: "The City and Racial Adjustment." *Social Forces* (October 1948).

Mayer, Kurt: "Small Business as a Social Institution." *Social Research*, Vol. XIV (September 1947).

Mayo, Elton: *The Human Problems of an Industrial Civilization*. New York: Macmillan Co.; 1933.

Meadows, Paul: *The Culture of Industrial Man*. Lincoln, Nebr.: University of Nebraska Press; 1950.

Meeting the Special Problems of Small Business: A Statement on National Policy. New York: Committee for Economic Development; 1947.

Merwin, Charles L.: *Financing Small Corporations*. New York: National Bureau of Economic Research; 1942.

Meusel, Alfred: "Middle Class." *Encyclopaedia of the Social Sciences*, Vol. X (1933).

Miller, John P.: *Unfair Competition.* Cambridge: Harvard University Press; 1941.

Miller, Raymond Curtis (ed.): *Twentieth-Century Pessimism and the American Dream.* Detroit: Wayne State University Press; 1961.

Mills, C. Wright: "The Middle Classes in Middle-Sized Cities." *American Sociological Review* (October 1946).

———: *The New Men of Power.* New York: Harcourt, Brace & Co.; 1948.

———: "Professional Ideology of Social Pathologists." *American Journal of Sociology* (September 1943).

———: *White Collar.* New York: Oxford University Press; 1951.

Morgan, Arthur: *The Small Community.* New York: Harper & Brothers; 1942.

Morison, S. E., and Commager, H. S.: *The Growth of the American Republic.* New York: Oxford University Press; 1942.

Morse, Arthur D.: "Who's Trying to Ruin Our Schools?" *McCall's Magazine* (September 1951).

Mund, Vernon Arthur: *Open Markets, an Essential of Free Enterprise.* New York: Harper & Brothers; 1948.

National Association of Manufacturers. Economic Principles Commission: *The American Individual Enterprise System, Its Nature, Evolution, and Future.* New York: McGraw-Hill Book Co.; 1946.

Newman, William J.: *The Futilitarian Society.* New York: George Braziller; 1961.

Nicholson, Joseph L.: "The Fallacy of Easy Money for the Small Business." *Harvard Business Review,* Vol. XVII (Autumn 1938).

Noyes, Charles E.: "Is Big Business Bad Business?" *The Nation* (August 6, 1949).

Nutter, G. W.: "Monopoly, Bigness and Progress." *Journal of Political Economy,* Vol. LXIV (December 1956).

Odiorne, George S.: "How Small Business Cuts Its Throat." *Harper's Magazine* (April 1960).

Osborn, Richard Clinton: *Effects of Corporate Size on Efficiency and Profitability.* Urbana, Ill.: University of Illinois Press; 1950.

———: "The Plea for Small Business." *The Accounting Review* (October 1951).

Oxenfeldt, Alfred R.: *New Firms and Free Enterprise.* Washington, D.C.: American Council on Public Affairs; 1943.

Packman, Martin: "Future of Small Business." *Editorial Research Reports,* Vol. II (August 1955).

Parrington, Vernon L.: *Main Currents in American Thought.* New York: Harcourt, Brace & Co.; 1927.

Patterson, S. Howard: *The Social Aspects of Industry.* New York: McGraw-Hill Book Co.; 1943.

Pepper, Roger S.: "Pressure Groups among 'Small Business Men.'" Unpublished M.A. thesis. Columbia University; 1940.

Perlman, Selig: *A Theory of the Labor Movement*. New York: Augustus M. Kelley; 1949.

Pflaum, Irving: "The Baffling Career of Robert E. Wood." *Harper's Magazine* (April 1954).

Phillips, C. F.: "Free Competition in Practice: Its Advantages and Risks." *Commercial and Financial Chronicle*, Vol. CXXCIV (September 13, 1956).

Phillips, Joseph D.: *Little Business in the American Economy*. Urbana, Ill.: University of Illinois Press; 1958.

Porter, Sylvia: "Your Money's Worth." *San Francisco Chronicle*, February 22, 1961.

Problems of Smaller Stores. New York: U.S. National Retail Merchants Association; 1959.

Prothro, J. W.: "Business Ideas and the American Tradition." *Journal of Politics*, Vol. XV (February 1953).

Quantius, Frances W.: "Corporate Versus Noncorporate Business Borrowers: A Case Study." *Current Economic Comment*, Vol. XVI (May 1954).

Quinn, T. M.: *I Quit Monster Business*. New York: Public Relations; 1948.

————: *Giant Business—Threat to Democracy*. New York: Exposition Press; 1953.

Riesman, David: *The Lonely Crowd*. New Haven: Yale University Press; 1950.

————: "The Study of the City." Reprinted in *City Lights* (Fall 1953).

Ripley, William Z.: *Main Street and Wall Street*. Boston: Little, Brown & Co.; 1932.

Robertson, D. H.: *The Control of Industry*. New York: Pitman Publishing Corp.; 1948.

Robinson, E. A. G.: *The Structure of Competitive Industry*. New York: Pitman Publishing Corp.; 1948.

Rose, Arnold: "Anti-Semitism's Root in City Hatred." *Commentary* (October 1948).

Rossiter, Clinton: *Conservatism in America*. New York: Alfred A. Knopf; 1955.

————: "Wanted: An American Conservatism." *Fortune* (March 1950).

Sanzo, R.: "Small Business Looks at Itself." *Dun's Review and Modern Industry*, Vol. LXX (October 1957).

Saulnier, R. J.: "Proper Role of Government in Fostering Small Business." *Commercial and Financial Chronicle*, Vol. CXXCVI (November 7, 1957).

Schmidt, Charles H.: *Analyzing the Effects of Business Size on Sources and Uses of Funds*. New York: Conference on Research in Business Finance, National Bureau of Economic Research; 1952.

————: "Member Bank Loans to Small Business." *Federal Reserve Bulletin*, Vol. XXXIII (August 1947).

Schmidt, Emerson P.: "The Role and Problems of Small Business." *Law and Contemporary Problems,* Vol. XI (Summer–Autumn 1945).
———: *Small Business, Its Place and Problems.* Postwar Readjustment Bulletin No. 7. Washington, D.C.: U.S. Chamber of Commerce; 1943.

Schrieber, Albert N., and others: *Defense Procurement and Small Business: A Survey of Practices and Opinions of Small Business Firms Selling to Defense Programs.* Seattle: distributed by University of Washington Press; 1961.

Schumpeter, Joseph Alois: *Capitalism, Socialism and Democracy.* Second Edition. New York: Harper & Brothers; 1942.

Schweiger, T.: "Adequacy of Financing for Small Business since World War II." *Journal of Finance,* Vol. XIII (September 1958).

Skaife, Robert A.: "They Sow Distrust." *The Nation's Schools* (January 1951).

Slesinger, R. E.: "What Are the Perils and Pitfalls of Small Business Today?" *Commercial and Financial Chronicle,* Vol. CXXCIX (January 15, 1959).

Sloan, Alfred P.: *Adventures of a White-Collar Man.* New York: Doubleday, Doran & Co., 1941.

"Small Business Consensus: No Crutches Needed." *Dun's Review and Modern Industry,* Vol. LXXII (December 1958).

Small Business Fights for Survival. Washington, D.C.: Public Affairs Institute; 1951.

Small Business: Its Role and Its Problems. Committee on Economic Policy. Washington, D.C.: U.S. Chamber of Commerce; 1953.

Small Business: Problems and Prospects. General Management Series, No. 184. New York: American Management Association; 1957.

Smuckler, Ralph H.: "The Region of Isolationism." *American Political Science Review* (June 1953).

Sorokin, P., and Zimmermann, C. C.: *Principles of Rural-Urban Sociology.* New York: Henry Holt & Co.; 1929.

Sparkman, John: "Why a Senate Small Business Committee?" *Advanced Management,* Vol. XII (June 1957).

Steindl, Joseph: *Small and Big Business.* Oxford: Basil Blackwell; 1947.

Stewart, W. Blair: "Does Large-Scale Enterprise Lower Costs?—Discussion." *American Economic Review,* Vol. XXXVIII (May 1948).

Stocking, G. W.: "Saving Free Enterprise from Its Friends; The Rise of Big Business." *Southern Economic Journal,* Vol. XIX (April 1953).

Strachey, John: *Contemporary Capitalism.* New York: Random House; 1956.

Stults, Walter B.: "The Place and Future of Small Business." *Iowa Business Digest,* Vol. XXVII (May 1956).

Sutton, Frances Xavier: *The American Business Creed.* Cambridge: Harvard University Press; 1956.

Thurber, James: "Soapland," *The New Yorker,* Part II (May 29, 1948).

Trow, Martin: "Small Business, Political Tolerance and McCarthy." *American Journal of Sociology* (November 1958).

United States Armed Forces Institute: *The Small Business.* Madison, Wisc.: South-Western Publishing Co.; 1944.

Wallich, Henry C.: *The Cost of Freedom: A New Look at Capitalism.* New York: Harper & Brothers; 1960.

Weddell, Kennard: *Aiding Small Industry Through Government Purchases.* Menlo Park, Calif.: International Industrial Development Center, Stanford Research Institute; 1960.

Weissman, Rudolph L.: *Small Business and Venture Capital.* New York: Harper & Brothers; 1945.

Wessels, O. Richard: *Small Business as a Career.* Syracuse, N.Y.: Syracuse University Press; 1946.

Winston, Clement, and Osborne, Reba L.: "Postwar Patterns of Chain and Independent Store Sales." *Survey of Current Business,* Vol. XXIX (January 1949).

Wirth, L.: "Urbanism as a Way of Life." *American Journal of Sociology* (July 1938).

Wishart, P. B.: "Automatic Production and the Small Businessman." *Commercial and Financial Chronicle,* Vol. CXXCII (September 1, 1955).

Wolfbein, S. L.: "Employment Statistics for Small Business, U.S. Bureau of Labor Statistics." Washington, D.C.: U.S. Government Printing Office; 1953.

Wood, Robert: *Suburbia; Its Peoples and Their Politics.* Boston: Houghton Mifflin, 1959.

Worthy, James C.: *Big Business and Free Men.* New York: Harper, 1959.

Zeigler, Harmon: *The Politics of Small Business.* Washington, D.C.: Public Affairs Press; 1961.

B.   U.S. GOVERNMENT DOCUMENTS

Bureau of the Census: *Census of Business, 1954,* Vol. I, Retail Trade—Summary Statistics; Vol. III, Wholesale Trade—Summary Statistics; Vol. V, Selected Service Trades—Summary Statistics. Washington, D.C.: 1957.

Department of Commerce: *Small Business—A National Asset.* Economic Series No. 24. Washington, D.C.: 1943.

"Federal Aid for Small Business—Pros and Cons," U.S. Congress, House of Representatives, Select Committee on Small Business, 84th Congress. *Congressional Digest,* Vol. XXXV (December 1956).

Federal Reserve System: *Financing Small Business,* report to the Committees on Banking and Currency and the Select Committees on Small Business, U.S. Congress, 85th Congress, 2nd Session. Washington, D.C.: 1958.

Small Business Administration: *Management Research Summary*.
Alyea, Paul E.: "Overlapping Sales Taxes and Small Business." No. 15 (March 1961).
Brown, James R.: "The Structure of Small Business in Alabama." No. 49 (October 1961).
Carpenter, Walter H., Jr., and Handler, Edward: "Small Business and Pattern Bargaining." No. 38 (June 1961).
Davidson, Thomas L.: "Small Store Opportunities in Planned Shopping Centers." No. 17 (March 1961).
Doerflinger, William A., Baeza, Marco A., and LaSale, Melchoire L.: "Small Wholesale Business in New Jersey." No. 26 (April 1961).
Eldridge, Paul L.: "Small Business and the Superhighway Era." No. 6 (January 1961).
Kaufman, Charles N.: "Financing Small Business in South Dakota." No. 28 (May 1961).
Kinnard, William N., Jr., and Malinowski, Zenon S.: "How Urban Renewal Projects Affect Small Business." No. 1 (November 1960).
———: "Small Plant Turnover and Failure." No. 4 (January 1961).
———: "Use of External Assistance by Small Manufacturers." No. 30 (May 1961).
Lesikar, Raymond V.: "Education for Leadership in Small Business." No. 36 (June 1961).
Lewis, Jerry L.: "Problems and Needs of Small Manufacturers." No. 18 (March 1961).
McKeever, J. L.: "Problems of Small Retailers." No. 9 (January 1961).
O'Neal, F. Hodge, and Derwin, Jordan: "The Squeeze-Out in Small Business Ownership." No. 7 (January 1961).
Pugh, Olin S.: "Facts about Small Business Financing." No. 10 (February 1961).
Wickesberg, A. K.: "Organizational Patterns in Small Business." No. 12 (March 1961).
———: *Semiannual Reports*. Washington, D.C.: 1954–61.
———: *Small Business Administration: What It Is, What It Does*. Washington, D.C.: 1959.
———: *Small Business Research Series No. 2*.
Mayer, Kurt B., and Goldstein, Sidney: *The First Two Years— Problems of Small Firm Growth and Survival*. Washington, D.C.: 1961.
———: *You and Manufacturing*. Washington, D.C.: 1959.
———: *You and Selling*. Washington, D.C.: 1959.
Temporary National Economic Committee: *Final Report of the Executive Secretary*. Washington, D.C.: 1941.
———: Monographs.
Bertrand, Daniel, Evans, W. Duane, and Blanchard, E. L.: *The*

302

Motion Picture Industry—A Pattern of Control. No. 43. Washington, D.C.: 1941.

Cover, John H., *et al.: Problems of Small Business.* No. 17. Washington, D.C.: 1941.

Federal Trade Commission: *Relative Efficiency of Large, Medium-Sized, and Small Business.* No. 13. Washington, D.C.: 1941.

Hoffman, A. C.: *Large-Scale Organization in the Food Industries.* No. 35. Washington, D.C.: 1940.

Wilcox, Clair: *Competition and Monopoly in American Industry.* No. 21. Washington, D.C.: 1941.

U.S. Congress, House of Representatives: Document No. 584, Message from the President of the U.S. *Some Major Problems of Small Independent Businessmen,* 81st Congress, 2nd Session. Washington; D.C.: 1950.

———: Committee on Banking and Currency, Hearings. *Creation of Small Business Administration,* 83rd Congress, 1st Session. Washington, D.C.: 1953.

———: Select Committee To Investigate Lobbying Activities, Reports, No. 3232, *Conference of American Small Business Organizations,* 81st Congress, 2nd Session. Washington, D.C.: 1950.

———: Select Committee on Small Business, Hearings. *The Aircraft Industry,* Subcommittee 4, 85th Congress, 2nd Session. Washington, D.C.: 1959.

Aluminum Industry, Subcommittee 3, 85th Congress, 1st and 2nd Sessions. Washington, D.C.: 1959.

Distribution Practices in the Petroleum Industry, Parts 1–5, 85th Congress, 1st Session. Washington, D.C.: 1957.

Distribution Problems, Parts 1–3, 84th Congress, 1st Session. Washington, D.C.: 1955.

Distribution Problems, Parts 4–8, 84th Congress, 1st Session. Washington, D.C.: 1956.

Effects of Foreign Oil Imports on Independent Domestic Producers, Part 1, 81st Congress, 1st Session. Washington, D.C.: 1949.

Effects of Foreign Oil Imports on Independent Domestic Producers, Parts 2–3, 81st Congress, 2nd Session. Washington, D.C.: 1950.

Effects of the Present Tax Structure on Small Business, 83rd Congress, 1st Session. Washington, D.C.: 1953.

Mergers and Unfair Competition in Food Marketing, 86th Congress, 1st Session. Washington, D.C.: 1960.

The Organization and Procedures of the Federal Regulatory Commissions and Agencies and Their Effect on Small Business. Part 1—Federal Trade Commission; Part 2—Federal Power Commission, 84th Congress, 1st Session; Part 3—Federal Communications Commission; Part 4—Civil Aeronautics Board; Part 5—Securities and Exchange Commission, 84th Congress, 2nd Session. Washington, D.C.: 1956.

Participation of Small Business in Foreign Trade and Foreign Aid, Subcommittee No. 3, 86th Congress, 1st Session. Washington, D.C.: 1959.

Price Discrimination—The Robinson-Patman Act and Related Matters, Parts 1–3 and Appendix, 84th Congress, 1st Session. Washington, D.C.: 1956.

Problems in the Metal Mining Industry, 83rd Congress, 1st Session. Washington, D.C.: 1953.

Problems of Small-Business Financing, Part 1, 85th Congress, 1st Session. Washington, D.C.: 1957.

Small Business in the Aluminum Industry, 86th Congress, 2nd Session. Washington, D.C.: 1960.

Small Business Organizations, 81st Congress, 1st Session. Washington, D.C.: 1950.

Small Business Problems in the Dairy Industry, Parts 1–3, 86th Congress, 1st Session. Washington, D.C.: 1959.

Small Business Problems in the Dairy Industry, Parts 4–5, 86th Congress, 2nd Session. Washington, D.C.: 1960.

Small Business Problems in Food Distribution, Subcommittee 5, Parts 1–3, 86th Congress, 1st Session. Washington, D.C.: 1960.

Small Business Problems in the Petroleum Industry, Part 1, 86th Congress, 1st Session. Washington, D.C.: 1960.

Small Business Problems in the Petroleum Industry, Part 2, 86th Congress, 2nd Session. Washington, D.C.: 1960.

Steel—Acquisitions, Mergers and Expansion of 12 Major Companies, 1900–1950, 81st Congress, 2nd Session. Washington, D.C.: 1950.

————: Select Committee on Small Business, Publications. *Banking Concentration and Small Business,* staff report, 86th Congress, 2nd Session. Washington, D.C.: 1960.

Status of Small Business in Retail Trade (1948–1958), staff report, 86th Congress, 2nd Session. Washington, D.C.: 1960.

————: Select Committee on Small Business, Reports. No. 2970, *Final Report,* 84th Congress, 2nd Session. Washington, D.C.: 1957. No. 2234, *Small Business Problems in Food Distribution,* report of Subcommittee 5 on Distribution Problems Affecting Small Business, 86th Congress, 2nd Session. Washington, D.C.: 1960.

U.S. Congress, Senate: Committee on Banking and Currency, hearings, *Credit Needs of Small Business,* Parts 1–2, 85th Congress, 1st Session. Washington, D.C.: 1957.

————: Committee on Interstate and Foreign Commerce, Hearings, *Mahaffie Nomination to Interstate Commerce Commission—1952,* 82nd Congress, 2nd Session. Washington, D.C.: 1952.

————: Select Committee on Small Business, Special Committee Report, *Small Business and Civic Welfare,* 79th Congress, 2nd Session. Senate Document No. 135. Washington, D.C.: 1946.

————: Select Committee on Small Business, Hearings. *Administra-*

tion of the Motor Carrier Act by the Interstate Commerce Commission, 84th Congress, 1st Session. Washington, D.C.: 1955.

Discount-House Operations, 85th Congress, 2nd Session. Washington, D.C.: 1958.

Food-Marketing—Report of the Federal Trade Commission, 86th Congress, 2nd Session. Washington, D.C.: 1960.

Government Procurement—1960, Lack of *Competition in Military Procurement and Its Impact on Small Business,* 86th Congress, 2nd Session. Washington, D.C.: 1960.

Government Procurement—1957, Case Studies in Government Procurement, 85th Congress, 1st Session. Washington, D.C.: 1957.

Impact of Imports on American Small Business, 86th Congress, 2nd Session. Washington, D.C.: 1960.

Material Shortages, Parts 1–4, 82nd Congress, 1st Session. Washington, D.C.: 1951.

Mergers and Unfair Competition in Food Marketing, 86th Congress, 1st Session. Washington, D.C.: 1959.

Military Procurement—1956, Small Business Problems in Military Procurement, 84th Congress, 2nd Session. Washington, D.C.: 1956.

Monopoly and Cartels, Part 1, 82nd Congress, 2nd Session. Washington, D.C.: 1952.

On Alleged Discriminatory Practices Against Small Business Concerns in Suburban Shopping Centers—1959, 86th Congress, 1st Session. Washington, D.C.: 1959.

Patent Policies of Departments and Agencies of the Federal Government, 86th Congress, 1st Session. Washington, D.C.: 1959.

Price Discrimination and the Basing Point System, Subcommittee on Price Discrimination and the Basing Point System, 82nd Congress, 1st Session. Washington, D.C.: 1951.

The Role of Private Antitrust Enforcement in Protecting Small Business—1958, 85th Congress, 2nd Session. Washington, D.C.: 1958.

The Role of Small Business in Defense Missile Procurement—1958, 85th Congress, 2nd Session. Washington, D.C.: 1958.

The Role of Small Business in Government Procurement—1961, 87th Congress, 1st Session. Washington, D.C.: 1961.

Small Business Administration—1961, 87th Congress, 1st Session. Washington, D.C.: 1961.

Small Business Administration—1960, Parts 1–2, 86th Congress, 2nd Session. Washington, D.C.: 1960.

Small Business Administration—1959, 86th Congress, 1st Session. Washington, D.C.: 1959.

Small Business Administration—1956, Progress Report of the Small Business Administration, 84th Congress, 2nd Session. Washington, D.C.: 1956.

Small Business and Credit, Reconstruction Finance Corporation—

The Degree of Availability of Reconstruction Finance Corporation Funds to Small Business, 81st Congress, 2nd Session. Washington, D.C.: 1950.

Small Business and War Program, 77th Congress, 1st Session. Washington, D.C.: 1941.

Small Business Exports and the World Market—1960, 86th Congress, 2nd Session. Washington, D.C.: 1961.

Small Business Investment Act—1960, 86th Congress, 2nd Session. Washington, D.C.: 1960.

Small Business Participation in Defense Subcontracting, 86th Congress, 1st Session. Washington, D.C.: 1959.

Small Business Participation in Government Procurement—1958, 85th Congress, 2nd Session. Washington, D.C.: 1958.

Small Business Problems in the Pacific Northwest—1957, 85th Congress, 1st Session. Washington, D.C.: 1957.

Tax Depreciation Allowances on Capital Equipment, 86th Congress, 1st Session. Washington, D.C.: 1959.

Tax Problems of Small Business, Parts 1–3, 85th Congress, 1st Session. Washington, D.C.: 1957.

Tax Problems of Small Business, Parts 1–2, 82nd Congress, 2nd Session. Washington, D.C.: 1952.

Trucking Mergers and Concentration, 85th Congress, 1st Session. Washington, D.C.: 1957.

————: Select Committee on Small Business, Mimeograph, *Statistical Data on Small Business,* 85th Congress, 2nd Session. Washington, D.C.: 1958.

————: Select Committee on Small Business, Publications.

Allen, Julius W.: *The Federal Agencies and Small Business,* 78th Congress, 1st Session. Washington, D.C.: 1943.

Civil Aeronautics Board: *Material Relative to Competition in the Regulated Civil-Aviation Industry—1956,* 84th Congress, 2nd Session. Washington, D.C.: 1956.

————: *The Role of Competition in Commercial Air Transportation,* for Subcommittee on Monopoly, 82nd Congress, 2nd Session. Washington, D.C.: 1952.

Mund, Vernon A.: *The Right To Buy—and Its Denial to Small Business,* 85th Congress, 1st Session. Washington, D.C.: 1957.

The Right To Buy, 1959, Staff Report, 86th Congress, 1st Session. Washington, D.C.: 1959.

Small Business—Access to Capital, 78th Congress, 1st Session. Washington, D.C.: 1943.

Small Business Act, Text, approved July 18, 1958, Public Law 536, 85th Congress, 2nd Session, as amended by Public Law 85–699 and Public Law 86–367. Washington, D.C.: 1960.

Small Business Investment Act, Public Law 699, 85th Congress, 2nd Session. Washington, D.C.: 1960.

Small Business Research and Education, 77th Congress, 1st Session. Washington, D.C.; 1941.

————: Select Committee on Small Business, Reports.

No. 1044, *Tenth Annual Report,* 86th Congress, 2nd Session. Washington, D.C.: 1960.

No. 6, *Ninth Annual Report,* 86th Congress, 1st Session. Washington, D.C.: 1959.

No. 1282, *Eighth Annual Report,* 85th Congress, 2nd Session. Washington, D.C.: 1958.

No. 1693, *Competition, Regulation and the Public Interest in the Motor Carrier Industry—Administration of the Motor Carrier Act by the Interstate Commerce Commission,* 84th Congress, 2nd Session. Washington, D.C.: 1956.

No. 2504, *Discount-House Operations, Summarizing Testimony on Competitive Impact of Discount-House Operations on Small Business,* 85th Congress, 2nd Session. Washington, D.C.: 1958.

No. 2819, *Fair Trade—A Study on Fair Trade, Based on a Survey of Manufacturers and Retailers,* 84th Congress, 2nd Session. Washington, D.C.: 1956.

No. 4, *Government Procurement—1960,* 86th Congress, 2nd Session. Washington, D.C.: 1961.

No. 1908, *Impact of Imports on Small Business,* 86th Congress, 2nd Session. Washington, D.C.: 1960.

No. 1016, *The Impact of Suburban Shopping Centers on Independent Retailers,* 86th Congress, 2nd Session. Washington, D.C.: 1960.

No. 47, *Small Business—Its Record and Outlook,* 79th Congress, 1st Session. Washington, D.C.: 1945.

No. 1441, *Mergers and Concentration in the Trucking Industry,* 85th Congress, 2nd Session. Washington, D.C.: 1958.

No. 1723, *Military Procurement, 1956—Military Procurement Practices—Case Studies,* 84th Congress, 2nd Session. Washington, D.C.: 1956.

No. 77, *Report on Material Shortage,* 82nd Congress, 1st Session. Washington, D.C.: 1951.

No. 586, *Report on Price Discrimination and the Basing Point System,* 82nd Congress, 1st Session. Washington, D.C.: 1951.

No. 438, *Report on Small-Business Manpower Problems—Industrial Manpower,* 82nd Congress, 1st Session. Washington, D.C.: 1951.

No. 1855, *The Role of Private Antitrust Enforcement in Protecting Small Business,* 85th Congress, 2nd Session. Washington, D.C.: 1958.

No. 2499, *The Role of Small Business in Defense Missile Procurement,* 85th Congress, 2nd Session. Washington, D.C.: 1958.

No. 206, *Small Business and Defense Subcontracts,* 83rd Congress, 1st Session. Washington, D.C.: 1953.

No. 46, *Small Business Finance and Taxation,* 81st Congress, 1st

Session. Washington, D.C.: 1949.

No. 716, *Small Business Participation in Defense Subcontracting,* 86th Congress, 1st Session. Washington, D.C.: 1959.

No. 2505, *Small Business Participation in Government Procurement,* 85th Congress, 2nd Session. Washington, D.C.: 1958.

No. 1017, *Tax Depreciation Allowances in Capital Equipment,* 86th Congress, 2nd Session. Washington, D.C.: 1960.

No. 1237, *Tax Problems of Small Business,* 85th Congress, 2nd Session. Washington, D.C.: 1958.

U.S. President's Conference on Technical and Distribution Research for the Benefit of Small Business: *Proceedings.* Washington, D.C.: 1957.

Index

A NOTE ON THE TYPE

THE TEXT of this book was set on the Linotype in a face called TIMES ROMAN, designed by *Stanley Morison* for *The Times* (London), and first introduced by that newspaper in 1932. Among typographers and designers of the twentieth century, Stanley Morison has been a strong forming influence, as typographical advisor to the English Monotype Corporation, as a director of two distinguished English publishing houses, and as a writer of sensibility, erudition, and keen practical sense.

Composed, printed, and bound by
Kingsport Press, Inc., Kingsport, Tennessee.
Typography and binding design by
S. NEIL FUJITA

A NOTE ABOUT THE AUTHOR

JOHN H. BUNZEL is Assistant Professor of Political Science at Stanford University. Born in New York City in 1924, he did his undergraduate work at Princeton University, graduating *magna cum laude* in 1948. He received his Master's degree from Columbia University in 1949, and his Ph.D. from the University of California at Berkeley in 1954. Before coming to Stanford, Professor Bunzel taught at San Francisco State College and Michigan State University. At present, he makes his home in Menlo Park, California.